Staying legal

A guide to issues and practice affecting the
library, information and publishing sectors

Staying legal

A guide to issues and practice affecting the
library, information and publishing sectors

Second edition

Edited by
Chris Armstrong
and
Laurence W. Bebbington

facet publishing

© The compilation: Chris Armstrong and Laurence W. Bebbington 1999, 2004
The articles: the contributors 2004

Published by
Facet Publishing
7 Ridgmount Street
London WC1E 7AE

Facet Publishing (formerly Library Association Publishing) is wholly owned by
CILIP: the Chartered Institute of Library and Information Professionals.

First published 1999
This second edition 2004

British Library Cataloguing in Publication Data

A catalogue record for this book is available from the British Library.

ISBN 1-85604-438-6

Typeset from editors' disks by Facet Publishing in 11/13 pt Elegant Garamond
and Syntax.
Printed and made in Great Britain by MPG Books Ltd, Bodmin, Cornwall.

Contents

The contributors

Stephen Adams is managing director of Magister Ltd, an information and training consultancy specializing in patents documentation. He trained as a chemist at the University of Bristol, then completed a Masters degree in Information Science at City University, London. He has worked in technical information for over 20 years, in central UK government, private research associations and industry, including nine years with Zeneca Agrochemicals (now Syngenta) as their principal patent searcher. He formed Magister Ltd in 1997. The company works closely with patent information users (and non-users), the major patent database producers, online hosts and industry lobby groups such as the Patent Documentation Group. He has been active in the UK Patent and Trade Mark Group, which represents patent searchers in industry, private legal practice and the public sector, as Chair, Secretary and Newsletter Editor. He is currently one of the Directors-at-Large of PIUG Inc., the International Society for Patent Information, and a member of the Editorial Advisory Board for the Elsevier journal *World Patent Information*.

Chris Armstrong is Managing Director of Information Automation Limited (IAL), a research, training and consultancy company in the library and information management sector which was established in 1987 and which runs the Centre for Information Quality Management (CIQM). He works regularly with the Department of Information Studies in Aberystwyth where he teaches a module on electronic publishing, and is currently involved with the department on several major research projects.

Chris publishes and speaks at conferences regularly. He is a Fellow of both CILIP: the Chartered Institute of Library and Information Professionals and of the Institute of Analysts and Programmers (IAP), and is currently Chair of UKOLUG – a Special Interest Group of CILIP that looks after the needs of users of all types of electronic resources. Particular interests are the quality and evaluation of information resources and information literacy. The company's website is at http://www.i-a-l.co.uk.

Laurence W. Bebbington is Law Librarian at the University of Nottingham. He has lectured in Information Science at the University of Strathclyde and has also worked at the universities of Birmingham, Cambridge and Glasgow, and at the Royal College of Physicians and Surgeons of Glasgow. He is a former Vice Chair of UKOLUG. He writes a regular column on legal issues in information work for the *UKOLUG Newsletter* and a column on 'IT and the Law' for *Legal Information Management*. He has written on various aspects of librarianship and information science and on subjects such as copyright, data protection and other legal issues in information work. He has also presented workshops and seminars on these topics.

Andrew Charlesworth studied law at the Universities of Warwick and Cambridge. He is currently Senior Research Fellow in IT and Law, and Director of the Centre for IT and Law (CITL) at the University of Bristol. The Centre for IT and the Law is sponsored by Vodafone Group Services Ltd, Barclaycard, Herbert Smith, Hewlett Packard Laboratories and the Law Society Charitable Trust.

He is a member of the Editorial Board of the *Journal of Information Law and Technology* and Associate Editor of the *International Yearbook of Law, Computers & Technology*. In the past, he has been a member of both the Executive Committee of the British & Irish Legal Education Technology Association (BILETA) and the General Council of the Society for Computers and Law (SCL).

He has provided consultancy services in Information Technology Law to a range of UK further and higher education organizations, and to other organizations as diverse as the British Computer Society, the Health Ministry of Ontario, and the Interior Ministry of the UAE.

He has presented papers on computer misuse, data protection, intellectual property, and legal issues relating to the internet, at conferences and seminars in Europe, North America, the Middle East and Australia. Recent publications include *Information Privacy Law in the European Union: e pluribus unum or ex uno plures?* and *Legal Issues Relating to the Archiving of Internet Resources in the UK, EU, USA and Australia* – a study undertaken for the JISC and the Wellcome Trust.

Allison Coleman is Director of Culturenet Cymru Ltd, a company funded by the Welsh Assembly Government, with the aim of promoting the culture and heritage of Wales online. She is also Director of Gathering the Jewels Ltd, a digitization company funded by the New Opportunities Fund.

Allison is a former Senior Lecturer at the University of Wales, Aberystwyth, where she lectured on Intellectual Property and International Copyright Laws. She is the author a number of books, including *The Legal Protection of Trade Secrets, Intellectual Property Law and Professional Issues in Software Engineering* and is currently writing a book on copyright exceptions.

Guy Holborn has been Librarian of Lincoln's Inn Library since 1985, having previously held posts at the House of Lords Library and the Institute of Advanced Legal Studies in the University of London. He has regularly lectured on the English legal system on courses for law librarians. His publications include *Butterworths Legal Research Guide* (2nd edn, 2001). He was awarded the Wallace Breem Memorial Award by the British and Irish Association of Law Librarians in 1992.

Richard McCracken is Head of Rights at the Open University. He is responsible for managing the protection of the University's copyright and related rights and trademarks. His department acquires and licenses third party content in course materials across all media, including broadcast programming commissioned from the BBC and independent production companies, printed course texts and co-published textbooks, multimedia and digital media.

Richard speaks widely on copyright and related issues at broadcast, publishing and educational conferences and was co-author with Madeleine Gilbart of the book, *Buying and Clearing Rights: broadcast, print and multimedia* (Blueprint). He has acted as an external reviewer of rights management projects funded under several European Commission funding programmes and was a member of the Higher Education Funding Council/Universities UK working group developing good practice in managing copyright in online higher education.

Gerry Power is from Ireland, and started his career in university libraries in Dublin and Limerick. From 1990 to 1992, he contributed to a human rights documentation project in the Gambia, West Africa, a post sponsored by the Irish Agency for Personal Service Overseas (APSO). Based in London since 1993, he has worked as systems librarian at the NSPCC, and project cataloguer in the Library of the Royal College of Surgeons of England. He has been Access Librarian at Institute for Advanced Legal Studies (IALS) since January 2001, working to promote awareness of IALS collections and services among law schools in the UK.

Heather Rowe specializes in advising in relation to companies in the fields of telecommunications and computers and is a partner in Lovells' Technology, Media and Telecoms Group. She drafts, on a regular basis, turnkey projects in the computer/telecommunications field, outsourcing agreements, agreements relating to hardware and software supply and development, and terms and conditions for a wide range of services in the information technology and telecommunications fields. Heather specializes in all aspects of electronic commerce. Another major part of her practice relates to data protection. She advises extensively on issues of concern such as the restrictions on exporting personal data from within Europe to countries outside.

She was Chairman of the International Chamber of Commerce's International Task Force on Data Protection and Privacy for over ten years, as well as ICC UK's Committee on Computing, Telecommunications and Information Policy. Heather is former Chairman of Committee R, the Technology & E-Commerce Law Committee of the International Bar Association.

Heather published *The Data Protection Act 1998 – a practical guide* for Tolley's Publishing in 2000.

Mark Taylor read physics at Oxford University and undertook the Common Professional Exam and Legal Practice Course at York College of Law. Prior to qualifying as a solicitor, Mark worked for IBM at its UK Scientific Centre in Winchester, as part of a team developing image processing software to assist doctors in the analysis of melanomas. He also worked for IBM in London developing 'intelligent' call centre processing software in C++.

Since qualification as a solicitor, Mark has worked in Lovells' Technology, Media and Telecommunications Group specializing in contentious and non-contentious work in the fields of IT, electronic commerce and data protection.

Mark has co-authored two chapters on security and electronic signatures for a forthcoming Butterworths book on online financial services and last year spoke at Secure IT Europe 2002. He is a member of the International Chamber of Commerce's UK Committee on E-commerce.

Dr Charlotte Waelde, Co-Director, Arts and Humanities Research Board (AHRB) Research Centre for Studies into Intellectual Property and Technology Law, is a senior lecturer within the School of Law at the University of Edinburgh. Her research interests centre around the role of intellectual property law within the digital environment. She has written widely in the field of intellectual property law, and is co-editor of *Law and the Internet: a framework for electronic commerce*. She is currently involved in a number of research projects focusing not only on the ways in which traditional intellectual property laws are being re-shaped in response to developments in technology, but also how those communities affected by the changing nature of both law and technology respond in practice to the challenges. In the field of intellectual property her current research projects include: a wide ranging investigation into the changing nature of the public domain on the internet; a practical examination of the effect of the changes to the law of copyright on the research and education sectors; an investigation of the legal implications of the digitization of archives and images used within the cultural heritage sector, and an analysis of the intersection between intellectual property, competition and human rights. For further details of the work of the AHRB Research Centre see http://www.law.ed.ac.uk/ahrb.

Introduction

Since the first edition of this book in 1999 there have been an increasing number of new laws and regulatory measures that impact directly on the information landscape. There has been new domestic legislation with yet more on the horizon; there have been developments at European and international levels; new cases have come before the courts, adding to our understanding of existing laws. One thing is certain – more developments are on their way.

This organic growth of the law is not surprising. Nearly three centuries ago John Arbuthnot, the Scottish mathematician, scientist and satirist, once observed that 'Law is a bottomless pit.' It is a sentiment that many who may read the collection of essays in this book would no doubt share. While lawyers have become reasonably used to dealing with the constantly expanding corpus of statute and case law which forms the staple of their profession (not to mention other sources of law and regulation), those engaged in many areas of information work now find themselves faced with a similar problem – the need to be aware of the legal and regulatory framework within which they operate and the associated need to maintain some awareness of ongoing key developments. Authors, publishers, software designers, librarians and information managers, academics, freelancers, web designers, website operators, IT consultants, students of librarianship, administrators of computing and information management courses – the potential list is lengthy – all increasingly operate in environments which are heavily regulated by law, and laws which are constantly changing and expanding at that.

This collection, however, is not a legal textbook. It does not purport to be so and that is not its aim. And it is not to be relied upon as such. For those who need a thorough treatment of some of the areas covered directly or indirectly in this book (such as copyright, e-commerce, contracts or data protection) then there are many good and easily accessible legal texts available. For those who have specific problems or issues that need solutions, then, this collection does not seek to provide legal advice or guidance. That is a role for solicitors and barristers. Any reader who feels that they may have a problem – or even the potential for a problem to develop – should seek appropriate legal advice and guidance. Rather, this book, like its predecessor, merely strives to raise awareness and provide an outline of some of the major areas of information work that are increasingly affected by developments in the law. It seeks to highlight the legal basics that now underpin many aspects and areas of work for the increasing number and variety of individuals now engaged in information work and the knowledge industries.

Chapter 1 deals with some legal fundamentals. For example, what are the sources of law? How are the courts that decide disputes structured? Why are the decisions of some courts more important than others? What is the difference between certain areas of law – such as contract and tort? If I actually want to look up the full text of an Act of Parliament, such as the Copyright Designs and Patents Act 1988, how would I go about it? And what kind of pitfalls might I need to be aware of? This first chapter seeks to introduce some key legal basics that are both fascinating and interesting in themselves and which will assist the reader in navigating and understanding the discussions in subsequent chapters.

Although we are all obliged to obey and observe the law, as Chapter 2 suggests this is often not easy. Access to the laws that govern us is a major issue. The best resources for accessing the law tend to be commercial databases. These are expensive and not easily accessible to the vast majority of the public. Although there are several initiatives to make the sources of the law available to the public, these are often incomplete and, again, not easily accessible to all. In addition, there is generally little or no training, advice or guidance open to the public at large in terms of understanding and using legal resources and materials. Neither is it fanciful to assume that many professional information workers are any more legally literate than are many members of the public. This may be becoming an increasing requirement in, and for, our profession, but much still needs to be done in educating information professionals in many spheres about legal basics, legal sources and legal research. Chapter 2 addresses some of the key issues associated with access to legal information such as access, costs, education and training, availability and the needs of some particular groups.

Copyright is a traditional mainstay of information work and no book of this type could be complete without a chapter on the subject. Chapter 3 provides an overview of the fundamentals of copyright. What does copyright protect? What exclusive rights does it confer? How long does it last? What are the exceptions to copyright? Why should we observe copyright? How is copyright infringed? At the time of writing (and indeed for months before it) the law of copyright has been in a state of flux owing to the UK's lengthy process of implementing the changes to copyright law introduced at European Union level. Where possible the main likely changes have been alluded to. In addition, a few other areas of current concern are also addressed – for example, ownership of copyright, digitization and aspects of licensing.

Chapter 4 deals with another area of intellectual property – trade marks. These are of long-standing interest in information work, where recognition and branding have been crucial in many areas. The emergence of the internet has brought a profound focus on trademarks in so far as they have also become intimately related to the use of domain names. This chapter provides a detailed overview of the main aspects of trademark law with many illuminating examples. As organizations and businesses seek to exploit their presences on the internet in new and different ways, this key area of the law will no doubt continue to develop rapidly, and in ways of which all sectors of the information profession will need to be aware.

Patents are dealt with in Chapter 5. Again, this is an area of law that is of historic interest to information professionals. The chapter provides an introduction to the main principles of patent law and to aspects of the patenting process. Since it confers a limited monopoly, a patent can be a particularly powerful and valuable piece of intellectual property, and this chapter provides guidance on many key areas and developments associated with this subject.

Articles in magazines and newspapers in the computing and information press frequently highlight major disputes in the specification and procurement of IT systems. They also point to a growing trend in managing IT systems, services and facilities in different ways, such as by outsourcing or facilities management. Chapter 6 looks briefly at these areas, and at some of the contractual issues involved in IT system procurement and outsourcing contracts. In doing so, it introduces some of the basics of contract law. As a further example of the increasing importance of contractual arrangements in information work, the chapter also highlights some of the contractual and copyright issues associated with authorship and ownership of intellectual property in academic institutions.

Information professionals encounter aspects of contract law in a number of ways but the most common is probably by way of licences and licensing arrangements that are entered into in database, e-journal and other information resource subscriptions. Chapter 7 provides an overview of aspects of the licensing process and the most important licensing terms and conditions. Essential aspects of licensing and licence negotiation are covered, together with pitfalls to be avoided.

Data protection is outlined in Chapter 8, which provides an overall view of the centrepiece of the data protection framework, the Data Protection Act 1998. The chapter outlines the Data Protection Principles, key terms and aspects of the Act, the rights of data subjects under the Act, some of the main offences and the penalties and sanctions for non-compliance. Much delegated legislation now exists under this Act and cases are beginning to emerge in the courts. In addition, high profile incidents are appearing in the newspapers. It is now an area with which all information professionals need to have a basic familiarity.

Criminal activity in the online environment is attracting increasing attention in the media – and increasing attention by legislators at national, supranational and international levels. In addition, new crime enforcement agencies are being established, and there is increasing cross-border co-operation between law enforcement agencies. Chapter 9 reviews the main areas of criminal liability in the online environment by introducing the key UK legislation and discussing the main offences. The chapter looks at the prominent advances during the last five years in legislating against cybercrime, and major developments and improvements in detecting, prosecuting and enforcing criminal laws on the internet.

Chapter 10 explodes the myth that the internet is somehow a law unto itself – an unregulated area of individual, group or corporate activity. Many general laws apply. Newer laws addressing specific issues have been introduced. Key areas of regulation include advertising, liability for content, jurisdictional issues, consumer protection, aspects of online contract formation, etc. Regulation is also apparent in the use and adoption of sectoral codes of practice. This is a complex and rapidly expanding area, and one of key concern for any organization operating a website and providing information and services from it.

The final chapter reviews some of the risks discussed or alluded to throughout the book. It offers some thoughts on managing the risks associated with the online environment. It is not intended to be a comprehensive approach to risk management. It seeks to encourage readers to begin thinking about the risks that may exist in their own organizations or activities, and to develop a strategy to address and manage them – by identifying risks, prioritizing them and controlling them through such initiatives as organizational training and awareness, and workplace IT and internet use policies.

As already suggested, this collection of essays is not intended to be a comprehensive companion or statement of the law on the topics covered in the book. It is compiled with the needs in mind of those who need to know something about the way that areas of the law now greatly influence and impact on information work. It will have succeeded to some degree if it in some measure advances the reader's awareness of the diverse range of legal issues confronting the information profession, or if it stimulates the reader to actively investigate and learn more about areas of particular interest. If the web designer realizes that he or she needs to know a bit more about copyright or data protection then we would count that as a success; if the e-resources librarian in a university or college learns a bit more about licences or contracts then we would count that as a success; or if a colleague working in a small company now understands more about aspects of e-commerce or can discuss areas of legal risk with IT managers and colleagues, then we would count that as a success. This book cannot make legal experts out of information workers. But hopefully it can help information workers in different sectors, roles and contexts to understand a bit more about the legal and regulatory environment in which they work. Staying legal in information work, especially in the online environment, is an ongoing battle. As part of that battle this book is merely an introduction.

Calvin Coolidge, the 30th President of the USA, once remarked that 'I sometimes wish that people would put a little more emphasis upon the observance of the law than they do upon its enforcement.' This is sound advice. An awareness of the law that binds you is the first step in observing that law – or in other words, the first step on the road to staying legal. We hope that this book might be a useful first step.

Chris Armstrong
Laurence W. Bebbington

1

The law and information work: legal fundamentals

Guy Holborn

Introduction

This chapter gives an overview of the legal sources, concepts and topics that information professionals might encounter both in their work and in reading the other parts of this book. The law rests on a vast base of sources, which are added to at an alarming rate every day. It is subject to rapid obsolescence, but in a wholly unpredictable way. If something potentially defamatory was posted on a website, the owner might need to be aware of the possible defence afforded by the Electronic Commerce (EC Directive) Regulations 2002, which only came into force on 21 August 2002. Yet whether the statement was indeed defamatory would rest on legal principles decided by the courts in the 16th century.

The United Kingdom and its jurisdictions

One preliminary matter to clarify for an understanding of the legal system (and also of the scope of this chapter) is how the law applies in the separate constituent parts of the United Kingdom. Subject to the qualification recently arising with regard to Wales, the United Kingdom comprises three separate jurisdictions – England and Wales, Scotland and Northern Ireland – each with a separate system of courts, separate legal professions and, frequently, different substantive law. The Government of Wales Act 1998 gave the new National Assembly of Wales the power to make secondary legislation (explained more fully below), so that the position is altered slightly. It might therefore be said that the UK now has three-and-a-half jurisdictions. But for nearly all legal purposes, England and Wales remains a single jurisdiction, and the expression 'English law' means the law of

England and Wales. The establishment of the Scottish Parliament by the Scotland Act 1998 merely extends Scotland's pre-existing separateness as a jurisdiction. The Scottish legal system has completely distinct historical roots, unlike Northern Ireland, which in most respects is similar to the English system.

Although there are three separate jurisdictions, the Parliament at Westminster can of course legislate for the whole of the United Kingdom, or for any of its constituent parts, and notwithstanding devolution still does. Furthermore, Scotland (in civil, though not criminal matters) and Northern Ireland share with England and Wales a final court of appeal in the form of the House of Lords, and a decision by it on the law of one jurisdiction may have a direct bearing on the law of another. It is thus important to distinguish 'UK law' from 'English law'. Unfortunately there are no hard-and-fast rules that allow one to predict whether the law on any particular subject is going to be the same throughout the UK or not. When using secondary legal sources, such as textbooks or journal articles, one should always bear in mind the provenance of publisher and author. If both hail from England, adopt the default assumption that they are only describing English law. Since this author and publisher are English, apply that assumption to this chapter too.

Sources of law

The primary sources of the law – what constitutes 'the law of the land' – are twofold: legislation on the one hand and the binding decisions of the courts on the other. But also considered in this section are quasi-legislation and non-statutory regulatory materials, secondary sources that describe the law, and international law and its sources. The section concludes with consideration of EU law, which as a source of law falls into a category of its own, being neither conventional domestic law nor conventional international law.

Legislation

Most legal systems distinguish between primary legislation and secondary legislation – that is, legislation made by the legislature and legislation made by the executive. In the UK, for most practical purposes, that boils down to Acts of Parliament on the one hand and Statutory Instruments (SIs) on the other.

Primary legislation

Called either 'Acts' or 'statutes' – the terms are interchangeable – this form of legislation is the result of a bill passing through both Houses of Parliament and receiving royal assent. The Acts that are normally encountered are 'Public General Acts' and are so labelled on the spines of the red, official Stationery Office annual bound volumes that you may see on a library shelf (and so listed on the HMSO website). There is a separate series of Local and Personal Acts, but they are of no practical significance for the matters discussed in this book.

Generally an Act may only be amended or repealed, either expressly or by implication, through another Act (though nowadays such constitutional purity is frequently compromised – some Acts contain express powers permitting them to be amended by SI, but usually only in matters of minor detail). There remain in force, or partly in force, Acts of considerable antiquity. Magna Carta is one, but to take a more everyday illustration, if a librarian were provoked by a troublesome reader into punching him on the nose, then the charge of assault occasioning actual bodily harm would be made under the Offences Against the Person Act, which dates from 1861. The same Act might even be invoked to cover the modern phenomenon of psychiatric injury resulting from harassment by offensive e-mails.

If there is a need to refer to the text of an Act, it is of the greatest importance to be aware of three considerations. First, is the Act still, wholly or partly, in force? The free availability of all Acts from 1988 to date on the HMSO website has of course been a welcome innovation, but seen there is simply the text as it was orig-inally enacted. Most lawyers use the commercially published *Halsbury's Statutes* (or its electronic equivalent *Legislation Direct*), which prints the text of statutes in force as amended, with an updating mechanism. For those without access to such a source, the problem will be greatly alleviated when the official Statute Law Database, which will provide text as amended, goes live – free access to the gen-eral public is promised.

Secondly, is the Act yet in force? Few Acts come into force immediately on being passed. Look for a commencement section at the end of the Act, before any schedules. If there is none, then the Act indeed came into force on the date it was passed (printed at its head). Otherwise the commencement section will either give a date or say that it is to be on a day to be appointed. In the latter case, a com-mencement order (or often a succession of commencement orders) in the form of an SI will in due course be made by the relevant minister. It is not unknown for several years to pass before an Act is brought fully into force.

There is also an important inter-relationship between the two points discussed above. Even if it is known that an Act has recently been repealed by a new Act, that is not the end of the story. It needs to be established whether the repealing Act has itself been commenced – until it is, the old Act remains in force. It will be seen that unless one is entirely confident that what is being read has not been amended or repealed, and has been commenced, it would make sense to seek the advice of a friendly law librarian.

The third point is usually more straightforward. What is the geographical extent of the Act? Does it apply to England, Wales, Scotland or Northern Ireland? Again look for an extent section at the end of the Act. If the Act is silent, it applies to the whole of the UK; otherwise its extent will be stated.

Secondary legislation

Although 'secondary' legislation is so labelled in contradistinction to 'primary' legislation, this form of legislation may also be referred to as 'subordinate' or 'subsidiary' or 'delegated' legislation, and it is perhaps the last of these terms that most accurately reflects its nature. An Act may delegate to a person or body other than Parliament a power to make further legislation. That person is usually, but not necessarily, a minister (the 'Secretary of State'). The important point is that the legislation can only be made strictly within the terms of the enabling power in the Act – otherwise, in contrast to an Act, its validity can be challenged in the courts.

Although delegated legislation may bear a variety of labels, such as 'rules', 'orders', 'regulations', 'schemes', etc., the generic form of publication is 'Statutory Instrument' (SI). As with an Act, one needs to know whether an SI has been amended or revoked (SIs are 'revoked' rather than 'repealed'). On the other hand, there is no need to worry about commencement – this is stated on their face.

Since 1999, Scotland has had its own series of Scottish Statutory Instruments (SSIs) – though a UK SI may apply to Scotland. The SIs made by the Welsh Assembly, on the other hand, are published in the main UK series, though readily discernible by being in Welsh as well as in English. The Welsh Assembly, unlike the Scottish Parliament, cannot make its own primary legislation, so all of its legislation must derive from some enabling power in a Westminster statute.

Quasi-legislation and other regulatory materials

Quasi-legislation refers to material that does not have the force of law in the same way that an Act or SI does, but nonetheless may have legal consequences. The clearest illustration is statutory codes of practice. Take as an everyday example the Highway Code, which is made under the Road Traffic Act 1988 and has to be laid before Parliament. A breach of its terms is not a criminal offence, nor does it directly give rise to any civil liability, but under Section 38 of the Act such a breach may be relied upon as evidence – of, say, negligence in a civil case. Other examples of quasi-legislation are departmental circulars, which in certain fields, such as local government, assume as much importance as legislation proper, and may have persuasive, if not legal, force in the courts if an issue on the performance of a statutory duty were to arise. Another good illustration is the guidance issued by the Commissioner under the Data Protection Act 1998, which is now voluminous and its extent exceeds the legislation itself. The statutory provisions in s. 51 of the Data Protection Act 1998 simply enjoin the Commissioner (i.e. the Information Commissioner, as the office has been called since the Freedom of Information Act 2000 – originally 'Data Protection Registrar' under the 1984 Act, and then 'Data Protection Commissioner' under the 1998 Act) to 'promote the following of good practice by data controllers', 'to promote the observance of the requirements of this Act' and 'to prepare and disseminate to such persons as he considers appropriate codes of practice for guidance as to good practice.' But though the Commissioner's materials are performing, legally, no more than those functions, it would clearly be unwise for anyone to ignore them if they are concerned that an enforcement notice might land on their doorstep. Likewise, there is a plethora of materials emanating from governmental or non-governmental bodies which may have relevance in legal proceedings, particularly where questions of standards or reasonableness are in issue.

Case law

Although legislation progressively encroaches, so that few areas of law are untouched by it, there remain substantial parts of the law governed by the principles laid down over the centuries by the courts (the 'common law' in one of its senses), notably the law of contract and tort. And even in criminal law there are still some common law offences, murder being the most prominent. Even where the common law has been supplanted by legislation, the role of the judges has not diminished since they have to interpret it. So most legal issues have to be resolved by looking at both legislation and case law.

The decisions of the courts act as a source of law through the doctrine of precedent. This dictates that, as a matter of fairness and consistency, like cases should be decided alike, and functions through the hierarchical structure of the courts so that the decisions of the higher courts are binding on the lower courts. It is simply enough stated, but two conceptual difficulties arise. The first is distinguishing fact from law. Most cases create no new law but simply apply existing law to the particular facts. The second difficulty, if a case does create law, is analysing what precise legal principle it does stand for – in technical language, finding the *ratio*. This difficulty is all the more acute in appellate cases where more than one judge gives reasons.

When using a case it is of course important to know which court gave the decision in order to assess its precedent value. For this reason, among others, the court structure is explained below. A decision of the County Court has little precedent value. A decision of the House of Lords, on the other hand, is binding on all other courts. The law created by the decision can only be changed by legislation, a contrary ruling by the European Court of Justice (ECJ) on a point of EU law, or by the House of Lords itself, in a later case, overruling its earlier decision, which is very rare.

One characteristic of case law, which distinguishes it from legislation as a source of law, may be apparent: whereas Parliament may change the law at any time by amending or repealing legislation if it chooses to do so, changes in the common law only arise through the random exigencies of litigation.

Secondary sources

In England, textbooks and other secondary sources are not a formal source of law, but nonetheless have relevance in the courts. As well as famous old works, such as *Blackstone's Commentaries* from the 18th century, modern writings by highly regarded authors, whether academics or practitioners, may be, and frequently are, cited in court as persuasive sources. A typical example will be found in the recent case concerning photocopying of newspaper cuttings, *Newspaper Licensing Agency Ltd v. Marks and Spencer plc*, where in the Court of Appeal (the case of course went on to the House of Lords), Mance LJ, wrestling with the meaning of 'typographical arrangement', says, 'I agree with the way in which *Copinger & Skone James on Copyright*, 14th ed (1999) . . . put the matter' ([2001] Ch. 257 at 284) and proceeds to quote from it.

International law and its sources

International law bears heavily on some of the matters discussed in this book. It is of two kinds. The first is public international law, which is the law governing the legal relations between *states* (or international organizations), and is distinct from internal domestic (municipal) law. Public international law thus embraces such topics as recognition of states, the law of war, treaty-making and diplomatic immunity. That is not to say it cannot relate to individuals, as does the international law on asylum or human rights or war crimes; but such protection of individuals, unless also given effect to in domestic law, operates only at the international level through international courts and tribunals.

Secondly there is private international law, which is perhaps better described by its alternative name, the 'conflict of laws', that is the law that applies when there is a foreign element. For example, the English subsidiary of a US computer firm is contracted to install a system in Germany – if there is a dispute, does English law, US law or German law apply? Each jurisdiction will have as part of its own domestic law rules for resolving conflicts of laws, but it is clearly helpful if the rules can be harmonized, and so there are a number international regimes to achieve this. They will usually be given effect by means of agreements between states, which are thus in the sphere of public international law, though their subject matter is private international law. It will be appreciated that electronic commerce and the internet have thrown up some quite acute problems in the field of the conflict of laws. The recent decision of the High Court of Australia (its final court of appeal) in *Dow Jones Inc v. Gutnick* [2002] HCA 56 is an illustration. Dow Jones had placed an article allegedly defaming Mr Gutnick, an Australian, on their website, which had a small number of Australian subscribers. It was held that the case should be heard in Victoria according to the laws of Australia, since that was the place of publication, and not, as Dow Jones contended, in New Jersey, where the server was located – an outcome with far-reaching implications for online publishers. If widely adopted, such a solution would mean that online providers have to be aware of the law of defamation and potential liability, not only in their own country, but also anywhere from Afghanistan to Zimbabwe. On the other hand, were the Dow Jones contention to be adopted, the danger would be the creation of 'server havens' like tax havens; an unscrupulous provider could avoid liability by the simple expedient of physically removing its server to a defamation-friendly jurisdiction. It should be further understood that in cross-border litigation, deciding the forum and applicable law is only one side of the coin; the other is the recognition and enforcement of foreign judgments. In a *Gutnick*-type situation, while liability and the amount of any damages may be decided according to Australian law, if a party in the position of Dow Jones had no assets in Australia and was unwilling to pay the damages, then the procedures and sanctions to make them do so would be a matter of US law.

The two most obvious sources of public international law are treaties, which equate with legislation in domestic law, and the case law of international courts and tribunals, such as the International Court of Justice at The Hague. But customary law and the writings of jurists are also recognized as sources of law.

Treaties may be bilateral, between just two states, or multilateral, between many states. They come with a bewildering variety of labels that are not generally of legal significance. 'Convention' is perhaps the most common for a multilateral treaty. A 'protocol' is most commonly used for an additional treaty amending a principal treaty. Typically, multilateral treaties come into effect in a three-stage process. First, representatives of each state, usually at the conclusion of an international conference (the location of which often gives it its name), will *sign* the treaty. The treaty is then concluded, but not binding. Secondly the treaty has to be *ratified* by each state, signalling consent to be bound. In the UK, ratification is not a parliamentary power, so is in effect exercised by ministers. There may be an interval of years between signing and ratification. Thirdly, in analogous fashion to the commencement provisions in an Act, the treaty may have to enter into force. This will depend on its terms, for example, after a certain number of parties have ratified. All treaties to which the UK is a party are published as Command Papers, usually twice: first on signing, then in the official UK Treaty Series on ratification.

Ratification and entry into force may not be the end of the story. The constitutional position in the UK (it is different in some other jurisdictions) is that a treaty, even if binding at the international level, has no direct effect, enforceable by the English courts, until it is incorporated into domestic law by means of an Act or SI. The European Convention on Human Rights is of course a famous example. Before the Human Rights Act 1998, redress was only available at Strasbourg. A more mundane example is the Contracts (Applicable Law) Act 1990, a conflict of laws measure, which incorporated the 1980 Rome Convention on the Law Applicable to Contractual Obligations. This example also illustrates the typical life cycle of a treaty. While it was concluded in 1980, the UK was not originally a signatory but signed in 1981. The Convention only entered into force three months after the seventh ratification was received, which was not until the UK's ratification in January 1991. In anticipation of ratification the 1990 Act was passed (but not commenced). On ratification an SI could be made commencing the Act in April 1991, on the same date that the Convention entered into force.

EU law

There were originally three 'European Communities' (in the plural): the European Economic Community (EEC or 'Common Market'), the European Coal and Steel Community (ECSC) and the European Atomic Energy Community (Euratom). The ECSC treaty expired on 23 July 2002, so now there are only two. The Maastricht Treaty of 1992 created the 'European Union', which extended European co-operation beyond the purely economic sphere. The Maastricht Treaty also renamed the EEC as simply the 'European Community' (EC), in the singular. The European Union is said to comprise three 'pillars': (1) the European Communities (EC, Euratom and, before 2002, ECSC); (2) common foreign and security policy; and (3) justice and home affairs. The *law* derives from the first pillar, and the roles of the Commission, the European Parliament and the ECJ relate almost exclusively to it. So it is not incorrect to refer to EC law rather than EU law. In so far as there is non-EC EU law, which is the province of the Council of the European Union, it only has the status of other conventional public international law, as discussed above. The Treaty of Amsterdam in 1997 transferred some matters relating to asylum and to private international law from pillar (3) to pillar (1), bringing them within EC law. The Treaty of Amsterdam, on a more pragmatic level, renumbered the articles of the original Treaty of Rome (and the Maastricht Treaty); but old habits die hard, so there has been a tendency to cite both old and new, for example, Art. 234 (ex Art. 177).

The European Parliament, which was first directly elected in 1979, has seen its powers to legislate, rather than merely be consulted on legislation, steadily increased by the treaties of Maastricht, Amsterdam and most recently Nice (2001). Most legislation is now made with the Parliament having a veto, but there remain areas where the Council can legislate on its own, as indeed occasionally can the Commission, whose role is otherwise merely to initiate legislative proposals (and provide the 'civil service' for the EC).

The sources of EU law are first the treaties establishing the communities and the Union, the subsequent amending treaties, and the treaties of accession of additional member states. Under the normal principles of public international law described above, the treaties required incorporation into UK domestic law. However, the novel feature of the European Communities Act 1972 was that it gave effect to all *future* obligations under Community law *without further enactment*. Thus the second source of EU law, secondary legislation made at Brussels, forms part of UK law, as does the third source, the decisions of the ECJ at Luxembourg.

Secondary legislation takes three forms. First are Directives. These require member states to enact their own legislation to give effect to them. In the UK this is almost invariably in the form of an SI, though implementation of major Directives is occasionally by means of an Act, as was the case with the Data Protection Act 1998. A deadline for implementation is set in the Directive. Failure to meet the deadline (as recently occurred with implementation of the Copyright Directive in the UK) not merely incurs the wrath of the European Commission, but may ultimately give the Directive direct effect. Secondly, there are Regulations. These have direct effect without further ado. In practice, however, adjustments in domestic legislation may be required, in matters such as procedure or enforcement, to accommodate a Regulation. So quite a number of SIs are made, not 'implementing' in the strict sense, but in connection with EU Regulations. Thirdly, there are Decisions, which are addressed to particular member states or particular undertakings. If they are directed to the UK an SI will usually be required.

The ECJ, broadly speaking, hears two types of case. One is disputes between member states or actions brought by the Commission against member states. The other is 'preliminary rulings', where a court in a member state refers a point of EU law – the case then returns to the court of origin for a decision in light of the ruling. As well as the ECJ itself, there has been since 1989 the Court of First Instance (CFI), with a limited jurisdiction (mostly certain competition cases), but which is to be enlarged following the 2001 Nice Treaty, which will also create a third tier of court, a 'judicial panel'.

The structure of the courts

The watershed creating the modern court structure was the Judicature Acts 1873–5, which abolished the four separate superior courts which had been in place for centuries (Common Pleas, King's Bench, Exchequer and Chancery), and replaced them with a single High Court, organized in Divisions; the Court of Appeal was also newly created by the 1873–5 Acts.

Today the High Court comprises three Divisions, Queen's Bench, Chancery and Family, which sit principally in the Royal Courts of Justice in the Strand, but also in the major provincial cities, such as Manchester, Leeds and Cardiff. Although there are minor differences in procedure between them, the three Divisions are distinguished simply by the subject matter of the cases they hear. The Queen's Bench Division (QBD) hears most ordinary civil claims involving tort, such as personal injury and other negligence actions, and contract, and is the largest in terms of business, and accordingly has the most judges – about 100. It also has an entirely separate and important role in the guise of what is now called the Administrative Court, which is described more fully below. The Chancery Division hears cases involving areas that were traditionally the province of the Court of Chancery, such as land, wills and trusts, but nowadays much else besides, including intellectual property, company and tax cases. The role of the Family Division is self-explanatory. Cases in the High Court are heard by a single judge without (except in libel) a jury.

The separate role of the QBD, other than hearing ordinary first instance cases, is to supervise inferior bodies and tribunals in their exercise of their powers. This supervisory jurisdiction is principally exercised today by means of the procedure called judicial review. The decisions of any inferior court, tribunal or other decision-making public body, or person – notably ministers – may be challenged in this way. Judicial review is not an appeal – the merits of the case, in theory at any rate, are not open to new enquiry – but is an investigation of the propriety of the decision-making process. That process may be impugned on three grounds. First is illegality, that is the decision-maker acted beyond their powers, which will usually be statutory. The second ground is unfairness, that is some procedural irregularity or breach of natural justice, such as not permitting applicants to put their case properly or bias. Lastly is irrationality – a decision was reached that no properly informed decision-maker could rationally reach. This last ground, also known as *Wednesbury* unreasonableness after a 1948 case of that name, is sometimes seen as a review of the merits of the decision by the back door. The case arising from certain public libraries refusing to stock *The Times* and other News International titles during the Wapping dispute, *R. v. Ealing London Borough Council, ex parte Times Newspapers Ltd* (1986) 85 LGR 316, is a typical illustration of judicial review. The decision to ban the publications was outside the local authorities' powers under s. 7 of the Public Libraries and Museums Act 1964, and thus illegal. Furthermore, no rational local authority could have thought that such a ban could be in discharge of their duty to service libraries. Judicial review cases are heard by what was called, and technically still is called, a Divisional Court of the QBD. A Divisional Court is the court sitting with more than one judge – either two or three – at least one of whom will be a Court of Appeal judge. The Divisional Court also hears some other categories of case apart from judicial review, such as appeals on points of law from magistrates' courts. The area of law dealt with by the Divisional Court, which is generally described as public law or administrative law (on which see further below), has in recent years assumed enormous importance because the decisions challenged before it are most frequently those of ministers. As a result of a recent review, the Divisional Court has been officially, though not statutorily, relabelled the Administrative Court.

Within the QBD, in its ordinary first instance capacity, and in the Chancery Division are a number of specialist courts. These do not have any separate status, but are simply a convenient way of arranging the listing of cases before a judge with the requisite specialist knowledge. The QBD has a Commercial Court and an Admiralty Court, and the Chancery Division has a Companies Court and a Patents Court.

Another specialist court is the Technology and Construction Court. Again this is not separate from the High Court as such and has no statutory status, but is tantamount to another Division. It has its origins in what was called Official Referees' business. Any claim brought in the QBD or Chancery Division could be so assigned if it involved lengthy investigation of technical documentation or scientific evidence. The bulk of Official Referees' business came from building and construction disputes, but with an increasing number of disputes involving information technology, such as contracts for the installation of computer systems, coming before it, it was renamed as the Technology and Construction Court in 1998 and its procedures revamped. Though having High Court status, and headed by a High Court judge, its seven other full-time judges are Circuit Judges.

Beneath the High Court in the civil court structure are the County Courts, created in 1846. Though local, they are misnamed since they are not county-specific – there are now about 220 in England and Wales. With certain exceptions, it is the claimant's option whether to start proceedings in the County Court or in the High Court. However, there are a number of disincentives, particular on costs, against bringing an inappropriate case in the High Court. Thus the bulk of cases, unless they involve large sums or complex matters, are brought in the County Court. Since 1998 there has also been a common procedural code, the Civil Procedure Rules (CPR), which replaced the separate County Court Rules and the Supreme Court Rules. There is also a specialist Patents Court at County Court level – currently the Central London County Court is so designated.

Whether a case starts in the County Court or High Court, appeal may be made to the Court of Appeal (Civil Division), which sits in panels of two or three judges. Appeals may only now be brought with permission – either from the judge hearing the original case or from a Court of Appeal judge. A decision of the Court of Appeal may in turn be appealed to the House of Lords – a third bite of the cherry. But permission is again required, and is naturally only rarely granted – while the Court of Appeal hears several thousand appeals each year, the House of Lords has only about 80 cases. The Law Lords usually sit in panels of five.

So far the courts with civil jurisdiction have been described. The magistrates' courts also have some civil jurisdiction, particularly in family matters and in licensing, but are otherwise the first rung in the ladder of the criminal courts. Offences triable only in the magistrates' courts are said to be 'summary offences'. More serious offences which are triable only in the Crown Court are said to be 'indictable offences', that is they are tried before a judge and jury. The Crown Court also hears appeals from the magistrates' courts. Certain offences, of which theft is perhaps the most common, may be tried either in a magistrates' court or in the Crown Court at the option of the defendant, and are said to be 'either-way' offences. Appeals from the Crown Court, against either conviction or sentence, go to the Court of Appeal (Criminal Division), and then to the House of Lords.

Tribunals

Alongside the court system is a plethora of tribunals. They vary greatly in their powers and procedures. Some, at one end of the spectrum, for example, the Employment Appeal Tribunal, are hardly distinguishable from courts of law proper. Others operate much more informally, may be limited to determining limited factual issues, may only comprise lay persons, and may not permit (at any rate publicly funded) legal representation. There may be a statutory right of appeal from the decisions of a tribunal to a higher tribunal or to a court. On the other hand, the decisions of many tribunals can only be challenged by way of judicial review. The ideal characteristics of tribunals, which distinguish them from courts of law, were classically identified in the *Franks Report on Tribunals* of 1957 as cheapness, accessibility to the parties, speedy dispute resolution, absence of the cost and technicalities of the court system, and the possibility of decisions being made by those with expert knowledge.

One tribunal worth mentioning specifically in the context of this book is the Copyright Tribunal, set up under the Copyright, Designs and Patents Act 1988 (as the successor to the Performing Rights Tribunal, which dated from the Copyright Act 1956) to regulate the granting of licences by licensing bodies. It has of course received particular prominence as a result of the case brought before it of *Universities UK Ltd v. Copyright Licensing Agency Ltd* [2002] EMLR 35. In terms of cost and complexity, the case illustrates that the tribunal, like others, does not necessarily live up to all of Franks's ideals – both sides were represented by leading city law firms and QCs.

Some legal concepts and topics
Civil law and criminal law

This basic distinction manifests itself in a number of ways. A civil claim results in a remedy, such as the payment of damages by way of compensation being granted to one party against the other. A criminal prosecution is instigated by the state and results in the punishment of the offender, but not (directly) compensation to the victim. The rules of evidence differ between a civil case and a criminal case, being more stringent in the latter, for example, as to the admissibility of hearsay evidence. The prosecution must prove their case to a jury beyond reasonable doubt, whereas a claimant in a civil case needs merely to convince a judge on the balance of probabilities. On a practical level, the terminology differs in the civil and criminal context, so that, for example, 'sue' in a civil case equates to 'prosecute' in a criminal one.

There are, of course, some qualifications. For example, an individual may bring a private prosecution instead of the Crown, where the legislation creating the offence permits it (as does, for example, the Copyright, Designs and Patents Act 1988 – a power not infrequently exercised). Some wrongs may give rise to civil liability and at the same time amount to the commission of a criminal offence. Infringement of copyright is again an example. A copyright holder may sue in the civil courts for damages or an injunction, but may consider it more effective (for example, if the alleged infringer is impecunious, or wider deterrence is sought) to bring a criminal prosecution. And an acquittal does not preclude also bringing a civil action, bearing in mind the differences in the standard of proof.

Public law and private law

While public law may be regarded as including criminal law, it more usually describes the civil law as it applies to the state and its emanations; 'constitutional and administrative law' is a synonym. The distinction between public law and private law assumes most importance in the context of judicial review. Applicants aggrieved by a decision of, say, a government department do not necessarily want, or would not necessarily be entitled to, damages – they would want the decision quashed. Yet the ambit of judicial review is strictly limited. For one thing there are very strict time limits for starting proceedings – six months, as opposed to six years for most ordinary civil actions. Furthermore, the application must be against a 'public' body, or a body that in the circumstances is exercising public duties. The point has been much litigated. A recent illustration is *R. v. British Standards Institution, ex parte Dorgard* [2001] ACD 86. The applicant made fire-door release mechanisms, and submitted them to the BSI for testing. The BSI erroneously issued a certificate to the effect that they complied with the relevant standard when they did not. When the applicant refused to return the certificate and stop using it for promotional purposes, the BSI circulated a letter to Chief Fire Officers. The applicant sought judicial review of the BSI's refusal to withdraw the letter. It was held that, while the BSI did exercise some public duties and so might in some circumstances be amenable to judicial review (notwithstanding that it is non-governmental company), the dispute was really about a private commercial transaction (the contract with BSI to have the product tested). The applicant thus failed to qualify for judicial review, a 'public law remedy', and would only have recourse to 'private law remedies', such as damages or an injunction, if they could show there had been a breach of contract, or if a tort (in this case malicious falsehood) had been committed.

Common law

This is a particularly troublesome expression to the lay person, since it means different things to lawyers in different contexts. It has (at least) four senses, each based on a contradistinction. Historically – going back to the Norman Conquest and the establishment of the English legal system as we know it – it was in contradistinction to 'local law'. The imposition of the King's law common to the whole realm was the essence. In turn, 'common law' became shorthand for the English legal system in general, and for the family of legal systems in other parts of the English-speaking world that followed it. In this sense it is used in contradistinction to 'civil law', which is the term used, in this context, to describe the Roman-based legal systems of the European continent. Thirdly, it is used in contradistinction to statute law, that is the decisions of the courts.

The fourth sense is the most technical to explain; this is when it is used in contradistinction to 'equity'. In origin, equity carried the same meaning as in ordinary usage, namely fairness. The King might personally grant relief to a petitioner where a decision of the ordinary courts, which became hidebound by procedural restrictions, had resulted in some harshness. The King in due course delegated this role to his Lord Chancellor, and in turn this developed into the jurisdiction exercised by the Court of Chancery, which became a court like any other. 'Equity' thus became simply the term for those parts of the law, both substantive and procedural, that were administered by the Court of Chancery. Until the Judicature Acts of 1873–5, when common law and equity were 'fused', the

law in many areas could thus be likened to playing rugby with Union rules and
League rules being both applicable at the same time. And even today there are
tricky corners of the law where differences in doctrinal origin can lead to competing solutions depending on whether the roots are taken from the common law or
from equity. An illustration is breach of confidence. There may be a contractual
duty not to disclose confidential information, and even where there is not an
express term (for example, in a contract of employment) the courts may readily
imply one. The obligation is then said to arise 'at law'. But in the absence of a
contract the right to confidentiality may still be imposed 'in equity'; confidence
has classically been described as the 'cousin of trust', and the trust is the foremost
creation of the Court of Chancery and equity.

Contract and tort

These are the two main species of civil liability. The nature of a contract is a
promise that is legally binding, whereas tort encompasses those civil wrongs
which are actionable even in the absence of any contractual relationship. The tort
of negligence is the most significant. At its most general it is the failure to exercise
care so as to cause foreseeable harm to others. Actions for personal injuries caused
in road traffic accidents are perhaps the most numerous to come before the
courts. But an action for negligence will lie in an enormous range of other circumstances, provided that the result was injury to the person or physical damage
to property. If the injured party is just out of pocket, suffering what is called 'pure
economic loss', there is no redress to be had under this tort (subject, as usual, to
controversial exceptions). Other torts include defamation, trespass, nuisance,
deceit, breach of statutory duty, as well as a whole range of 'specialized' torts such
as malicious prosecution.

Many contracts will be in writing and signed, but with a few exceptions (for
example, assignment of copyright) that is not a legal requirement (notwithstanding the Samuel Goldwyn quip that 'an oral contract is not worth the paper it is
written on'). One fundamental of the law of contract (conventionally, at any rate
– there have been recent statutory modifications) is that any cause of action arising from a breach of contract can only be brought by a party to the contract. To
take the paradigm case, if an individual bought faulty goods, he or she might sue
the retailer for a breach of the contract for the sale of the goods, but could not sue
the manufacturer (who might have a deeper pocket than the retailer) *in contract*,
simply because they were not party to the contract of sale. However, if the faulty
goods caused injury or damaged property, an action against the manufacturer
might be possible, but in tort. From this example, it will seen that if an individual
is injured a cause of action against the retailer in both contract and tort could
arise. Such concurrent liability is quite common, and might apply, for example, to

the liability of a computer consultant who caused damage to a library system (though whether mere data loss would amount to property damage might keep the lawyers arguing). But there are some significant differences between contract and tort, even when the same facts may give rise to both. One is the remedy available. In contract, an order to perform the contract, as opposed to awarding monetary damages, may be made; and only in tort are exemplary damages available. Another is any defence available – for example, contributory negligence, where the winning side was partly at fault – which is not generally applicable to breach of contract. And yet another is the limitation period for bringing proceedings: though the standard period in both contract and tort is the same, in contract time begins to run when the *breach* occurs, even if the resulting damage only arises later, whereas in tort it begins only when the damage occurs.

Conclusion

It is clear why lawyers can earn a living. The law *is* complex in its structure and terminology. Reading this chapter is obviously not a short cut for seeking legal advice. Furthermore, an in-depth understanding of some of the topics covered in this book, such as intellectual property, cross-border rights and EU law, is only within the competence of relatively few specialist lawyers. So legal advice must always be sought from an appropriate source. But having said that, there is no reason why information professionals, with the little demystification that this chapter has sought to provide, cannot have an intelligent grasp of the legal matters that impinge on their work – their work is likely to be more productive and more interesting, with such an understanding.

Further reading

Berlins, M. and Dyer, C. (2000) *The Law Machine*, 5th edn, Penguin.

Clinch, P. (2000) *Legal Information: what it is and where to find it*, 2nd edn, Aslib.

Darbyshire, P. (2001) *Eddey & Darbyshire on the English Legal System*, 7th edn, Sweet & Maxwell.

Harris, P. (2002) *Introduction to Law*, 6th edn, Butterworths.

Holborn, G. (2001) *Butterworths Legal Research Guide*, 2nd edn, Butterworths.

2

Public access to legal information

Gerry Power

Introduction

This chapter concerns public access to legal materials – in other words, how ordinary people with no legal training are aware of, and get hold of, primary and secondary legal materials to meet their information needs. Primary and secondary materials include current legislation, reports of decisions of the courts and materials which explain or comment upon these, such as journal articles, leaflets or guidance. This chapter focuses upon certain groups of people, such as public library users, school children and prisoners, because it was possible to discuss and research these. It would be equally appropriate here to discuss people with disabilities, carers, those on low income, young offenders, etc., but this would have extended the chapter too much.

There has been some popularization of the law in mass media, and the body of legal information has certain overlaps with this consumer-oriented information, which may suggest another approach. However, it should be noted that the Consumers' Association has collaborated with the Community Legal Service to produce a series of leaflets,[1] available to all through community outlets or by post.

The following pages first explore the context of the changing legal landscape since 2000. In so doing they offer a glimpse of the big picture and how this impinges on end-users. The next section considers some of the salient newer services and offers an assessment of these to help identify some elements of good practice in providing legal information to the public. The final section – on libraries, schools and prisons – looks at some of the challenges facing these services in dealing with legal information. This is not an exhaustive survey, but rather a series of snapshots, and thanks are due to the librarians who were interviewed, for their time and thoughts.

Image, language and interpretation

One of the traditional images of the lawyer sees him or her seated comfortably at a desk in a nicely furnished office. A nice lamp sheds a studious light. Elegantly bound and expensive-looking volumes, reports and legislation, perhaps, form a backdrop which signifies the learned profession. The atmosphere is professional, studious, but rather remote. Remote, especially, if we try to deconstruct the image a little and get our hands on some of those volumes. Firstly, they are very expensive! As anybody who has ever purchased some books for library collections knows, law books do not come cheap. Secondly, will a non-lawyer with some of those fine volumes be able to understand what is printed in them? Is it possible to gain a sufficient understanding, or must it be left to our learned friend? The dilemma is that members of the public are supposed to know the law, and ignorance of the law is no excuse, as the legal maxim goes. An interesting quotation comes from Cicero:

> It is ignorance of the law rather than knowledge of it that leads to litigation.[2]

Such words are well worth remembering in our new millennium of supposedly enhanced access.

But readers of this volume are trained as information professionals, not as lawyers. Librarians and information professionals follow CILIP's code of practice in working for our users. They do their utmost to facilitate the flow of information and ideas, and to promote free and equal access to them, as much as possible. On the other hand, librarians and information professionals must be very careful in dealing with litigants in person, because their expertise lies in finding legal information, not in interpreting that information. Providing legal materials to lay people, be they litigants or consumers or public library users, calls for caution and due diligence. Users need to be informed that they should know if a piece of legislation is in force, if they have the updated version, and if any subsidiary legislation also applies. If they are looking for case law, it must be pointed out that decisions as reported can have direct and indirect histories.

Librarians are increasingly involved in instructing users in how to use new technologies to help themselves to information. Librarians are involved in developing content for, and adding value to, web services. Increasingly, librarians and information professionals in academe and in public libraries develop these roles, and this will inevitably mean developing a more acute knowledge of legal sources. It is necessary to review our training and keep our skills and knowledge up to date.

The context

The new millennium has brought new resources and new visions for the delivery of legal services and legal information to ordinary people. Public access to legal information has been enhanced by new initiatives from governments and parliaments, as well as from the voluntary and educational sectors, and from the legal profession. There is much talk of modernization, transparency, access to justice for all, and user-friendliness. But are all these visions and new resources permeating down to people in their daily lives, to help them solve problems and to know the legal system better? Or are they still the preserve of the professionals and those in the know, with little relevance yet to most people's lives? How well are libraries and information services coping in this new landscape? Do librarians and information professionals have the skills and awareness to help members of the public, and are their services seen by users to be attractive and worthwhile? Before answering these questions it is necessary to consider the context.

In 2001, the Irish Attorney General, Michael McDowell, spoke very favourably of the librarian's role in elucidating the law for the public.[3] He reviewed various measures taken by his Office to promote clarity of, and access to, the law:

- a statute law restatement bill to help towards the annual consolidation of Irish statues
- a CD-ROM project to document pre-1920s statutes
- the possibility of making the electronic version the authoritative version.

In his vision, the electronic agenda for government is a necessity and not an option. Smaller jurisdictions like Ireland need to embrace this kind of change to keep up with international competition and the imperatives of e-commerce.

At another meeting in 2001, Michael Wills MP, Parliamentary Secretary at the Lord Chancellor's Department (LCD), spoke[4] of the importance of the electronic agenda for the UK government, and of opening up access for the public. He outlined the Lord Chancellor's Department's strategy to modernize the justice system. It is a vision which encourages increased awareness of legal rights and responsibilities, as part of lifelong learning.[5] It seeks to ensure that citizens can reap the benefits which the law confers, and encourages the avoidance of disputes, or if they happen it encourages their early resolution, with the most appropriate forms of dispute resolution.

Another landmark change in public access to information was, of course, the implementation of the Freedom of Information Act 2000 (FOI, 2000). Freedom of information is recognized as a key professional issue by CILIP, the Chartered Institute of Library and Information Professionals. CILIP values freedom of information as a core responsibility for its members, and believes that its members have the skills to help deliver it. CILIP's main concerns, in its response to the government on freedom of information,[6] were:

1 *Information management*: do public bodies have the necessary skills and training to store and retrieve information and provide it to the public?
2 *Equality of access*: charging for access will not guarantee equality of access, as better-off citizens can afford to pay more.

By 2005, public bodies need to have issued a publication scheme or guide to the information they hold, and from 2005 they will need to supply information to members of the public on request. Some categories of information are exempt and need not be released.

The Lord Chancellor sees the new freedom of information legislation as ushering in a new era of the openness of public administration. However, there is no room for complacency for the information profession, and we need to monitor the implementation very closely. To quote from a recent journal article[7] on the subject:

> Librarians are in the front line as facilitators who provide access to both existing official publications and the range of information that should become available under FOI. It is vital to the health of democracy that they assist citizens in holding governments to account for their actions and decisions – after all, the price of liberty is eternal vigilance.

Many librarians will be familiar with the UKOnline and HMSO websites. Now both the Scottish Parliament[8] and the Welsh Assembly[9] offer websites containing many parliamentary documents, current and archived, available for everyone. Documents and FAQs on the Human Rights Act 1998 are also available, from both official and voluntary organizations. (Home Office, LCD, Liberty). The commencement of this Act, in October 2000, was seen by many as a landmark legal event.

The year 2000 also saw the introduction of a new legal aid regime, with the creation of the Community Legal Service (CLS – discussed in more detail in the next section on new services). Many different types of community organization, including public libraries and Citizens Advice Bureaux, can supply basic legal information to their users under the CLS scheme, and can apply for the

CLS quality mark as an information provider. On 25 October 2000, the Lord Chancellor awarded the CLS quality mark (information level) to the ten library services in the east of England, at an event in Hethersett Library, outside Norwich.[10] The event underlined the importance of libraries in improving people's access to legal information and help.

Using new technologies, to help in service and information delivery, is not only a concern of government, but has been discussed at inter-governmental level also. The Council of Europe issued recommendations[11] in 2001 on the delivery of court and other legal services to the citizen through the use of new technologies.

The Council considers new technology as a tool of justice necessary for good democracy, and highlights the importance of facilitating access to legal information. Better communication with the courts and other legal agencies enables people to have better participation in their community and national life. The Council also argues that the delivery of court services through ICT will facilitate the access to law required by international human rights instruments.

The recommendations set forth a number of principles and guidelines, which should be disseminated and applied in the justice systems in member countries of the Council of Europe. The recommendations consider the policy issues for legal information, freedom of information and court proceedings, and tackle all the key issues: availability, accessibility, timeliness, accuracy, authenticity, copyright, charging, privacy and transparency. While the recommendations are not legally binding on member states, they form a useful blueprint for citizen access to legal information, and a useful touchstone, along with Susskind (see below), in evaluating current services.

Information and communication technologies (ICTs) play a vital role in enhancing public access to legal information. Technology has enabled the National Association of Citizens Advice Bureaux (NACAB) to publish their Advice Guide[12] on the web, which offers basic advice and information on people's rights and entitlements. The information files are regularly updated. The interface and browsing screens are very straightforward, and plain English is used throughout.

Some commentators, however, are sceptical about the benefits of internet services because they are outside the reach of people with no computers. A cautionary note is sounded by Ardill,[13] who points out that users need literacy in English and some level of curiosity to make sense of the websites. She also states that most poorer households do not own a computer, and this section of the population includes many vulnerable and excluded people. She argues that information services and leaflets can be useful as a follow-up to interactive advisory sessions.

Ardill's paper also questions whether the government has done enough to promote the Human Rights Act 1998, which ushered in a new legal culture. Promoting legal literacy means more resources for public legal education. She also suggests that family and criminal legislation could be made easier to understand for ordinary people. The new era of education for citizenship, from August 2002, is discussed briefly below under the heading Education for citizenship.

One author who strongly advocates ICTs is Susskind. He suggests[14] that ICT can promote public access to the law in ten ways, among which are:

- providing legal services and legal information via the web
- a portal model in plain English, reflecting people's real life events and needs (e.g. debt, housing, education, employment), and which avoids legal jargon
- an e-mail enquiry service on legal matters, answered by lawyers
- online graphical help on using the courts
- free public access to primary materials, including legislation, Statutory Instruments and case law
- online guidance to help citizens understand their rights and obligations, with preventive legal guidance as well.

His discussion on public access to the law gives us these useful points of analysis for the next section, to help assess some of the newer services emerging in the last few years.

Newer services

BAILII

BAILII stands for the British and Irish Legal Information Institute. This web service aims to give free access via the internet to a comprehensive collection of the full text of British and Irish primary legal materials. BAILII's website[15] currently offers case reports and legislation for the jurisdictions of the UK and Ireland. In this way, BAILII provides ready access to information provided by the legislatures and the courts, and thus supports the agendas of open government and access to justice.

BAILII's philosophy is that all citizens have the right to free access to comprehensive and understandable sources of legislation and case law. As well as providing the materials on its website, the Institute also encourages the courts, legislatures and law reform bodies to make their information available for free on the web, and to follow good standards of text formatting and presentation in doing so. BAILII promotes a system of vendor- and media-neutral citation of case law, and a list of the neutral citations already assigned by courts in the UK can be seen at http://www.bailii.org/bailii/citation.html.

At the October 2001 launch meeting,[16] tributes were paid to the remarkable co-operation between different sectors, individuals and agencies which go towards producing and supporting BAILII. The list includes the legal profession and its professional associations and bodies, law schools and the academic sector, AUSTLII (the Australasian Legal Information Institute), and court services in the UK and Ireland.

The BAILII pilot project started in April 2000, and BAILII registered as a charity in December 2000. Its current business plan[17] identifies the priority developments for the next few years, and among them are:

- developing the free internet database of legal materials
- improving the quality of the data
- promoting the service and free access to law in general
- conducting a user survey and some research into legal information retrieval.

In an address to the Freeing the Law meeting launch on 10 October 2001, at Linklaters, Silk Street, London, Laurence West Knights QC stressed the need for BAILII to be steady, reliable and transparent. He outlined the challenges facing the fledgling new service in gaining resources, conducting research and lobbying the government.

An interesting point raised in the discussion at the same meeting was the need for some structured form of user feedback, such as a user forum, for BAILII. This would help to inform and evaluate the service, and as noted above, a user survey is a priority for the next few years. The service receives many messages from users, and it would be useful if these could be analysed to produce a report on issues raised.

BAILII does an admirable job in providing web access to a comprehensive collection of primary legal materials for the UK and Ireland. In time, perhaps, user feedback and research may reveal what kind of extra online help users need in using the materials – for example, a glossary of legal terms, or an outline of formats used to process the documents.

The files of legislation for the UK on BAILII need some updating. This requires a lot of hypertext linking between sections of acts. But the future of the Statute Law Database, under development at the Lord Chancellor's Department, will be a major deciding factor in the public domain availability of updated files of statutes in the UK. The Statutory Publications Office of the Lord Chancellor's Department 'is exploring various business and technical options for delivery of the service to users both inside and outside the public domain.'[18]

BAILII's website receives over 200,000 page views per week, according to its promotional leaflet. This usage breaks down approximately as follows:

- 25% educational institutions
- 25% legal profession and business
- 15% general public
- 10% government
- 25% overseas.

Just Ask!

Just Ask! is the website[19] of the Community Legal Services (CLS). The CLS was set up by the Government in 2000 to help provide a good legal service locally. It aims to provide information and help to people to enable them to know and exercise their rights effectively and in time, and in their own area.

The CLS works through a network of local organizations, which include solicitors firms, Citizens Advice Bureaux, law centres, public libraries and other community organizations. The CLS replaces the previous legal aid scheme. It exists to help people who cannot afford to pay for legal services themselves. It operates a quality mark to ensure that people using the service get adequate standards of help and information from service providers, or to ensure that they can be referred from one service to another if further help is needed.

The Just Ask! website offers users a directory of service providers as well as a facility to search for advice on the internet.

The directory contains details of over 15,000 solicitors and other service providers who are committed to the CLS quality mark. Users can search by their postcode, or by the name of the nearest town or city, to get a listing of local providers. They can also search by category (debt, employment, family, etc.) or by target group (carers, children, older people, etc.) or by language spoken. Help files for the site are available in a number of different languages, including Bengali, Urdu, Chinese and Gujerati.

Directory entries give the following details for each service provider:

- address and contact details
- hours
- charges
- services
- categories of law
- target groups
- accessibility
- a location map.

The directory is easy to use, and the JustAsk! site uses plain English throughout. Just Ask! won the Plain English Campaign's award for the best website of 2001. Keeping the site easy to use and accessible is a top priority. Steve Orchard, chief executive of the Legal Services Commission, was quoted, in the press release about the award, as follows:

> The Community Legal Service provides people with information on the legal world, which has not traditionally been known for its use of plain English. We hope the site will be an easy to use route into advice and help.[20]

Usage of the site appears to be on the increase. The Just Ask! web administrator said in 2003 that the service had been receiving approximately 12,000 page impressions a week during recent months, compared with approximately 6500 page impressions when the site first went live in April 2000.

Just Ask! is easy to use, and contains a wealth of information about getting legal help. As a web service it is clear and tailored to reflect the way people live in communities.

Adviceguide

This web service[21] provides basic information on legal rights, consumer matters, the legal system, benefits and other topics. Adviceguide is produced as an online guide by the National Association of Citizens Advice Bureaux (NACAB). Citizens Advice Bureaux (CAB) also offer free confidential advice from their 2000 outlets in England, Wales and Northern Ireland.

The information provided by the service is regularly updated, to incorporate changes and developments in law and consumer affairs. The information presented, and the interface, are in plain English. An interface in Welsh, with information files in Welsh, is also available. The topics of information relate to people's real lives, from benefits and civil rights, to family matters, health, the legal system and travel. If people have complicated queries for the service, they are encouraged to contact their local CAB for more in-depth advice. An online directory of the CAB is provided.

Users are offered three ways in which to find the information they need:

- by picking a topic from the basic list, grouped under four headings:
  — your money
  — your family
  — your daily life
  — your rights
- by clicking on the site map, for an overview of content

- by doing a text search on a word or phrase.

Users make the initial choice, once they have logged on to the site, of information on England, Northern Ireland, Scotland or Wales. There are no distractions or gimmicks on the site, and only a few relevant links to other sites. The design is clear, clutter-free and easy to use. Users can contact the publishers with comments and suggestions about the site. According to NACAB's annual report for 2000/2001, approximately 30,000 people use Adviceguide each month.

SOSIG Law Gateway

The SOSIG Law Gateway[22] is designed primarily to support research and teaching in the UK higher education sector. However, it is useful to consider it here for two reasons:

1 As a web service free at the point of use, it offers guidance, links and an online tutorial on free legal resources published in the UK and from around the world.
2 It has devised a number of evaluation and feedback mechanisms to keep the service relevant and responsive to users.

The Law Gateway is provided as part of the Social Sciences Information Gateway, known as SOSIG for short. It is funded by the Joint Information Systems Committee of the Further and Higher Education Funding Councils and the Economic and Social Research Council. It aims to identify and evaluate good legal resources from around the world, and thereby to offer guidance and access to such resources. SOSIG presents the information it compiles as a database, which users can browse or search.

Browsing

Users can choose to follow a range of broad categories from the Gateway's front page, and then to scan and select from subcategories thereunder. If UK law is chosen, the screen offers a long list of over 100 resources, but these are grouped conveniently under useful categories (articles, law reports, legislation, journals, organizations, resource guides, etc.). Users can choose to read a description of a particular resource and then link to it directly on the web, or to refine their selection further.

Searching

Users can choose to do simple or complex searches. Simple searches can be done using a keyword or phrase. More complex searches allow users to be more analytical in their strategy, with options to specify the database field on which they wish to search (e.g. title or description) or the type of resource (e.g. law reports, legislation, organizations or resource guides, to name a few).

Evaluation and feedback

Since its beginning in 1994, the SOSIG service has conducted various evaluation and feedback exercises[23] with users and funders. This has helped to keep it relevant to users' needs and has contributed to the service's strategic direction. Research has been done on users' search behaviour, their preferences for searching or browsing, their perceptions of the service, and their research needs. Also, useful feedback has been gained from advisory and user groups, from funders' reports, from training events and from unsolicited feedback. All of this research and feedback has helped, in various ways, towards redesigning the interface and browsing screens, identifying new resources, promoting the service more effectively and engaging different user communities more effectively.

Education for citizenship

Citizenship became a foundation subject for key stages 3 and 4 in secondary schools in England from 1 August 2002.[24] A new attainment target and programme of study in citizenship took effect from the new school year in 2002. Schools have some flexibility in the way they deal with citizenship as a subject, and can introduce variations, once the basic requirements are met.

The programme of study [25] for key stage 3 states that pupils should be taught about their legal and human rights and responsibilities, and how these relate to young people. They will also learn about diversity in the community, central and local government, the electoral process and the role of voluntary organizations.

The programme of study for key stage 4 states that pupils should be taught about the legal and human rights and responsibilities underpinning society, and how they relate to citizens, including the role and operation of the criminal and civil justice systems. They will also learn about local and central government, the freedom of the press, the role of voluntary organizations, the electoral process and democratic participation.

This new subject obviously has implications for teachers and for school librarians. One would expect a lot of guidance from the Department for Education and Skills, but apparently not a lot is forthcoming. Heater[26] explains that any guidance from the Department must be very circumspect to avoid the possibility or semblance of government interference in citizenship education, and to keep it politically clean. He also discusses the challenges facing schools and teachers in dealing with citizenship. For change to be comfortable, it will need to be gradual. The lack of a firm tradition of this form of education in England, and the lack of government involvement, puts a lot of strain on the voluntary bodies to produce resources. Heater commends the Citizenship Foundation and the Politics Association for making a vital contribution in supplying teaching materials and courses. He raises the question of how citizenship education can be examined, and wonders how teachers and schools can approach the concept of 'world citizenship'.

The Citizenship Foundation[27] present different case studies on their website. These examples of good practice in citizenship education include projects which have made a difference in their local school and community, and schools are encouraged to submit their own examples of good practice. The project cover a wide range of topics, including anti-bullying, culture/media, human rights, diversity, political and financial literacy, and law-related education. Some whole school policies and audits are also available.

Tackling Political Literacy is a classroom resource in PDF format designed to help make young people more politically aware and effective. The materials focus on developing political ideas rather than on a knowledge of political organizations. Materials from key stage 1 to key stage 4 are included. Other publications, which can be purchased from the Citizenship Foundation, are listed on its website, with some free sample materials available from some of the featured titles (PDF).

Books and packs available to order from the Politics Association on their website[28] include material on devolution, pressure groups, the EU, Parliament, the electoral system, constitutional change and the mass media. Another useful website is Citizen21,[29] presented by Charter88, which is a resource on citizenship for teachers who are getting to grips with the National Curriculum. Teaching resources are available on voting, human rights, Europe and other issues.

An interesting new development, about which we may hear more, is street law. Briefly, street law involves law students (including trainee barristers and solicitors) in preparing and delivering courses on rights and responsibilities to community and school groups. The courses show young people how the law affects them. Prof. Richard Grimes of the College of Law stated recently[30] that the College had done street law projects from its branches in Birmingham, Chester, Guildford, London and York. Students had given presentations in schools, prisons, a drug rehabilitation clinic and other community settings.

The US website Street Law Online[31] offers some sample materials and rationales for street law, which favour a 'practical, participatory education about democracy, law and human rights'. Some collaboration between the Citizenship

Foundation and Street Law Inc. took place in 2002, and this is reported and discussed in the *Citizenship Foundation Newsletter*, available on their website.

To sum up, teachers and school children have been busy since Autumn 2002 as they have tackled the new curriculum on citizenship. Non-profit organizations are providing some materials to support this, and trainee lawyers can help in certain settings.

Hammersmith Public Library

Hammersmith Public Reference Library, in West London, has an extensive legal collection comprising statute law, UK law reports and several journals.[32] This collection has been built up over many years, and forms an important resource in the reference service in this public library. Many users of the law collection are litigants in person, doing research on topics such as bankruptcy, landlord and tenant, insurance, employment and taxation. People also ask to see the legislation on parking fines and unsafe vehicles; health and safety is another popular topic. The *Industrial Relations Law Reports* are a highly valued and much-used series at Hammersmith. The law collection is one of the best publicly available law collections in London, and on average three or four members of the public per day are referred to the library by the Law Society.

People sometimes have unusual enquiries. More than one author has asked to see legislation from days gone by, on topics like divorce, to help them write historical novels. Users sometimes ask for back runs of directories of solicitors to help them compile their family history.

Reference library staff can help users to track down the more obscure citations, and to use the *Digest*. Many law students from West London use the library, and get regular help from the reference staff in deciphering their citations. The reference librarian is a little concerned that so many students have no idea what the citation means, or how to find out what it means. A photocopying service is available for the public and for solicitors.

The reference librarian helps people to find other sources of information and advice in the area, if they cannot get the information they require in the library. People are often referred to the Hammersmith Law Centre, and sometimes to the Citizens Advice Bureau. 'There is always another source of help to refer people on to', she states. After its commencement in October 2000, there were lots of queries about the Human Rights Act 1998, but these have declined.

The library has subscribed to Lawtel since 1982, and staff use this service frequently. The reference library now has five personal computers linked to the People's Network. These are always in demand. However, many users still prefer to have hard copy in hand, if it is available. The former reference librarian pointed out that public libraries depend upon visitor numbers as a basic justification of their existence. Web services can present public librarians with a dilemma. Should they promote good free services on the web to their users? And if users are satisfied with web resources, will access to the web mean that they use the library less? Or should librarians continue to promote the print and leaflet resources and not promote the web resources as actively?

At Hammersmith, law is perceived by many library users, and by some public library staff, as an intimidating and difficult subject, and one to be avoided. Many people are reluctant to enter the reference library because of this. This points, perhaps, to a marketing opportunity. Susskind[33] argues that citizens need to know that the law confers benefits on them, even if they do not have a legal problem. The law is about preventive remedies as well as about resolving disputes. Perhaps there is an opportunity for public libraries to promote the range of subject guides on rights, leaflets and web-based services which people can use there.

Similarly, a study published in 2000 concluded that approximately 45% of the respondents were unaware that information concerning legal rights, politics and welfare benefits was held in most public libraries.[34] It also concluded that a lack of information poses difficulty in solving problems in employment, housing and welfare. Is this perhaps a marketing opportunity for our public libraries to promote materials for basic public legal education?

Reference library staff at Hammersmith have attended courses on legal research organized by BIALL, the British and Irish Association of Law Libraries, and check regularly for new training opportunities on handling legal information.

Wormwood Scrubs Prison Library

The Prison Library at HM Prison Wormwood Scrubs in West London provides a library service for a prison population of approximately 1200 inmates.[35] Library services cater for prisoners' recreational, educational and, to a certain extent, informational needs. Prisons are required by law to provide a library to inmates.

There are lots of requests at Wormwood Scrubs Library for information on appeals and how to appeal. Occasionally, prisoners ask for law reports, and these can usually be supplied from the law collection in Hammersmith Public Library, nearby. Archbold's *Criminal Pleading* is in demand a lot, as is the annual *Prisons Handbook*, published by Waterside Press.

A document of fundamental importance to prison libraries is the Prison Service Order number 6710, entitled *Prison Libraries*. This order stipulates that a number of publications must be provided in all prison libraries, and all of these are available at Wormwood Scrubs. This list includes:

- a number of Acts and guides to Acts, mainly covering criminal justice, the prison service, human rights and the police
- rules, standing orders and prison service orders
- prison service manuals and instructions
- prisoners' information books, of which one is for males, one for females, one for prisoners serving life sentences, and one on visiting and keeping in touch (these are available in English and in a host of other languages)
- education and training manuals
- Council of Europe documents, including the European Convention on Human Rights
- prison reports and enquiries
- books of legal guidance, including *A Guide to Proceedings in the Court of Appeal Criminal Division* [36]
- a textbook on prison law.

By and large, prison libraries are not well equipped with ICT. Provision of computers depends on the resources of the local authority and of the prison. Mobile phones are not allowed anywhere in the prison. Inmates can currently use phone cards of low denomination, which they purchase from their allowances. The Prison Service is moving over to a PIN phone system, where inmates get an account and pin number to make calls. It is sometimes possible for prisoners to have PCs in their cells, but this is under discussion and at the discretion of the prison governor. An intranet for the Prison Service is under consideration, and two of the major factors in this development are costs and information security.

In principle, prisoners are entitled to all the materials they could get from a public library, subject to resources. There is no censorship in prison libraries. Prisoners can get what they want, within reason.

Other services are provided within the prison to cater for prisoners' legal needs, and these include a citizens' advice bureau, a representative of NACRO, the National Association for the Care and Resettlement of Offenders, and a legal services officer.

Conclusion

Susskind advocates a portal to offer advice relevant to people in their daily lives, in plain English. The basic question is whether it should be one single portal, when in practice basic legal information comes from a plurality of sources. Organizations from the not-for-profit sector, such as NACAB, the Citizenship Foundation and Liberty, have been providing information of a high standard for some time, and recent technology has allowed them to publish their files on the internet. Contributions from these organizations are to be valued for their independence and their relevance to people in need, and also for their clear communication and plain English. Free access to primary materials is enabled by services like BAILII. Thus, at least some of Susskind's desiderata are already being met in various ways.

The newer services outlined above all demonstrate points of good practice in handling and disseminating legal information. But as Ardill points out, more evaluation of these services is needed if they are to continue to be effective. As library and information professionals, we need to remember that many people have no access to computers, and that English is not the first language for everyone.

Many of our public libraries have good basic collections of legal material, and can apply to the CLS to be basic legal information providers. We can identify two significant challenges facing public libraries in the provision of legal information: image, and the balance between print and electronic. There is perhaps an opportunity for libraries to promote the collections and skills they have, and to give people a more fully rounded picture of the law and the benefits it confers. As more and more legal information is being published on the web, it may be advisable to consider the development of print collections in tandem with an exploration of the range of information now available on the web.

Notes

1 Available at http://www.legalservices.gov.uk/leaflets/cls/index.htm.
2 From *De legibus*, bk. I, ch. VI, included in James, S. and Stebbings, C., (1987) *A Dictionary of Legal Quotations*, London, Croom Helm.
3 Keynote speech at the BIALL Annual Conference, British and Irish Association of Law Librarians, 9 June 2001, Cork, Ireland.
4 Freeing the Law: BAILII launch meeting, 10 Ocober 2001, Linklaters, London.
5 *Civil Justice 2000: a vision of the civil justice system in the information age*, Lord Chancellor's Department. Available at http://lcd.gov.uk/cj2000/cj2000fr.htm.·
6 Available at http://www.la-hq.org.uk/directory/prof_issues/yrtk.html.
7 Picton, H. and Coburn, A. (2002) The Price of Liberty . . . : freedom of information and access to government information, *Refer*, **18** (3), 11–16.
8 Available at http://www.scottish.parliament.uk/.
9 Available at http://www.wales.gov.uk/index.htm.
10 Reported in *Focus* (2001) Legal Services Commission, (January), 18.
11 Available at http://cm.coe.int/ta/rec/2001/2001r3.htm.
12 Available at http://www.adviceguide.org.uk.
13 Ardill, N. (2002) Public Legal Education: unfinished business?, *Legal Action*, (February supplement), 1–4.

14 Susskind, R. (2002) *Transforming the Law: essays on technology, justice and the legal marketplace*, Oxford, Oxford University Press, ch. 12,

15 Available at http://www.bailii.org.

16 See note 4 above.

17 BAILII (2002) *British and Irish Legal Information Institute business plan, 2002–2004.*

18 Reported at http://www.lcd.gov.uk/lawdatfr.htm.

19 Available at http://www.justask.org.uk.

20 Available at http://www.justask.org.uk/about/news.jsp?lang=en.

21 Available at http://www.adviceguide.org.uk.

22 Available at http://www.sosig.ac.uk/law/.

23 Summarized in a paper 'Evaluation and feedback from user communities', given to the SOSIG Consultation Day, Bristol, 8 March 2002.

24 Education (National Curriculum) (Attainment Target and Programmes of Study in Citizenship) (England) Order 2000 SI 2000/1603.

25 Department for Education and Employment (1999) *The National Curriculum for England: citizenship, key stages 3–4*, London, Stationery Office.

26 Heater, D. (2001) The History of Citizenship Education in England, *Curriculum Journal*, **12** (1), 103–23.

27 Information available at http://www.citfou.org.uk/.

28 Available at http://www.politics-association.org.uk/about-frameset.htm.

29 Available at http://www.citizen21.org.uk/index.html.

30 See press release on the College website at http://www.college-of-law.co.uk/news/street_law_conf.asp.

31 Available at http://www.streetlaw.org/.

32 I would like to thank Kamla Butcher, reference librarian, and Vernon Burgess, former reference librarian (now retired), for showing me round and for their time in discussing legal information.

33 See note 14 above.

34 Marcella, R. and Baxter, G. (2002) Citizenship Information Needs in the UK, *Aslib Proceedings*, **52** (3), (March), 115–23.

35 Thanks to Tracy Coombes, librarian at HMP Wormwood Scrubs, London, for showing me round and discussing the prison library service.

36 *A Guide to Proceedings in the Court of Appeal Criminal Division* (1997), London, Criminal Appeal Office. Also available at http://www.courtservice.gov.uk/forms_and_guidance/forms/pro_guide.pdf.

3

Copyright in the information age

Allison Coleman

Copyright law is currently in a state of flux. The Copyright, Designs and Patents Act 1988 (CDPA) has been amended many times, and at the time of writing is about to be amended again, this time by regulations implementing the EU directive on copyright and related rights in the information society (the 'Information Society Directive'[1]). The plus side of the regular changes to copyright law is that it is constantly being updated to take into account technological change. The downside is that it makes it much more difficult to 'stay legal'.

One of the most practical pieces of advice is never to look at an original version of the 1988 Act – much of this is now legal history, not law. Only look at a copy of the CDPA which has been updated by the latest set of regulations; and always consult the most recent edition of any book on copyright. Anything more than 12 months old can be unreliable. All references in this chapter to the 1988 Act are to the version of the CDPA in force at the date of writing and to the amendments proposed in the Consultation Paper on the Implementation of the Information Society Directive.[1] Many practitioner works on copyright contain an amended version of the 1988 CDPA in their appendices[2] and are updated regularly by supplements or are online.[3]

Why abide by copyright laws?

This is a question often asked of lawyers and information professionals alike. It is easy to cheat. Very few private users are caught, so why should they abide by copyright? Why not cheat? In some ways this is much the same type of question as 'Why obey a speed limit?'; 'Why not park on my neighbour's driveway without permission?'; 'Why pay for a television licence?' or 'Why not fiddle my tax return?' Laws are set up for a purpose and society depends on the law being observed by most of the people, most of the time. In a society where infringement of copyright is rife, the cultural heritage suffers. In a country where all CDs/DVDs are copied illegally, no indigenous singer, songwriter, sound recording studio, film company or software house would survive, for their income is dependent on receipts from legitimate sales, showings, rental, etc., and it is copyright which controls these forms of use.

On the other hand it is desirable that copyright materials should be used, read and circulated, and that an information-rich society should not just be a society of the rich. The aim of copyright laws is to set up a system which operates in the public interest, allowing the education, reading, use, and the reproduction, distribution and communication of copyright works, with due regard being paid to the rights of copyright owners to an economic return and the preservation of the integrity of their work.

The question takes on another complexion where the information professional is an employee. Employers are vicariously liable for the acts of their employees and are liable for infringements of copyright committed by their employees in the course of employment. Thus, they can have injunctions served upon them to prevent infringement of copyright taking place on their premises, or they can be required to pay damages, and they can also be criminally liable under the provision relating to secondary infringement (see below). Whilst it may be superficially attractive to think of the boss sewing mailbags, this will do nothing for the job prospects of the errant employee, as an employee is under a contractual duty of fidelity and that means, among other things, not committing illegal acts in the course of employment. Disciplinary action is likely and this might include dismissal in appropriate cases. Readers who infringe copyright using library equipment usually fall foul of library regulations and can have permission to use the library revoked.

The web: a copyright-free zone?

One important point to note at the outset of this chapter is that copyright applies not just to paper-based products, but to digital ones and to materials on the internet. It is a common misconception that the internet is in some way a copyright-free zone. It is true that in many instances text, software, etc. are put on the web and expressly stated to be free from any restrictions on use, reproduction, etc. That does not, however, mean that copyright laws do not apply. All that it means is that the owner of copyright has declared that copyright will not be enforced. In all other cases, copyright rules should be observed. These include the rules relating to fair dealing, for example, when downloading and printing, for these are acts of copying (see below). Many sites contain a copyright notice. Users of the site should read this and abide by its terms, for these constitute the licence between the owner of copyright in the information and the reader/user. In many instances, the licence may give greater rights to the user than the minimum allowed by law (e.g. a right to copy the whole document, not just a part), but it may also assert other rights (e.g. the moral rights to be identified as author and not to have the work subject to derogatory treatment). In this chapter, copyright principles should be assumed to apply to materials stored electronically, as well as to paper-based ones, unless the contrary is stated.

A further complication is that it is difficult to enforce copyright in materials on the web. The copyright owner may not know that a work has been copied; and the owner and the infringing user may well be in different countries. Cross-border litigation is complex and expensive. Governments, international organizations and the courts are wrestling with these problems. In many ways, technical protection measures, such as copyright management systems and copy protection schemes, may provide better protection for owners who do not have the time, the inclination or the resources to sue, but this is no reason to ignore the law or to write it off as totally ineffective.

What is protected by copyright?

Copyright protects only certain categories of items, called 'works'. There are nine categories of works,[4] but some of these are subdivided. If an item does not fall within the list, it is not protected by copyright. This often necessitates reform. There was a long debate on how to protect computer programs. Eventually it was decided to include them under the umbrella of copyright laws and to categorize them as literary works[5] – not the ideal solution, but one which had practical attractions.

The nine categories of copyright works are:[6]

- original literary, dramatic, musical or artistic works
- sound recordings, films, broadcasts or cable programmes
- the typographical arrangement of a published edition.

As an example of the subdivisions within the CDPA, the term 'literary work' includes – apart from the obvious items such as books, journal articles and letters – a table or compilation, a computer program and a database;[7] and 'artistic work' is widely defined as including photographs, sculptures, collages, maps, paintings, drawings, engravings, etchings and works of architecture.[8] Copyright therefore applies to most items held as stock by a library, archive, museum or gallery, and to the documentation and computerized data gathered or generated by a business.

Databases

Databases can be protected in two ways: by copyright and/or by an independent database right. Firstly, in copyright law, Section 3A of the CDPA 1988 defines a database as a collection of independent works, data or other material which (a) are arranged in a systematic or methodical way, and (b) are individually accessible by electronic or other means. This covers both electronic databases and, for example, a traditional paper-based card indexing system. But a database will only constitute a literary work, and attract copyright protection as such, if the database is original; and for these purposes 'original' is given a special meaning. Under Section 3A(2) of the 1988 CDPA, 'a database is original if, and only if, by reason of the selection or arrangement of the contents of the database the database constitutes the author's own intellectual creation.' Protection is unlikely to be given to an alphabetical listing of telephone numbers in a geographical area;[9] or to a comprehensive or complete database of historical records; but is given to a database of poetry selected thematically, because thematic selection is likely to satisfy the requirement of 'intellectual creation'.

This is clearly not fair to producers of telephone directories and comprehensive databases. These fulfil valuable social, economic and educational needs, and take time and cost money. To get around this, and to reward and encourage the producers of the databases which fall outside the range of copyright, we now have a new property right, called the database right, which subsists in a database 'if there has been substantial investment in obtaining, verifying or presenting the contents of the database.' This right is also given to owners of databases protected by copyright, but as copyright is more comprehensive and lasts longer, few copyright owners are likely to rely on it.

The database right is to be found in the Copyright Rights in Database Regulations 1997 (the '1997 Regulations'). It is a standalone right given to databases only, in contrast to copyright, which can apply to the whole range of works listed in Section 1 of the CDPA (see above). It is also called a *sui generis* right, because it is a specially invented right, outside the normal categories of intellectual property law, such as patents, copyrights, trade marks, etc. The database right is given to the maker of the database, or if it is made by an employee, to the employer; and the right is infringed by anyone who, without the consent of the owner of the right, extracts or re-utilizes all or a substantial part of the contents of the database. The right lasts for 15 years, but if the database is substantially revised, time may start running afresh. Copyright, by way of contrast, lasts for the life of the author or creator, plus 70 years (see further below). The distinction between the length of protection under copyright and under the database right is perhaps unfortunate in the case of so many digitization projects, where considerable sums of money will be spent digitizing entire collections (without selection) in return for only the shorter term of protection. This is something that should be borne in mind at the planning stage.

What are the rights of a copyright owner?

Copyright law grants six economic rights and four moral rights.[10] The six economic rights[11] of a copyright owner are the exclusive rights to:

(i)   copy the work
(ii) issue copies to the public
(iii) rent or lend the work to the public
(iv) perform, show or play the work in public
(v)   broadcast the work or include it in a cable programme service
(vi) make an adaptation of the work or do any of the above in relation to an adaptation, e.g. to translate a work from English to French and to publish the translation.

These are the 'acts restricted by copyright', but each is narrower than might at first sight appear. For example, it is possible for an individual to copy a literary work (other than a database) or a dramatic, musical or artistic work[12] for the purposes of private study or research[13] without infringing copyright, so long as the amount copied is reasonable ('fair dealing'); it is also possible to exhibit a work of art in public without the consent of the copyright owner, because the copyright owner's exclusive right to show a work does not apply to an artistic work. Copyright laws require careful construction. In particular, attention should be paid to which types of works are covered by any restriction; to the length of time a work is in copyright; and to the defences to infringement, which are otherwise known as 'acts permitted in relation to copyright works' (see further below).

The EU directive on copyright in the information society[13] is designed to cover copyright in the electronic environment. The directive was heavily criticized for extending the rights of copyright owners without sufficient regard to the rights of users. That was particularly the case when the directive was wending its way through the EU legislative process and amendments were introduced, largely at the behest of the copyright industries. However, the final version of the directive is more balanced. It is to be hoped that, when the UK government is exercising its discretion over whether to adopt certain clauses in the directive, it will take a balanced view, having regard to the rights of users and to the public domain, as well as to the rights of the owners of copyright; and that it will include as many of the directive's exceptions as possible, and also draft those exceptions in terms that are as broad as possible. One change of terminology is that the rights of a copyright owner are referred to in the directive as the right of reproduction, the right of communication and the right of distribution, but those three rights are already enshrined in UK law, albeit in the form of the six rights set out above. However, right (v) above will be redefined so as to cover any electronic communication to the public. The new 'right to communicate the work to the public' will apply to, and restrict, both broadcasting the work (including it in a non-interactive service) and including it in an on-demand service or other interactive service.

The economic rights of a copyright owner are described in the CDPA[14] as being exclusive rights. That means that only the copyright owner has these rights. Only a copyright owner has the right to copy a work, which in practice means that only a person who has the consent of a copyright owner can copy a work. Consent is sometimes given in response to a direct request – for example, a request by a library to an artist for permission to digitize a painting and to display it on their website – but more often than not it is given by licence, such as the licence given to a purchaser of software to download from CD-ROM or from the internet onto the hard drive of a PC.

The CDPA also gives four moral rights. These are the right to:

(i)   be identified as the author or director
(ii) object to derogatory treatment of a work
(iii) object to false attribution of a work
(iv) privacy in certain photographs and films.

The emphasis in this chapter will be on the six economic rights of a copyright owner set out on page 38, and on the exceptions to those rights which permit, for example, copying. Information providers are more likely to be faced with questions from readers concerning the economic rights. Care should, however, be taken not to infringe moral rights if materials are to be digitized, for digitization and digital enhancement can easily change a work. Specialist works should be consulted for further details of moral rights.

Who owns copyright?

The first owner of copyright is the author or creator of a work.[15] However, where a literary, dramatic, musical or artistic work, or a film, is made by an employee in the course of employment, the employer is the first owner of copyright, subject to any agreement to the contrary.[16] It should, however, be noted that consultants are not employees, and thus copyright belongs to them and not to any commissioning body, unless there is a term in the consultancy contract to the contrary and that contract is signed by the consultant. This complicates matters considerably when trying to trace the owner of copyright in order to get permission to copy or to do any of the other acts restricted by copyright.[17]

The position of academics is interesting. As stated above, the normal rule is that where a literary, dramatic, musical or artistic work, or a film is created by an employee in the course of employment, copyright belong to the employer. However, this is stated to be subject to any agreement to the contrary. In the present author's own university, there is an agreement between the university and its academic staff that copyright in most works created by academics belongs to the academics. The reason for this is academic freedom. If the position were otherwise, the university could use its copyright to prevent the publication of works written by academics, and this could amount to censorship. Censorship is condemned by the academic community, no matter how unpopular the views expressed.

Joint authorship sometimes confuses. This book comprises a set of essays by different contributors. Under agreement with the publisher, each contributor retains copyright. The work as a whole is not, however, a work of joint authorship, for that applies only where a work is produced by the collaboration of two or more authors in which the contribution of each author 'is not distinct from that of the other author or authors'. Each case will depend on its facts.

Copyright belongs to the Crown where a work is made by an officer or servant of the Crown in the course of his or her duties. Crown copyright also covers every Act of Parliament, Act of the Scottish Parliament, Act of the Northern Ireland Assembly or Measure of the General Synod of the Church of England. A work made by, or under the direction or control of, the House of Commons or the House of Lords is covered by Parliamentary copyright.[18]

Copyright can be transferred by assignment, by will or on bankruptcy.[19] Generally, copyright passes on death either under the terms of the will, or to the next of kin if there is an intestacy (where there is no will).[20] Publishing contracts often require a transfer of copyright by assignment. However, an author faced with a contract requiring an assignment of copyright would do well to question whether that is necessary, or whether it would be in his or her interest merely to give the publisher a licence to copy and to issue copies to the public (to publish). Assignment of copyright has become fashionable in academic publishing, but it rarely happens when a novel is published. Why the distinction? An author who assigns copyright to a publisher should certainly amend the contract to permit reasonable re-use, otherwise an author who draws on his or her previously published work in order to write about that subject matter again, may be faced with a complaint that copyright has been infringed, even though he or she wrote both works!

If a company that owns copyright goes out of business and its business is not transferred to another, there may be no owner of copyright, and thus no one to object to an infringement of copyright. However, it may not be that simple. For example, a publishing company might agree with its authors that copyright reverts to them on cessation of business; and in a case of bankruptcy or insolvency, copyright is transferred to the trustee in bankruptcy or official receiver, who may then assign (transfer) it to another. All of these matters can make copyright difficult to trace.

How long does copyright last?

This question has never been an easy one to answer, but it has certainly become much more difficult since UK law was amended to implement the 1993 EU directive on the term of copyright and related rights.[21] There are now too many different rules, which in itself is quite ridiculous and makes it impossible to carry all of them around in one's head. The best advice is to consult a table, such as is to be found in A User's Guide to Copyright[22] (5th edn) or one of several specialist books such as Padfield's Copyright for Archivists and Users of Archives; or Copinger, or Laddie, Prescott and Vitoria.[23] Much will depend on the type of work, the date of death of the author or authors, the date when the work was created, whether it is published or unpublished, and if published, the date of publication.[24]

Following the EU term directive, copyright in literary, dramatic, musical and artistic works was increased as of 1 January 1996 for works still in copyright, from the life of the author plus 50 years, to the life of the author plus 70 years. The duration of copyright protection in sound recordings, films, broadcasts and cable programmes remained at 50 years, with various start dates set out in the legislation. Those start dates will again be changed for sound recordings when the Information Society Directive is brought into force in the UK, but not for other categories of works. Copyright in the typographical arrangement of a work lasts for 25 years from the year in which the edition is first published.

The aim of the EU duration directive was to harmonize the term of copyright protection throughout the Union. To avoid continuing disharmony, some copyrights which had previously expired, such as the musical works of Elgar, were revived. The rule is that, if a work was in copyright in any member state (often Germany) on 1 July 1995, copyright would be extended to life plus 70 years. However, the law is discriminatory and the extended term of copyright applies only to works originating in the European Economic Area (EEA). When calculating the duration of copyright in non-EEA works (e.g. Australian works), the EU directive states that it is necessary to look to the term of copyright granted by Australian law, etc. The US has extended the term of copyright protection in line with EU laws in order to obtain reciprocal protection, but the law is being challenged as being unconstitutional. It may therefore change again. The job of a copyright officer is not an easy one, and the duration rules make it especially difficult.

How are the rights of a copyright owner infringed?

There are two types of copyright infringement. If a work is in copyright, any breach of the copyright owner's six economic rights can amount to a primary infringement of copyright.[25] Permission to copy, or to issue copies to the public, etc., must therefore be sought from the copyright owner, unless the act in question falls within one of the defences to copyright (permitted acts) set out in the next section – and of course the copyright owner can demand a fee. There is no statutory control over the level of the fee. It may therefore be tempting, when contemplating a digitization project, to digitize only those items and artefacts which are clearly out of copyright.

Primary infringement of copyright is a civil matter, not a matter for regulation by the criminal law. The remedies for primary infringement are the usual ones available to a successful litigant in a civil action, most commonly damages, an injunction and/or an account of profits. Similar remedies are available for infringement of moral rights.

One common act of infringement of the economic rights is copying without the consent of the copyright owner. Copying is widely defined in Section 17 of the CDPA. For instance:

1　Copying in relation to a literary, dramatic, musical or artistic work means reproducing the work in any material form. This includes storing the work in any medium by electronic means; and thus the act of scanning or digitizing is itself an infringing act unless permission has been given beforehand.
2　In relation to an artistic work, copying includes making a copy in three dimensions of a two-dimensional work (and vice versa).

One recurrent problem under the CDPA is that many normal uses of an electronic system involve acts of copying which are transient or are normal incidents of the use of the technology. Also copying by caching has become commonplace. The Information Society directive recognizes that there is nothing wrong with transient and incidental copying and duly legitimizes it. Article 5(1) of the directive, which will be included in the new regulations amending the CDPA, provides that

... temporary acts of reproduction ... which are transient or incidental, which are an integral and essential part of a technological process and the sole purpose of which is to enable:

(a) a transmission in a network between third parties by an intermediary, or
(b) a lawful use

of a work or other subject-matter shall be exempt from the reproduction right.

Copyright is also infringed (in general terms[26]) by

- issuing copies to the public
- renting or lending the work to the public[27]
- performing, showing or playing a work in public
- broadcasting a work or including it in a cable programme (soon to become 'communicating the work to the public' – see page 39
- making an adaptation of a work[28] or doing any act restricted by copyright with an adaptation.[29]

Copyright is infringed if the act relates to the whole of the work or to a substantial part of it.[30] In essence, a substantial part means an important part, and a substantial part may therefore be quite a small part of the work as a whole. The test is qualitative rather than quantitative. Thus copying an important part of a work is an act infringing copyright, as is publishing it or broadcasting it or including it in a cable programme. There is no need for an infringer to know that he or she is infringing copyright in order to be liable for primary infringement of copyright. Innocent infringement is still infringement, but innocence is taken into account when a court is deciding which remedy to grant. By way of contrast, flagrant infringement can attract a higher award of damages.

Another type of infringement of copyright is secondary infringement.[31] This is much more serious and can amount to a breach of both the civil law and the criminal law. Secondary infringement involves acts in the course of trade, and unlike primary infringement, requires the perpetrator to know or to have reason to believe that the act infringes copyright. Secondary infringement covers:

(a) importing an infringing copy other than for private and domestic use;
(b) possessing or dealing with an infringing copy in the course of business;
(c) providing the means (e.g. equipment) for making infringing copies;
(d) permitting the use of premises for an infringing performance; or
(e) providing apparatus for an infringing performance.

Secondary infringement can be punished by a fine or imprisonment for up to two years, or both.

What are the defences to copyright infringement?

This is an area of the law that will change when the EU directive on copyright and related rights in the Information Society is brought into UK law. At the time of writing we have the directive, a consultation paper and a draft set of implementing regulations. However, the Department of Trade and Industry, who have responsibility for drafting the regulations, have indicated that they intend to do the minimum necessary to implement the directive, which means making as few changes as possible to the CDPA; but some are inevitable, and a few, most notably the change to the definition of research in the fair dealing provisions, will have considerable impact on the library community (see further below). The consultation paper indicates the main changes to UK law, but tells us that more will be made. These are said to be minor, but the definition of minor is one of perspective, and what is minor to one sector of the copyright-using world may be of major importance to another.

Chapter 3 of the CDPA contains a list of 'acts permitted in relation to copyright works'. These are akin to a set of defences to an action for breach of copyright, for the doing of any of the acts listed in Chapter 3 will not infringe copyright. The Chapter 3 permitted acts are meant to balance the rights given to a copyright owner. For example, fair dealing with a work for the purposes of research or private study is permitted, which means that a student can photocopy a reasonable proportion of a copyright work for the purposes of his or her studies without infringing copyright or needing permission to copy. The permitted acts form the parameters of copyright and have been framed to reflect various public policies, such as education, the provision of copies by libraries and archives, public administration, and the lawful and reasonable use of computer programs. However, there is nothing in Chapter 3 which permits digitization plus dissemination over the web or by e-commerce; and hence all digitization projects involving libraries, museums and archives need permission to copy and to disseminate any work which is still in copyright.

Research and study

If we take the permitted acts in the order they appear in the Act, the first set of provisions concerns fair dealing for the purposes of:

- research and private study
- criticism or review

- the incidental inclusion of copyright material in an artistic work, sound recording, film, broadcast or cable programme.[32]

The biggest change, which will come with the implementation of the directive, concerns the definition of research, which until now has covered research for any purpose, be it commercial or non-commercial. Attempts were made, when the 1987 Copyright Bill was wending its way through Parliament, to define research in a way which covered only private research, for it was felt that anyone undertaking commercial research should pay for the privilege of copying. However, this was defeated after a concerted campaign by the library sector over the difficulty in administering the distinction and the unfairness of holding a library liable for the infringement by a reader of copyright laws through the secondary infringement. Those arguments held sway in 1987, and hence the CDPA was free from the distinction. However, unfortunately the copyright owners were able to persuade those taking part in the EU legislative process of the unfairness of the current position and the directive now allows the fair dealing provisions to be used only by those undertaking private (non-commercial) research or private study.

It will not be easy to tell if a researcher is engaging in commercial or non-commercial research. Often the line will be difficult to draw. However, the new regulations will inevitably require the redesign of the forms that library users must complete when requesting copying by a librarian, and the form should include a declaration that the research is either non-commercial (so that no permission is needed) or commercial and that permission to copy has been obtained (or will be obtained – see below) from the copyright owner. That should protect the librarian from liability unless he or she has reason to believe the declaration to be untrue. When a reader uses a self-service photocopying machine, the notice beside the machine should make clear the change in the law. More difficult to police will be the use of hand-held scanners, but prominent written notices or other forms of warning may well suffice. In each case the librarian should use all reasonable endeavours to police the new laws. No more can be expected. No doubt CILIP will issue guidance notes. [See Editor's note.[33]]

It is not clear to the present author just how copyright clearance by a commercial researcher will be administered. Will the researcher be expected to provide evidence of permission to copy before copying can take place? Or will the librarian charge a higher fee for copying to commercial as opposed to non-commercial researchers, then pass a proportion of the fee on to the copyright owner? Or will there be a licensing scheme? If there is a licensing scheme, who will run it – the Copyright Licensing Agency (CLA)? Who will agree terms – CILIP and the CLA?

Education

The second sub-division of permitted acts concerns education.[34] These cover:

- things done for the purposes of instruction or examination
- anthologies for educational use
- performing, playing or showing a work in the course of activities of an educational establishment
- recording by educational establishments of broadcasts and cable programmes (off-air recording)
- reprographic copying
- lending of copies by educational establishments.

A feature of these sections of the Act is the use of licensing to control recording off-air and reprographic copying (photocopying) by and for the purposes of educational establishments. Some students claim that they may copy under the education sections, but this is not the case. They must rely on the fair dealing provisions described above.

Reprographic copying in higher education came under the spotlight recently with the reference to the Copyright Tribunal of the Higher Education Copying Accord, the licence that governs photocopying in the HE sector. The case was brought on behalf of the universities by Universities UK (UUK) against the CLA, which was acting on behalf of the publishers and major copyright owners. The complaints were the fact that the licence was too expensive, the unsatisfactory nature of the system for clearance of copies for course packs, and the uncertainty over which artistic works were included in the licence and which were excluded. The parties had been in negotiations for some time, but had failed to come to any agreement as to the way forward. The only course of action was to refer the dispute to the Copyright Tribunal, which is empowered under the CDPA to make a determination that is reasonable in the circumstances. In the event, the Tribunal ruled in favour of UUK, removing the restriction on course pack copying and the cumbersome clearance system which accompanied it, clarifying the definition of artistic works included in the licence, and setting a fee per student per year by way of royalty for reprographic copying at HE institutions. Since this case was decided, a new licence has been agreed. Licensing schemes are available for schools and for further education. They must be observed in order to 'stay legal'.

Libraries and archives

The third set of permitted acts relates to libraries and archives.[35] Despite a merger of functions and moves towards cross-sectoral working in the domain of libraries, archives, museums and galleries, the CDPA is very traditional and retains a rigid distinction between the institutions and the tasks they perform. The Act permits:

- copying by librarians of single copies of articles in periodicals, or of parts of published works, for users who require them for research or private study
- lending of books within the public lending right scheme
- supplying copies of articles or published editions to other libraries for stock, and making surrogate/replacement copies for preservation purposes
- supplying copies of unpublished works
- making a copy of an article of cultural or historical importance or interest before export from the UK.

As has been suggested, the change in the definition of research will of course impact considerably on library practice under the first of the exceptions listed above. In future the exception will apply only to copying for non-commercial researchers. Commercial researchers and librarians copying on their behalf will need permission to copy.

As stated above, the CDPA draws strange distinctions in this modern world of merged functions and cross-sectoral working. Some of the exceptions in Chapter 3 apply to both libraries and to archives, others only to libraries, but none to archives alone. Museums and galleries are not mentioned at all. This means that different copyright rules apply to different institutions. Copyright law is difficult enough without these added complexities. However, in practice, an archive, a museum or a gallery with a library section holding books on art, architecture, family history, etc. may well be treated as a library, at least in relation to its library collection; and an archive section may be treated as an archive. But information professionals working in these mixed institutions need to be aware of the differences and how different rules apply to different materials under their care – an even worse position! Under the directive, these distinctions may be set aside and a uniform set of exceptions may be developed to apply to the sector as a whole.[36] This would be a very welcome development. However, at the time of writing it seems likely that this change will not take place. The government has the option of implementing certain sections of the directive, this being one, but it is thought unlikely to disturb the status quo, desirable though this may be from the perspective of the institutions themselves and of their searchers. It is also thought that the definition of prescribed libraries[37] will not be changed.

This chapter does not deal with the sections of the CDPA concerning public administration or computer programs, except to state that public records[38] which are open to public inspection may be may be copied, and a copy may be supplied, subject to certain conditions, without infringement of the Act; and generally, users of public records which are Crown copyright and which are publicly available may copy them without seeking formal permission or payment of a copyright fee.[39]

Copy protection devices

Given the ease of copying and the distribution of works in electronic form, it has become increasingly common to use technical devices and electronic management systems to protect copyright works and/or to trace their use. Examples include Electronic Copyright Management Systems (ECMS), Electronic Rights Management Systems (ERMS) and Digital Rights Management Systems (DRMS). Indeed, some see technical protection as a much more effective mode of protection than copyright itself, especially given the difficulty in actually enforcing copyright laws.

Section 296 of the CDPA gave to copyright owners a certain measure of protection against those who dealt in devices specifically designed or adapted to circumvent copy protection, or who published information intended to enable or assist others to circumvent copy protection. Later development of the internet focused attention on the need to harmonize the rules on an international basis. Updated provisions were included in two treaties agreed in 1996 – the World Intellectual Property (WIPO) Copyright Treaty and the WIPO Performances and Phonograms Treaty – and these are now to be received into EU law and thus into UK law through the Information Society Directive and the UK implementing regulations. There is to be a new civil remedy to protect against deliberate circumvention without authority of 'effective technological measures' which protect computer programs or other copyright works. It will also be criminal offence, *inter alia,* to sell, hire, import, possess or distribute any device, product or component which is primarily designed to facilitate the circumvention of a technological measure.

One problem with technological measures is that they can prevent users exercising their lawful rights without permission and without payment, e.g. to copy under the permitted acts. Unfortunately the consultation paper is rather weak on this point, and it merely makes a recommendation that if this happens, a complaint may be made to the Secretary of State, who may encourage voluntary measures to combat this abuse, or if this fails, give directions. This is unsatisfactory and drives a coach and horses through the whole system of user rights in the electronic environment. This will undoubtedly be one of the battle grounds of the future.

Conclusion

Copyright is in a constant state of flux. The laws are complex and it is not easy for information providers to 'stay legal'. Life was much easier when readers just read books, borrowed books and sometimes took notes, and before the photo-copier, scanner and digitization came on the scene. Life was also less litigious. But we cannot move back to those days. The information revolution is here to stay and part of the price to be paid is legal and technical complexity. Copyright is important. It is important for the authors, for the publishers and distributors, and no less so for the readers and researchers. A balance has to be struck between the competing rights and interests, but that balance can only be struck against a fundamental premise of major players, such as information professionals, oper-ating within the framework of rights created by law and by 'staying legal'.

The changing role of the information professional

Information professionals are likely to be faced with questions concerning copy-right in a variety of contexts: when advising users, for example, on the use of the photocopier, or more modern copying devices such as hand-held scanners; and increasingly nowadays when creating their own or their employer's web pages, websites based on links, or when planning digitization projects. Traditionally, information professionals such as librarians have been the users of copyright materials and advisors of users. Now they are also creators and publishers.

Digitization changes the role of the information professional from user or advisor to publisher, and it changes considerably the perspective from which copyright laws are viewed. Advising those who read, or readers who copy, is quite different from planning a major publishing venture such as a digitization project. The digitization team might consider the use of technical copy protec-tion systems and digital watermarking to protect rights in the newly created work. Also, appropriate administrative arrangements for copyright clearance must be made before digitization can go ahead, and the costs thereof, and copy-right fees, must be included in the cost of the project. Obtaining permission to copy (digitize) and to make available to the public via the web or on CD-ROM, as well as for any associated e-commercial use of images, is time-consuming work, but it is work which cannot be avoided. Copyright litigation is expensive, and adverse publicity highlighting ignorance or abuse is damaging in much wider terms.

Notes

1   Directive 2001/29/EC of the European Parliament and of the Council of 22 May 2001 on the harmonization of certain aspects of copyright and related rights in the information society. This chapter anticipates the changes to UK law, drawing on the amendments contained in the Consultation Paper on Implementation of the Directive in United Kingdom Law, published by the Patent Office on 7 August 2002.

2   For example, Garnett, K., James, J. R. and Davis, G. (eds) (1999) *Copinger and Skone James on Copyright*, 14th edn, London, Sweet and Maxwell; and Laddie, H., Prescott, P. and Vitoria, M. (1995) *The Modern Law of Copyright and Designs*, London, Butterworth. See also the latest edition of *Blackstone's Statutes on Intellectual Property*, by Andrew Christie and Stephen Gare.

3   *Copinger and Skone James on Copyright* (see note 2) is available online on Westlaw (subscription only).

4   Section 1, CDPA.

5   Copyright (Computer Software) Amendment Act 1985. See also Section 3, CDPA.

6   Section 1, CDPA.

7   Section 3, CDPA.

8   Section 4, CDPA.

9   As in the US Supreme Court decision in *Feist Publications Inc. v. Rural Telephone Service Inc.* 113 L Ed 2d 358 (1991).

10 In addition, performers are given rights under the CDPA, but these are not discussed further in this chapter. Their rights should be taken into account, e.g. when digitizing sound and moving images.

11 Section 16, CDPA.

12 But not a film, sound recording, broadcast or cable programme. Note however, that copying a literary, dramatic, musical or artistic work also does not infringe copyright in any typographical arrangement of the work.

13 The definition of research will change when the Information Society Directive comes into force. Only non-commercial research will be exempt for copyright infringement. Those engaging in commercial research will not be able to rely on the fair dealing exception and will have to obtain express permission from the copyright owner (and presumably have to pay a fee) before copying may take place.

14 Section 16. CDPA.

15 Section 9(1), CDPA. Note that the author is quite different from the owner of the physical carrier, such as the canvas on which a picture is painted. This may be a museum or gallery. They may object to copying, e.g. by photographing, but they

must do so on legal grounds other than copyright, e.g. contract-agreed terms of entry onto the premises.

16 Section 11, CDPA. Note again that this does not apply to all categories of works. It applies only to literary, dramatic, musical and artistic works, and films. It does not apply to sound recordings, broadcasts or cable programmes, or to the typographical arrangement of a published edition. Copyright in a sound recording belongs to the producer; in a broadcast, to the person making the broadcast, e.g. the BBC; in a cable programme, to the person providing the cable programme service, e.g. NTL; and in the typographical arrangement of a published edition, to the publisher. Therefore, with the exception of the sound recording, the 'person' who owns copyright in these types of works will normally be a company or corporation. There is thus no need to transfer copyright from the employee to the employer.

17 Note that the duration of copyright is determined by the date of death of the employee or consultant, and is not related in any way to the employer. Thus in the case of a literary work, copyright lasts for life of the author (employee) plus 70 years.

18 See generally Chapter X, CDPA.

19 See Chapter V, CDPA.

20 There are special rules relating to the passing of copyright on a specific or general bequest of unpublished papers – copyright can pass with the papers, depending on the date of death.

21 Council Directive 93/98 EEC of 29 October 1993.

22 Flint, M., Fitzpatrick, N. and Thorne, C. (2000) *A User's Guide to Copyright*, 5th edn, London, Butterworths.

23 Padfield, T. (2001) *Copyright for Archivists and Users of Archives*, London, UK Public Record Office [new edition awaited from Facet Publishing, 2004]. For *Copinger and Skone James on Copyright*, and Laddie, Prescott and Vitoria, see note 2 above.

24 Sections 12–15A, CDPA.

25 Sections 16–21, CDPA.

26 See the next section for examples of acts permitted in relation to copyright works.

27 Lending by libraries is generally exempt and lending a book to a friend is not an infringing act.

28 For example, translating it from one language to another.

29 For example, publishing (issuing copies to the public of) a translation without the consent of the copyright owner.

30 Section 16(3), CDPA.

31 Sections 22–6, CDPA.

32 Sections 29–31, CDPA.

33 Editor's note: Sandy Norman's *Practical Copyright for Information Professionals* is awaited from Facet Publishing in early 2004. Sandy was until recently Copyright Adviser to CILIP.

34 Sections 32–6A, CDPA.

35 Sections 37–44, CDPA.

36 For a detailed analysis *see* Coleman, A. and Davies, S. (2002) Copyright and Collections: recognising the realities of cross-sectoral integration, *Journal of the Society of Archivists*, **23**, 223–32.

37 These are defined in Copyright (Librarians and Archivists) Copying of Copyright Material) Regulations 1989.

38 This means public records within the meaning of the Public Records Act 1958, the Public Records (Scotland) Act 1937 or the Public Records (Northern Ireland) Act 1923, or in Welsh Public Records (as defined in the Government of Wales Act 1998).

39 A full account of the law is to be found in Padfield – see note 23.

4

Trade marks and passing off

Charlotte Waelde

Introduction

The laws of trade marks and passing off have always had relevance for the information industry. A publisher may make a portfolio of works available under a specific name – for instance, 'Penguin' or 'Facet Publishing'. Equally, providers of information may combine a name with a particular look, such as the 'European Intellectual Property Review' or the 'New York Times'. The purpose is to build recognition in a name or image associated with the product in the mind of the consumer. In this way, the consumer will associate the product with a particular producer (whether or not the consumer actually knows who the producer is), and the consumer will also come to associate a particular quality with that name or image. Goodwill will also be generated in the association between the get-up under which the products are sold and the producer.

Once recognition and goodwill have been built up, the trader will want to make sure that other participants in the industry do not 'free-ride' on or damage that investment. This is where the law of registered trade marks under the Trade Marks Act 1994 and the common law of passing off for unregistered marks step in. What these laws do is to give a measure of protection to those who have registered trade marks, or built up goodwill in their business.

Having said that, a balance always has to be struck between the legitimate interests of the original trader, and the encouragement of competition. If the protection granted by the law were too strong, it would prevent third parties from legitimately entering the market with competing products. Equally, if the law were too lax, it would allow third parties to enter the market to the detriment of the established business.

With the advent of the information society, both the law of registered trade marks and that of passing off have been used in ways that would have been unforeseen when they were developed. Notable examples are the application of these laws to the practice of optimizing the returns made on search engines using meta tags and banner advertising, and to domain names. Further problems arise because of the global nature of the internet compared with the territorial nature of the intellectual property laws. A trade mark may be used validly in connection with the digital dissemination of information over the internet in one jurisdiction, but that use may conflict with the use of a trade mark in another jurisdiction where the use is equally valid.

This chapter will first examine basic aspects of the law of trade marks and of passing off. Particular note will be taken of the ways in which infringement can occur and defences that may be raised in an action for infringement. The second part of the chapter will look at ways in which the UK courts have applied trade mark law and passing off to search-engine optimization techniques, to domain names and to the territorial conflicts that can arise when trade marks are used on the internet. The purpose of the chapter is to give participants in the information industry a broad overview as to when trade mark law and passing off may be relevant to their activities.

Registered trade marks

Sources of law and major institutions

The current legislation in the UK governing registered trade marks is contained in the Trade Marks Act 1994 (TMA). The TMA was introduced as a result of the EC Council Directive of 21 December 1988 to approximate the laws of the Member States relating to trade marks.[1] The TMA governs those trade marks registered in the UK Register with the Patent Office in Newport, Gwent. The Patent Office has a website at http://http://www.patent.gov.uk.

This chapter will focus on UK law. However, it is essential to note that in 1993 an EU regulation was finalized establishing a community trade mark (CTM).[2] This regulation has created an EU-wide trade mark normally effective throughout all Member States of the EU, and is the first example of a supranational trade mark right. In addition, a number of international organizations, including the World Intellectual Property Organization (WIPO) and the World Trade Organization (WTO), both based in Geneva, have oversight of a number of treaties which affect trade marks. These include the Paris Convention for the Protection of Industrial Property 1883 (WIPO) and the Agreement on Trade-Related Aspects of Intellectual Property Rights (TRIPS Agreement) 1994 (WTO).

The definition of a trade mark

A trade mark is defined in Section 1 of the TMA as: 'any sign capable of being represented graphically which is capable of distinguishing goods or services of one undertaking from those of other undertakings.' The mark may 'consist of words (including personal names), designs, letters, numerals or the shape of goods or their packaging.'

Simple word marks that have been registered include 'Puffin'.[3] Phrases which have been registered as trade marks include 'A Mars a day helps you work, rest and play.'[4] Many words are registered in combination with a device or a graphic such as that shown in Figure 4.1.

EDINBURGH LAW SCHOOL

Fig. 4.1   *The trade mark of the Edinburgh Law School*[5]

Fig. 4.2   *The signature of Marilyn Monroe*

Numbers have been registered, including the number 1010.[6] Personal names (in signature form) which have been registered include that shown in Figure 4.2.

The shape of the packaging of goods has been registered (see Figure 4.3), as has the shape of goods (see Figure 4.4).

Both gestures – 'The mark consists of a gesture made by a person which comprises tapping a pocket of an article of clothing worn below the waist of the person'[7] – and colours have been registered (see Figure 4.5). Sounds – 'The mark consists of the sound of a dog barking'[8] – and smells – 'The mark comprises the strong smell of bitter beer applied to flights for darts'[9] – have also been registered.

Fig. 4.3   *A Coca Cola bottle* [10]

Fig. 4.4   *The shape of the Mini, now owned by BMW* [11]

All of these types of marks are relevant for the information industry, and could be used in connection with dissemination of information goods and services. The one possible exception is smells, although in principle there would seem to be no reason why a distinctive smell could not be registered in conjunction with, say, a children's book!

The value of these marks to the information industry should not be underestimated. Many educational institutions already have registered a logo and/or a combination of words as a trade mark. Many information products, such as the legal information databases compiled by Butterworths (LexisNexis) and Sweet & Maxwell (Westlaw), are sold in connection with a mark which has come to be known by those in the field. As new products and services are launched, such as distance learning, it will be vital to sell these in conjunction with a distinctive image in order to differentiate them from those sold by others. The value of the mark then lies in the fact that users of the service will come to know and to trust the services and products sold in connection with the mark.

Marks have to be registered in a particular class of the trade mark register in connection with specified goods and services for which the mark is or will be used. The trade mark register contains 46 classes altogether, covering a diverse range of goods and services. As examples, class 9 includes apparatus for use in

> PURPLE as a colour applied overall to and subsisting in the goods, the colour purple being definable within chromacity coordinate parameters, according to the CIELAB system, of L, between 0 and 90, a between +5 and +100, and b between –5 and –100.

Fig. 4.5   *The colour purple* [12]

desktop and electronic publishing, class 35 includes compilation of directories for publishing on the internet, and class 41 includes advisory services relating to publishing.

Trade marks can give a monopoly for an unlimited period of time. Registration of a trade mark in the UK lasts for ten years from the date of registration.[13] Successive ten-year periods of registration may be applied for thereafter, with the result that, if timeously renewed, registration may be perpetual. Bass plc registered the red triangle shown in Figure 4.6 on 1 January 1876.

Fig. 4.6   *The Bass trade mark*

It was the first mark to be registered in the trade mark register and is still a valid registered trade mark. The 1994 Act sets out the grounds on which a mark will be refused registration on both absolute and relative grounds. However, more important for this discussion is an appreciation of when a registered mark will be infringed.

How can a trade mark be infringed?

Section 9 of the TMA provides that the proprietor of a registered trade mark has exclusive rights in the registered trade mark, which are infringed by the use of the trade mark in the UK without his consent. A sign is 'used' when a person affixes it to goods or packaging,[14] supplies or markets goods or services under the sign,[15] imports or exports goods under the sign,[16] or uses the sign on business paper or in advertising.[17] The Act makes no reference to the types of use that may be made of a trade mark in connection with digital dissemination of information, such as domain names, meta tags or in banner advertisements. However, that is unsurprising as the TMA (and the directive on which it is based) was drafted long before the internet was a popular means of dissemination. This has left the courts to apply the existing law to these new uses, sometimes with some difficulty.

The grounds on which an action for infringement of a registered trade mark may be taken under the 1994 Act are to be found mainly in Sections 10 (1) to (3).

Section 10(1)

When an *identical sign* is used in conjunction with *identical goods and services* for which a mark is registered, then the registered mark will be infringed.

For instance, if 'Puffin' were to be used by a party unrelated to Penguin, the publishers, in connection with the sale of printed publications, that would infringe Penguin Books Ltd's registered trade mark in 'Puffin'.[18]

Both the mark and the goods or services must be identical for this section to be relevant. In *Avnet Inc. v. Isoact Ltd* [19] on the question of 'identity of goods and services', it was found that the activities of an internet service provider who offered customers the opportunity to create their own web pages were not identical to the provision of advertising and promotional services.

The marks themselves, however, do not have to be absolutely identical to fall within this section. For instance, the typeface in a word or words can be different. So when Bravado Merchandising Services wanted to put the words 'Wet Wet Wet' on the cover of a book, the fact that the script differed from the registered mark (reproduced in Figure 4.7) did not mean the marks were not identical for the purposes of this section.[20]

Section 10(2)

If an *identical mark or similar* mark is used in connection with *identical* or *similar goods and services* and in each case there is a likelihood of *consumer confusion* then the registered mark will be infringed.

It will be recalled that a trade mark must be registered in the trade mark register in conjunction with the goods or services for which it is to be used. Thus, you might have a logo of a black cat stretching itself, and register that in con-

WET WET WET

Wet Wet Wet

Fig. 4.7   *The registered mark of Wet Wet Wet and the type identified with it*

nection with slippers. A competing trader might then use a picture of a black cat stretching itself in connection with gloves. Are the goods similar? They are both items of clothes – but one is for use on the feet, and the other on the hands. The same question arises in relation to the similarity of the marks. If one trader has registered a logo of a black cat stretching in relation to slippers, would that prevent a competing trader from using a picture of a dog or a lion stretching in connection with slippers? Are the cat, the dog and the lion to be regarded as similar?

In a series of cases the European Court of Justice (ECJ) has found firstly that the more distinctive a mark is considered to be, the wider the protection conferred by the trade mark over progressively more dissimilar *goods*.[21] Secondly, the court has held that the more distinctive a mark is, the greater protection it gives over similar-sounding marks, particularly where they are used in connection with similar goods and services.[22] The broad rule from these cases is that the more distinctive the mark, the greater the protection is that it confers.

The difficulty for the trade mark lawyer advising those in the information industry is to work out how to measure the distinctiveness of the mark and similarity of goods and services. Is Puffin to be treated as similar to Penguin? Are children's books to be treated the same as adults books? E-books the same as hard copies? Databases the same as e-books? In *Bonnier Media Ltd v. Greg Lloyd Smith and Kestrel Trading Corporation*,[23] the court found that the provision of a hard-copy financial newspaper performed a similar service to a website giving financial and market information.

It is also important to note that under this section it is not enough that there might be a likelihood of association between the marks; confusion must also be present. You may *associate* 'Persil' and 'Ariel'. Both are used for soap powders in the marketplace. But if the marks are only associated, but confusion is not present, then there will be no infringement.

Section 10(3)

If an *identical mark or similar mark* is used in connection with *dissimilar goods and services* and if the earlier trade mark has a *reputation* in the UK, and the use of the later mark would take *unfair advantage* of or be *detrimental* to the distinctive character or repute of the earlier mark, then the earlier mark will be infringed.

The issue of the use of a sign being detrimental to the *distinctive character or reputation* of a mark, has been referred to generally as 'dilution'. This can occur when advantage is taken of the reputation that a mark has, when that reputation is tarnished, or when the distinctive character of a mark is blurred.

Taking advantage of the reputation (free-riding)

One of the earliest cases to consider whether a mark took advantage of an existing one was *Oasis Stores Ltd's Trade Mark Application*.[24] The case concerned the application to register 'Ever Ready' for condoms (under nearly identical wording to the infringement provisions). This was opposed by Ever Ready plc, who had a registration for 'Eveready' in connection with *inter alia* batteries. Would the later registration take unfair advantage of the repute of the earlier trade mark? Here the Trade Mark Registry said that 'simply being reminded of a similar trade mark with a reputation for dissimilar goods [does not] necessarily amount to taking unfair advantage of the repute of that mark.'

This is an important limitation on the test of 'taking advantage' of the earlier mark. If merely being *reminded* of an earlier mark amounted infringement, the protection enjoyed by the earlier mark would be very broad (so long as it had a reputation).

Tarnishment (detrimental to the reputation)

The Registry and the courts have been willing to accept tarnishment as a ground for infringement of these provisions. In *C. A. Sheimer (M.) Sdn Bhd's Trade Mark* Application,[25] it was felt that the use by Scheimer of the word 'Visa' for condoms would be detrimental to the distinctive character or repute of the earlier trade mark. Registration was thus refused.

Blurring (detrimental to the distinctive character)

Blurring occurs where the distinctive character of the mark with the reputation becomes 'blurred' by overuse, such as by the use of the same or a similar mark on dissimilar products. This was considered in *Premier Brands UK Ltd v. Typhoon*,[26] where the attempted registration by Typhoon of the mark 'Typhoon' for kitchenware was opposed by Premier Brands, who had the registration of 'TY.PHOO' for tea.[27] The court opined that: 'The use of the sign in such circumstances will lead to blurring, as it will reduce the uniqueness of the TY.PHOO mark as a brand name in the kitchen.' This was, however, subject to the proviso that the association had to be such as to be 'detrimental as to the character or repute of the mark'. The action for dilution through blurring failed. However, there appears to be a suggestion in this case that, given the right conditions, such an action could succeed.

As might be gleaned from the foregoing discussion, it is essential to have an appreciation of those circumstances under which a registered trade mark will be infringed. Before a mark is chosen, careful research should be carried out to ascertain whether a proposed mark might be considered too close to an existing right. Equally, once the mark is chosen and is being used, it is essential to monitor what is happening in the marketplace to ensure that others are not using either the same or a similar mark in such a way that consumers would be confused, or the mark diluted. That said, there are legitimate ways in which a mark might be used by a third party, notably by way of comparative advertising. In addition, there are a number of defences that might be relevant. These are considered below.

Comparative advertising

Comparative advertising is the use of another's trade mark in advertising which compares the relative advantages and disadvantages of the products with that of the rival. Under the TMA it will only infringe the rights of the proprietor of the registered trade mark if it is contrary to honest practices in industrial or commercial matters and without due cause takes advantage of, or is detrimental to, the distinctive character or repute of the trade mark.[28] Such a practice is clearly of relevance to the information industry where, as with other industries, there will be a temptation to compare the relative merits and demerits of one product with those of another. There are, however, limits on what can be done.

One of the earliest cases to consider comparative advertising was *Barclays Bank plc v. RBS Advanta*.[29] RBS Advanta advertised a new credit card and in the advertisement made adverse comparisons with Barclaycard. The court refused to grant an injunction. The court considered that the primary objective was to allow comparative advertising so long as the use of the competitor's mark would be considered honest by a reasonable audience. Honesty was to be tested against what was reasonably to be expected of advertisements for that kind of goods or services by the relevant public.[30]

One case that might be considered to be on the margins is *British Airways plc v. Ryanair Ltd*.[31] An advertisement by Ryanair headed 'Expensive BA----DS' and 'Expensive BA' was found to constitute honest comparative advertising. In considering the actual wording of the slogan itself, the court found that this amounted to no more than vulgar abuse.

There are those traders who overstep the boundaries, and the courts have shown themselves willing to step in to moderate the practice. In *Emaco Ltd v. Dyson Appliances* Ltd,[32] both parties alleged trade mark infringement in relation to a flyer in which vacuum cleaners manufactured by the other party were described unfavourably. The court found the flyers thoroughly misleading. On an objective test this was 'otherwise than in accordance with honest practices in industrial or commercial matters'.[33]

Defences to an action of infringement

A number of defences to an action of infringement are contained in the TMA. The first is the 'own name defence', whereby a person may use his own name or address without infringing a registered mark. This must also be in accordance with honest practices. One may question a move by a software programmer called James Microsoft who wanted to start producing his own software and sell it under the name 'Microsoft'. On this point, the court has said in *Asprey & Garrard Ltd v. WRA (Guns) Ltd (t/a William R Asprey Esquire)*[34] that an own name defence is subject to the proviso: 'however honest . . . subjective intentions may be, any . . . own name [use] which amounts to passing off cannot be in accordance with honest practice in industrial or commercial matters.' (For discussion on passing off, see next section.)

The second defence is designed to allow traders to use registered trade marks where they might wish to describe some of the characteristics of their own products or services. For example, the maker of chairs might want to describe the fabric in which they were covered, and to do so may use a registered trade mark belonging to the maker of the fabric. Such use must also be in accordance with honest practices. In one case the court found that a sign 'Independent Volvo Specialist' used by a garage which mended Volvo cars but otherwise had no trading relationship with Volvo went beyond honest practices.[35]

The final defence provides that the use of a registered trade mark will not infringe that mark where it is necessary to indicate the intended purpose of a product or service (in particular, as accessories or spare parts). It may be that a computer programmer selling computer software wants to advertise by stating 'compatible with Microsoft 95 software'. So long as this is in accordance with honest practices in industrial or commercial matters, then such use of the registered trade mark is be permitted.

Honesty in commercial practice would appear to be the touchstone of liability under both the comparative advertising provisions and the defences discussed above. Perhaps one question that participants in the information industry might like to ask when considering a use that might infringe a registered mark is whether, if the tables were turned and that use was being made of the mark by a third party, that would be objectionable.

Passing off

The second branch of the law that has relevance to this discussion is that of passing off. The purpose of this section is to examine the main elements of passing off, highlighting the areas where trade mark law and passing off diverge.

Passing off concerns unregistered marks, and the legal redress that can be claimed if a third party encroaches too closely on the goodwill that has been built up in association with a particular mark or get-up used in connection with goods or services. Passing off protects the trader's ownership of goodwill and sometimes reputation, which may be damaged by a misrepresentation made by a third party. One difference between trade mark law and passing off is that trade mark law is based on statute whereas passing off is a common law tort whose origins lie in deception. Another difference is that in passing off there is no property in the name or get-up in question, whereas under trade mark law there is a property right in the registered mark. Although there are substantial overlaps, the protection given by passing off may in some circumstances be wider than that under trade mark law. For instance, in *United Biscuits v. Asda*,[36] Asda marketed a biscuit, Puffin, with packaging similar to that used by the United Biscuits for its biscuit, Penguin. A claim for trade mark infringement failed because the marks – Puffin and Penguin – were not sufficiently similar. However, considering the entire get-up of the products, the claim under passing off succeeded.

Passing off involves three essential elements: goodwill, a misrepresentation and damage.

Goodwill

Goodwill has been defined as *'the attractive force which brings in custom'*.[37] Goodwill is a form of property and can be assigned and licensed, but it cannot be separated from the business to which it is attached. What is protected by passing off is the goodwill attached to the goods or services which the claimant supplies by association with the identifying name or get-up, and *not* the brand name or get-up itself. Goodwill can become associated with a variety of trade indicia, including names, packaging, get-up, slogans and visual images. In *Reckitt & Colman Products Ltd v. Borden Inc.*,[38] Reckitt had sold lemon juice in yellow plastic squeeze packs which carried the word 'Jif' and had a green label attached. The product was known as the 'Jif Lemon'. Borden started selling lemon juice in yellow lemon-shaped containers with a green cap. Reckitt obtained an injunction. The House of Lords held that Reckitt *did not* have a proprietary right to the lemon-shaped container. Rather, it had acquired goodwill in the product, which was known to its buyers by the get-up in which it was sold.

Where a business is located in another jurisdiction and acquires an international reputation, this may lead to the setting-up of the business in the UK. The courts have said that simply having customers in the UK is not enough, and that the business must also be carried on in the UK:

[A] trader cannot acquire goodwill in this country without some sort of user in this country. His user may take many forms and in certain cases very slight activities have been held to suffice . . . I do not think that the mere sending into this country by a foreign trader of advertisements advertising his establishment abroad could fairly be treated as a user in this country.[39]

These points are important when considering whether the existence of a website accessible in the UK is sufficient to generate goodwill, or whether something more is needed. At present it would appear that there has to be more.

Misrepresentation

The second element in a passing off action is misrepresentation. The person seeking to establish a passing off claim must demonstrate that it is a reasonably foreseeable consequence of the defendant's misrepresentation that his business or goodwill will be damaged.

The most common form of misrepresentation is where the trader passes off his own goods as those of another. In these circumstances the misrepresentation is made to the public and leads the public to believe that the goods or services offered by him are those of the claimant. However, confusion itself does not amount to a misrepresentation. Thus, if all that a trader does is to carry on trade in his own name and does no more than to make a true statement that the goods are his goods, then no other trader is entitled to complain.[40] Having said that, it is not necessary for the claimant to deliberately intend to deceive the public. In other words, fraud is not necessary.

It is also possible to obtain an injunction where defendants equip themselves with the means of passing off. This occurred in the domain name case, *BT v. One in a* Million,[41] where One in a Million registered a large number of domain names which included the names of well-known businesses such as BT, Virgin and Marks & Spencer. The court found that the registrations had been made with the purpose of appropriating the defendant's goodwill. Thus the registrations were instruments of fraud. The court also found a case of passing off to be made out. When the name was typed into a search engine, the owner would be shown to be One in a Million. That would lead the searcher to believe that there was a connection between the two. This misrepresentation would lead to damage because it would erode the exclusive goodwill in the name.

There are a large number of cases where misrepresentation has been found. For example, *McDonald Hamburger v. Burgerking*[42] involved the use of a similar name and get-up. Burgerking ran an advertising campaign for its 'Whopper' hamburger. The posters said 'It's not just Big, Mac'. The court found that a significant number of people reading the advertisement would find it a misrepresentation as to the possible source of the 'Big Mac'. A misrepresentation as to quality can also be actionable. For instance, if a trader indicates that second-hand goods are in fact new [43] or that goods are fresh when they are actually past their sell-by date.[44]

Damage

The final head necessary to establish for a successful claim of passing off is damage or the likelihood of damage. The damage is to the goodwill, which is the property protected by a passing off action. A common type of damage is damage by association caused by the misrepresentation that there is some connection between the parties. For instance, in *Annabel's v. Schock*,[45] the complainant, who ran a respectable night club, obtained an injunction against the defendant, who had set up an escort agency also named Annabel's. There are other heads of damage – for instance, damage caused from lost business if the parties are in competition and one represents his goods as those of the other.

Defences

As with registered trade mark law, there are a number of defences to an action of passing off. Two of these are the own name defence and the defence of honest concurrent use.

Under passing off, the general rule is that a trader may not use his own name if the effect would be to pass off goods as those of another, even if the use is innocent. From the discussion above on registered trade marks, it would appear as if that defence might be wider, although it will be recalled that such use has to be in accordance with honest practices in commercial matters.

The second defence is that of honest concurrent use. If two traders have honestly used the same name or mark in trade concurrently, and it is distinctive of both traders, then both traders may continue such use. This again might be an important defence when considering dissemination over the internet, notably where traders are located in different jurisdictions.

As will be apparent from the discussion above on registered trade marks and passing off, these areas of the law may be used as a sword and a shield for those involved in the information industry. On the one hand, participants will want to protect their own get-up within the market-place by building up goodwill and, where possible, registering a variety of signs as trade marks. Equally, once these elements are protected, participants will want to ensure that others do not encroach too closely on the rights that have been acquired. However, as can be seen, there are limits on what can be achieved. It is also worth stressing at this stage that the laws of registered trade marks and passing off overlap quite substantially. The two should thus not be looked at in isolation.

The use of trade marks on the internet

Having given a brief outline of the main elements of the law relating to registered trade marks and passing off, the purpose of this part of the chapter is to examine a number of cases where those laws have been relevant in internet related disputes. Three specific areas will be discussed: the first is the 'invisible' use of trade marks in meta tags and banner advertisements; the second is the interaction between trade marks and domain names; the third is the general use of trade marks on the internet where there may be conflicting rights in other territories.

Invisible use of trade marks in meta tags and banner advertisements: search engine optimization

Words and increasingly images can be used in a variety of innovative ways on the internet to attract the attention of a consumer. Many of these practices are aimed at ensuring that a particular website comes high up on the list of 'hits' when search terms are put into a search engine by a surfer. Often hundreds of 'hits' are returned in response to a request. However, a surfer will only look to the first few of those in seeking relevant information, and therefore it is important to be ranked as high as possible in the list of 'hits' returned by a search engine. A number of practices have emerged to facilitate this process, among them the inclusion of certain search terms in meta tags and the use of banner advertisements. However, these practices might involve the application of trade mark law and passing off. The question, then, is what practices are lawful?

Meta tags

A meta tag is hidden information within a website that contains a synopsis of the information contained in the website, either in the form of single words or as sentences. As an example, the meta tags on the website for the AHRB Research Centre for Studies in Intellectual Property and Technology Law at the University of Edinburgh include the following:

> <META name = 'keywords' content = 'copyright, intellectual, property, technology, Scots, Scottish, Scotland, Edinburgh, University, system, law, Law, legal, links, lawschool, school, index, UK, English, national, best, principal, launch, biotechnology, patent, patents, genome, design, publication, international, Europe, European,

firms, internet, computer, computers, research, cyber, cyberspace, attorney, collo-
quia, trademark, trade, mark, conference, seminar, lecture'>

The search engines work by sending out 'spiders' to crawl over information in
the web and index web pages. A database is then created, which consists of a list
of words and information on where the words are to be found. The hits are usually rated, with the highest scoring hits displayed at the top of the list of hits
found by the search engine. If a term is found in the meta tags, it is likely to be
rated by the search engine as more relevant and so displayed more prominently
in the search result.[46]

Traders have been using trade marks (both registered and unregistered)
belonging to others in their meta tags to generate business.[47] The most useful
guidance on the acceptability of the practice has come in *Reed Executive plc v.
Reed Business Information Limited*,[48] which concerned not only meta tags, but
also a variety of other optimization practices. Reed Executive provide employment agency services (the Employment Agency) and have a registered mark
'Reed' in connection with these services. Reed Business Information are publishers (the Publishers). Both are well known in their respective fields and entitled to use their names. Problems arose when the Publishers decided to set up a
website, http://www.totaljobs.com, containing details of the advertisements
they carried in their hard-copy publications. The question arose as to whether
they carried out the function of an employment agency. If they did, then they
could be infringing the registered trade mark belonging to the Employment
Agency by virtue of the fact that the word 'Reed' was used in certain ways on the
website. In the event, the court did consider the services supplied to be identical, or at least sufficiently similar for a finding of infringement. In addition, the
court found that goodwill, misrepresentation and damage were present, sufficient for a passing off case to succeed. But how did this apply to meta tags and
banner advertisements?

On the question of meta tags, the judge considered that the use of a trade
mark in meta tags, albeit invisible to the eye of the surfer, constitutes trade mark
use for the purposes of the TMA. The purpose or effect of the use was to indicate the trade origin of the services. As the court was grappling with a strict
application of the tests of infringement under trade mark law, it was suggested
that the short test (which must be applied with caution) is whether the sign
'tells the truth about the site'. In the instant case it was decided that it did not,
because the use of the word 'Reed' by the Publishers in the meta tags suggested
a connection with the Employment Agency that did not exist.

The general advice as a result of this case is that marks belonging to others
should not be used in meta tags if such use would result in suggesting a connection which does not exist. But can a trade mark defence be relevant? In principle

it would appear that there should be no objection. However, in the instant case on the 'own name defence', the court found that such use was not in accordance with honest practices in industrial and commercial matters, as the Publishers knew that there was a chance of deception. But what of the other two defences? It will be recalled that a trade mark can be used where a third party wants to describe some of the characteristics of their own products or services, or where the use of a registered trade mark is necessary to indicate the intended purpose of a product or service. Thus, a bookshop such as amazon.co.uk should be able to use registered marks, such as Puffin, Penguin, Reed Elsevier or any other similar name, in their meta tags as descriptive of the products sold. Interestingly, however, the court suggested that these defences would not be available in a meta tags case because meta tags are invisible. However, it is hard to reconcile that with the view that such use would also be an infringement. Perhaps the rough test that was suggested for infringement – whether the sign tells the truth about the site – should also be available in relation to a defence to that infringement. Whether this view will prevail remains to be seen. Meanwhile, caution should be exercised as to the extent of the defences in meta tag cases.

Banner advertisements

The use of banner advertisements was also discussed in the above case, where a useful description was given:

> One of the things a search engine can do is display advertising in the space on its pages not occupied by the search results themselves. Alternatively it may provide pop-up advertisements (windows which open on the user's desktop to display an advertisement). These advertisements are generally called banners because they are shaped to occupy the area at the top, bottom or sides of the page. An advertiser can agree with a search engine provider for the display of a certain number of 'page impressions' of his advertisement in respect of prescribed keywords. The advertisements (up to the contracted maximum number) are displayed when a user searches for the word reserved. Thus, if the word 'jobs' is reserved for 10,000 impressions, the prescribed banner will be displayed to 10,000 users who search using the word 'jobs'.[49]

Having decided the meta tag issue (that the use of the marks should tell the truth about the site), the court found the issue concerning banner advertisements easy to answer. Only those advertisements triggered by a registered trade mark (or unregistered mark) belonging to another *and* specified by the claimant would be objectionable. Thus, if the Publishers did not specify 'Reed', the fact that they purchase 'jobs' and come up in a search for 'Reed jobs' with a banner is not due to any use of the sign 'Reed' by them and therefore cannot be infringement.

This will give some comfort to the information industry. It would appear that, so long as trade marks or other unregistered indicia that attract goodwill are not included, then purchasing words from search engines is a lawful practice. To echo the defences to trade mark infringement discussed above, a rough test might be to ask what is honest in industrial and commercial matters.

Trade marks, passing off and domain names

A domain name is part of the address of the location of a site on the internet. For instance, harrods.com is the domain name of the London department store Harrods. The portion of the address taken by 'harrods' is the part that often equates to the registered or unregistered trade mark of the person seeking to use the domain name. The next part is the top level domain (TLD), and .com, .net, .org, .info, .biz, .coop, .museum, .name, .aero and .pro. are all generic top level domains (gTLDs). There are also country code top level domains (ccTLDs), which include .uk and .fr. Different rules apply to registration of a domain name in the gTLDs and the ccTLDs. Each domain name is maintained by a registry (for instance, .name is managed by http://www.nic.name/ and .uk is managed by Nominet).You can check to see if a domain name is registered in any of the ccTLDs or gTLDs by going to http://www.whois.org.uk/.

The .com, .net and .org gTLDs are 'open' in the sense that any business or individual can make an application to register a domain name using those gTLDs. The policy is broadly to register on a 'first come first served' basis. It is, however, different for the new gTLDs. For instance the .biz gTLD must be used primarily for *bona fide* business or commercial purposes and not exclusively for personal use. Most registries operate dispute resolution policies in the event of a conflict between the holder of a trade mark and the holder of a domain name. Those who register in the gTLDs all operate under the same dispute resolution policy, which is known as the ICANN Uniform Domain Name Dispute Resolution Policy (UDRP), and has been in operation since late 1999. Nominet, the register for the .uk ccTLD, has had a dispute resolution procedure in place since December 2001.

Why have there been conflicts over domain names?

Disputes over ownership of domain names have arisen for a number of reasons. A domain name has been considered as akin to a trade mark (whether registered or unregistered) and so those who own the mark for the non-internet business wish to use the same name on the internet; it is seen as a valuable addition to the branding of goods and services, or of the business as a whole. However, as discussed above, trade mark law is territorial whereas the internet is global. Therefore different businesses in various parts of the world may have what they consider to be legitimate 'claims' to a particular domain name. As no two domain names can be identical, only one business can have a particular name.

Disputes have also arisen where internet participants have registered domain names which are the same or similar to the trading name or registered mark of a company that is well known or famous, or which has a reputation. Generally, the intention has been to do one of two things, the first being to offer it to the owner of the registered trade mark or trading company in return for some payment. If it is a name that is similar to the well known name, such as porsche-girls.com, the intention might be to use the domain name in an effort, not necessarily to confuse, but to draw people to the site – in other words, to draw on the magnetism that attaches to the mark. The name that has been given to this type of activity is 'domain name hijacking' or more commonly 'cybersquatting'. Parallels can be seen with the notion of dilution discussed above. Finally, disputes have also arisen where someone, perhaps a disgruntled consumer, registers a domain name that includes a derogatory addition – normally 'sucks'. Examples include natwestsucks.com, and guinessbeerreallyreallysucks.com.[50]

How are the disputes resolved?

The disputes considered by the courts have looked to the law of both trade marks and passing off in determining the issues. Of those, section 10(1) of the TMA was in issue in *Avnet Inc. v. Isoact Limited (Avnet)*,[51] a case that has been discussed earlier in this chapter. It will be recalled that the court found that the goods and services covered by the registration of the mark 'Avnet' were not identical to those being offered by the internet service provider who had the domain name avnet.co.uk. Thus there was no infringement under the 1994 Act. The outcome was that the principle of 'first come first served' in relation to domain name registration was upheld.

The UK courts have also considered the application of the law in the context of cybersquatting. The first of these cases, *BT v. One in a Million*,[52] has also been discussed above. This case was decided primarily by looking to the law of passing off, and by some extension of existing principles, the court determined that by registering the domain names the defendants had created *instruments of fraud*. Thus the domain names had to be handed back to the trade mark and brand owners. The court also considered infringement under Section 10(3) of the 1994 Act, and found that the domain names were registered to take advantage of the distinctive character and reputation of the marks, which was both unfair and detrimental. The court thus made clear its dislike of these practices but did not really elaborate on how that section applied. Suffice it to say that the courts have shown a dislike of the practice of cybersquatting, even though that has involved some extension of the law of both registered marks and passing off.

Alternative dispute resolution

Surprisingly few domain name disputes have reached the courts. One reason for this is that many are referred for resolution to the arbitrators applying the ICANN UDRP or one of the national dispute resolution procedures. The dispute policies can be found on the websites of ICANN at http://www.icann.org, or for the .uk TLD at http://www.nominet.org.uk. The rules in these policies do not mirror registered trade mark law, but tend rather to focus on abusive domain name registration. Most provide that the policy will apply where an element of 'bad faith' has been found in the registration of a domain name. For instance, bad faith can be found where a domain name has been acquired for one or more of the following purposes: primarily for selling or renting the name; to prevent the owner of a trade mark from acquiring it; to disrupt the business of a competitor; to attract a competitor's customers to the site; to cause confusion with the public.

Thousands of cases have been heard by the arbitrators of the ICANN UDRP – fewer under policies run by national registries, but the numbers are increasing. Names in dispute have included generic names such as 'allocation' and 'concierge', place names such as 'Barcelona' and 'Heathrow', personal names such as 'BillyConnolly' and 'Madonna', business names such as 'BankofNewZealand' and 'Easyjet', and additions such as 'Directlinesucks' and 'Easymaterial'. Of the '.sucks' cases that have been arbitrated, the majority have been transferred to the complainant broadly on the basis that the domain name is confusingly similar to the trade mark even though there is an addition to it.[53] However, there have been exceptions, and it is noteworthy that some arbitrators have sought to balance the competing interests of the trade marks owners with considerations of free speech.[54]

From the above, the advice when choosing a domain name is firstly to look carefully at the rules governing registration. Second, it would be prudent to carry out a search in the both the UK and the CTM register to see if there might be competing rights. The domain name should then be used fairly. To return to the test for infringement under the TMA, as a rough rule of thumb, 'is the domain name being used honestly in commercial practice?'

The use of trade marks on the internet

Moving on from domain names to the use of trade marks within websites, it has been suggested above that it is perfectly possible, and indeed likely, that different traders in different jurisdictions own the same trade mark for the same goods and services. For instance, the mark 'ABC' might be owned by A in country Z, registered for X goods. That same mark might be owned by B in country Y, also registered for X goods. Given that trade mark law is territorial, that is perfectly acceptable. What then happens when those marks are used on the internet? Does the mere *accessibility* of a web page containing a trade mark in any country of the world also mean that the mark is *used* in that country in a manner sufficient to bring in the application of territorial laws?

Three UK cases have considered the question of accessibility of marks on the internet. Two of these revolved around the question of when a mark was *used* in the UK – a test set out in the 1994 Act as a prerequisite for infringement.

In *1-800 Flowers Inc. v. Phonenames Ltd*,[55] the question was whether the defendant had *used* or had the *intention to use* the trade mark 800 FLOWERS in the UK for the purposes of registration. The applicant had argued that the trade mark had been used in the UK by its use on a website. The court considered that, merely because an internet website could be accessed from anywhere in the world, that of itself did not mean that it should be regarded as having been *used* everywhere in the world. *Use*, for trade mark purposes, depended on all the circumstances of a particular case, particularly the intention of the owner of the website and the understanding that a person using the internet would gain from reading the website. On the facts of this case, there was insufficient intention shown to use the mark in the UK.

The second case, *Euromarket Designs Inc. v.* Peters,[56] concerned alleged acts of infringement of a registered trade mark in the UK by the use of a sign by Peters on a website emanating from Ireland. Euromarket had a UK and CTM for 'Crate & Barrel' in class 21.[57] Peters ran a store in Dublin called 'Crate & Barrel'. Peters advertised their shop in Dublin on a website. It was alleged that two kinds of goods sold in the Irish store, a hurricane lamp and a beaded coaster, fell within the specification of Euromarket's trade mark. On the question of use, the court considered that an apt analogy was that of peering down a telescope towards Dublin, and being invited to visit the shop in Dublin. This would not amount to *use* in the UK. This was different from other internet selling activities, such as those carried out by Amazon.com, who had gone out actively seeking world-wide custom. In those circumstances, a sign would be 'used' on a website.

Thus the question of *use* needs to be examined closely for the purposes of trade mark infringement. The merit of taking this approach is that it allows trade mark owners to use the internet as a method of dissemination of information about products without immediately running the risk of infringing trade mark rights in other territories where the same or similar trade mark exists owned by an independent entity.

However, a third case to consider this and related points was *Bonnier Media Limited v. Greg Lloyd Smith and Kestrel Trading Corporation*.[58] Bonnier Media are the owners, printers and publishers of a newspaper known as 'business a.m.'. They have a registered mark, which includes that name in classes 16, 35 and 41 of the register. They also run a website using the domain name http://www.businessam.co.uk. Lloyd is resident and domiciled in Greece and the managing director of Kestrel, a company incorporated in Mauritius. Lloyd and Kestrel registered a number of domain names, including businessam.uk.com and businessam.info. Bonnier feared that the defenders would set up and run a website passing themselves off as Bonnier as well as infringing their trade mark. The court found that 'the person who sets up the website can be regarded as potentially committing a delict in any country where the website can be seen, in other words in any country in the world.'[59] In other words, the marks could be considered as potentially being used in any country in the world. However, the judge went on to narrow this by saying that a website should not be regarded as having delictual consequences (i.e. being used) where it is unlikely to be of significant interest to consumers. In this case, there had been a history of some animosity between the parties. Bonnier had run a series of stories about the defender, as a result of which libel proceedings were under way in England. As a consequence it was considered that there was a likelihood that the domain name and website would be used to confuse customers of Bonnier resulting in both trade mark infringement and passing off.

The implications of this case – that a trade mark is used in any country where the website is accessible – is thus narrowed by the need to show that there is likely to be a threatened wrong in the country where jurisdiction is claimed. Nonetheless, the case does illustrate what might happen if there are competing claims in different countries. This case was decided under UK law. The laws of other EU countries are similar. Countries further afield, such as the USA, have their own rules on jurisdiction. It should, however, be stressed that the external factors in this case (the animosity between the parties and the litigation in England) had a powerful influence on the decision of the judge. Comparing this with the other two cases mentioned above, it appears that the courts are much more circumspect in deciding that a trade mark is actually used (or potentially used) in a jurisdiction where such factors are absent.

Conclusion

Trade marks are of great relevance to the information industry, and with the increase in the use of the internet and other forms of digital dissemination, that importance is growing. The purpose of this chapter has been to give an overview of just some of the areas where industry participants should consider the implications of the law in their activities. Finally it should be stressed that the focus of this chapter has been on UK law, and trade mark law, like other intellectual property laws, is territorial. To the extent that information products are disseminated overseas, whether by way of hard copy, digital products or other services, then it may well be worth considering registering a trade mark in those countries where the products are likely to find a market. Apart from the CTM which gives protection throughout the EU, simplified procedures exist for registering marks in other countries under the Madrid Agreement and Protocol administered by WIPO where countries have incorporated those treaties into their domestic laws. In addition, laws of other countries may have to be considered in determining whether a particular course of action will be acceptable. For guidance on those issues, interested parties should consult specialized texts.

Notes

1   89/104/EEC, OJ [1989] L40/1.
2   Council Regulation (EC) No 40/94 of 20 December 1993 on the Community Trade Mark.
3   Trade Mark No. 648226. Class 16. Proprietor Penguin Books Ltd.
4   Trade Mark No. 1438989. Class 30. Proprietor Mars UK Ltd.
5   Trade Mark No. 2101409. Classes 41, 42. Proprietor The University Court of the University of Edinburgh.
6   Trade Mark No. 2142860. Classes 3, 4, 16, 18, 25. Proprietor Acheson and Acheson Limited.
7   Trade Mark No. 2048673. Classes 29, 30, 31. Proprietor ASDA Stores Limited.
8   Trade Mark No. 2007456. Class 2. Proprietor Imperial Chemical Industries plc.
9   Trade Mark No. 2000234. Class 28. (flights for darts). Proprietor Unicorn Products Limited.
10   Trade Mark No. 2000546. Proprietor The Coca Cola Company.
11   Trade Mark No. 2002390. Classes 6, 12, 16, 28. Proprietor Bayerische Motoren Werke Aktiengesellschaft.
12   Trade Mark No. 2009633. Class 3. Proprietor Chemisphere UK Ltd.
13   Section 42(1) of the 1994 Act.
14   Section 10(4)(a) of the 1994 Act.
15   Section 10(4)(b) of the 1994 Act.

16 Section 10(4)(c) of the 1994 Act.

17 Section 10(4)(d) of the 1994 Act.

18 Trade Mark No. 648226. Class 16. Proprietor Penguin Books Ltd.

19 [1998] FSR 16; [1997] ETMR 562.

20 *Bravado Merchandising Services Ltd v. Mainstream Publishing Ltd*, 1996 SLT 597, 1996 SCLR 1, [1996] FSR 205.

21 *Canon Kabushiki Kaisha v. Metro Goldwyn Mayer Inc.* (C39/97) [1998] All ER (EC) 934; [1999] 1 CMLR 77.

22 *Lloyd Schuhfabrik Meyer & Co. GmbH v. Klijsen Handel BV* (C342/97) [1999] All ER (EC) 587; [1999] 2 CMLR 1343.

23 Court of Session, 1 July 2002.

24 [1998] RPC 631, 1998 WL 1045122 (TMR), [1999], ETMR 531.

25 [2000] RPC 484 1999 WL 1706052. (Appointed Person), [2000] ETMR 1170.

26 [2000] ETMR 1071, [2000] FSR 767.

27 In class 30.

28 Section 10(6) of the 1994 Act.

29 [1996] RPC 307.

30 See also *Vodaphone Group plc and Vodaphone Ltd v. Orange Personal Communications* [1997] FSR 34.

31 [2001] ETMR 24; [2001] FSR 32.

32 [1999] ETMR 903.

33 See also *Cable & Wireless Plc v. British Telecommunications Plc* [1998] FSR 383.

34 [2002] ETMR 47, [2002] FSR 31.

35 *Aktiebolaget Volvo v. Heritage (Leicester) Ltd* [2000] FSR 253.

36 [1997] RPC 513.

37 *IRC v. Muller.*

38 [1990] 1 All ER 873, [1990] RPC 341.

39 *Bernadin v. Pavilion* [1967] RPC 581.

40 *Marengo v. Daily Sketch* [1948] 1 All ER 406.

41 [1999] 1 WLR 903, [1998] 4 All ER 476, [1999] ETMR 61.

42 [1987] FSR 112.

43 *Gillette v. Diamond Edge* 1926.

44 *Wilts United Dairies v. Thomas Robinson* [1957] RPC 220.

45 [1972] FSR 261, [1972] RPC 838.

46 Typing the word 'Disney' into Google on 9 August 2002 returned 6,010,000 hits. Typing 'Pamela Anderson' in returned 891,000 hits.

47 To find out if a competitor is using your registered or unregistered mark in their meta tags, enter your trade mark as a search term in one of the search engines. Then note the websites upon which the mark does not visibly appear. Once you have accessed one of these pages, you can view the HTML version of those pages

(using the Netscape navigator browser by clicking on 'view' and then 'document source'). This will show the terms included in the meta tag.

48 HC Ch D 20 May 2002.
49 Ibid., Para 52.
50 WIPO Arbitration Centre D2000-0996.
51 [1998] FSR 16.
52 [1999] 4 All ER 476, [1999] RPC 1.
53 WIPO Arbitration Centre D2000-0996 – guinessbeerreallyreallysucks.com and variations.
54 WIPO Arbitration Centre D2000-0636 – natwestsucks.com.
55 [2000] ETMR 369, 1999 WL 1578359 (Ch D), [2000] FSR 697.
56 [2001] FSR 20 Ch D.
57 Trade Mark No. 1331917.
58 OH Court of Session 1 July 2002.
59 Ibid., Para 19.

5

Patents: exploitation and protection

Stephen Adams

Introduction

This chapter provides an introduction to some of the main principles of patenting and patent law, and highlights the areas to which non-specialist information workers need to pay attention, in order to remain within the law in the course of their own work and when giving advice to library or information centre users. It is divided into five sections: the first three discuss patents as property, technical documents and legal documents; section four discusses how an average library can assist inventors and patent researchers; and the chapter concludes with some points on forthcoming changes to the patent scene.

Patents as property
Principles of patent protection

A modern patent provides a limited-duration trading monopoly to the patent holder, in return for a general public benefit in the form of published details about how the invention works. The documents which are printed as part of this 'laying-open' process are strictly 'patent specifications'; the true patent usually consists of a single-page certificate issued by the granting authority to the patent holder (patentee). The specifications can be consulted during the lifetime of the patent, and freely exploited after its expiry.

The mechanism of patent granting

Most countries today operate a procedure called 'deferred examination'. This splits the process of obtaining a patent into two distinct stages, each associated with a published document. An idealized procedure is as follows:

1 *Initial application*: the local patent office completes minimal formal checks and conducts an official search of the literature, which is compiled as a 'search report' – a list of other documents to be considered during the later examination process. *First publication* of the unexamined application and its search report takes place approximately 18 months after filing.

   Applicants now have an *option to withdraw* the application. They may do so if the search report has identified significant prior publications (which suggest that the invention is unpatentable) or if their efforts to develop the invention since filing suggest that it is unlikely to succeed commercially.

2 If applicants wish to proceed, they *request 'substantive examination'*. The application is then examined in detail, as discussed below. This process will typically last at least two years. If successful, the *grant* of the patent is accompanied by a simultaneous *second publication* of the specification, incorporating any amendments which may have been imposed by the examination procedure.

The fact that the deferred examination system leads to two distinct documents – one at 18 months and a second one at grant – has clear implications for the information worker, and will be discussed in more detail later. However, before tackling the documentation issues, it is worth reviewing what factors are considered by the patent office during the substantive examination stage.

Patentability criteria

Most patent offices require that four general criteria must be satisfied in order for a patent to be granted. These criteria are discussed below. Failure to prove one or more of them will result in the application being rejected. It should be noted that the exact standards used for each criterion vary between countries; this discussion refers to the UK situation.

Novelty

The Patents Act 1977[1] at Section 2(1) and (2) requires so-called 'universal novelty' – that is, *any* form of publication (book, report, thesis, conference proceeding, pamphlet, patent specification, slide set, photograph, audiotape, videotape . . .) –

irrespective of its language or origin, which discloses your invention prior to the first filing of your patent application, may result in rejection.

Inventive step

Inventive step (Section 3) requires that the application should have some inventive merit and should not be such a trivial development that (as one Master of the Rolls put it in somewhat unjudicial language) 'any fool could do it'.[2] The intention is to prevent patents being granted for obvious extensions or re-applications of known technology.

Industrial utility

The third criterion requires that the invention can be made or used in any kind of industry (Section 4). Most of the time, this can be fairly clearly established, and may be asserted in a simple one-sentence description within the patent specification. The test for utility has recently been made more rigorous in the USA, and it should not be assumed that this aspect will always be easy to prove.

Excluded subject matter

Sections 1(2), (3) and (4) and 4(2) define certain things which are not regarded as 'inventions' or 'being capable of industrial application'. Amongst these, in the UK, are discoveries, scientific theories or mathematical methods, methods of doing business and computer software. The definition of excluded subject matter can change; the principal amendment has allowed certain biotechnological inventions as patentable.[3]

Patentee rights and exploiting an invention

Every patent granted in the UK has to satisfy the above criteria, whether the inventor is a multinational company or an individual, and ultimately the same legal rights may be granted or denied. Until a case is granted, the applicant has no more rights over the invention than anyone else.

The patent grant confers a range of rights which the holder can enforce in the courts. These consist principally of the rights to *prevent others* from making, selling or offering for sale, using and importing a patented product. Most importantly, a patent does not in itself entitle the patentee to do anything; it is a *negative right* enabling them to prevent someone else doing certain acts without their permission.

Manufacture and sale

Inventors have a number of options when deciding how to exploit their patent. They may:

- make and sell the product or use the process themselves
- sell the patent to someone else (re-assignment)
- mortgage the patent, using it as security for a loan
- license someone else to work the invention, having negotiated a royalty rate on the sale of the products.

Note that a manufacturer, whose name may be strongly linked in the public mind with a certain product, is not necessarily the patentee. For example, the well known 'Workmate'® folding work-bench is usually regarded as a Black & Decker product, but in fact the inventor was an individual, who licensed the patent to the tool company. Many companies are starting to make more active use of licensing opportunities; some interesting examples are discussed in Rivette and Kline.[4]

Use

The sale of a product by the patentee (or with their authority) gives an implied licence to the purchaser to use that product. However, if the supplier is an unauthorized source, the purchaser can be held liable for unlawful use. If hitherto expensive goods are offered at an unrealistic price, it is worthwhile checking whether the seller is actually authorized to act for the patentee.

The right to restrict use only applies once. Generally, once goods are sold by legitimate means, the rights of the patentee are deemed 'exhausted'. Hence, a library which buys patented equipment second-hand cannot be charged with infringement.

Importation

The territorial extent of patent protection is a complicated area, particularly within the EU. A patent normally confers the right to sue for infringement in a single country. Hence, if a company has a UK patent but no corresponding French patent on the same invention, there is nothing that they can do to prevent a rival company in Paris producing and selling the same product *within* France. However, if the rival then attempts to export and market their product in the UK, they would infringe the UK patent.

The complicating factor in Europe is that the EU is considered as a single trading territory, leading to the phenomenon of 'parallel importation'. A company which holds two patents, one in a high-priced country and a second in a low-priced country, cannot use its patent rights in the higher-priced country to prevent importation of *the same patentee's* proprietary product bought legitimately in the lower-priced country. This is particularly controversial in the area of pharmaceuticals, where large price differentials may still occur for the same patented product across EU states.[5]

Infringement

The patentee's basic right is to control the working of their invention – if someone is carrying out any of the above acts without permission, they are said to be infringing the patent. The principal definition of infringement is in section 60 of the Act, although there are special cases where acts which would normally have been considered infringing may be allowable.

Legal proceedings in patents often proceed in pairs. If company A sues company B for infringement of company A's patent, then company B will often counter-sue for invalidity of the same patent. The basic philosophy is 'kill the patent before it kills me' – if the alleged infringer can show that the patent should never have been granted in the first place, there is no case to answer when the patentee attempts to enforce their rights.

Business methods and software patents

A prominent case in the USA[6] has led to a substantial increase in filings for patents in these two technical areas in that country. Interest is also increasing in Europe and Japan.

There are two consequences for the information worker. Firstly, users must be aware that any software purchased for their organization (stock control, periodical circulation, catalogue search software, etc.) may now be the subject of patent rights, as well as or instead of other restrictions such as copyright or contract law. To avoid the possibility of infringement, software must only be purchased from legitimate sources and only used in compliance with the licence terms.

The second aspect relates to business methods. Many business method patents in the USA have been attacked for lack of novelty – critics can sometimes produce prior publications which should have been a bar to patentability. The difficulty of this line of attack is that software and business method developments are notoriously poorly documented, and it may be very difficult in practice to prove exactly when a piece of 'common knowledge' actually entered the public domain.

The implication is that record-keeping processes need to be improved, both as potential evidence to contest an infringement case, and to assist one's own patenting effort. Managers should ensure that the processes and decisions surrounding the development of bespoke software are well documented, and all in-house software developers should be encouraged to document their procedures and to archive copies of their source and object code. For further information, the Patent Office has produced a small booklet in co-operation with the Universities of Sussex and of Sheffield, funded by the European Commission's DG Enterprise.[7]

Patents as technical documents

Patents represent a unique source of rapidly-published information on technical developments. Various studies[8–11] have shown that a large proportion of the information contained in patents, sometimes as high as 80%, did not appear in other scientific literature forms such as journal articles or reports. Despite the difficulty of conducting objective studies in this area, the general trend is clear, namely that patent specifications form an extremely valuable source of teaching in most technical arts.

Gazettes and specifications

There are two principal forms in which patents may be found in a general library: the periodical gazette and the patent specification.

Patent gazettes from most major patent offices issue weekly. Their content will always include a list of newly granted patents, with a description ranging from a simple title to an extensive abstract. Listings are often sorted into classes, so that patents in the same technical field will be found within a few pages of one another. With a little practice, it is possible to run a weekly scan to monitor patents which have been obtained by a particular inventor or company.

Internet versions of patent gazettes are becoming very common. Smaller patent offices often load these as PDF files, which are convenient to view but very difficult to scan rapidly or to search. By contrast, the internet version of the *Patent Cooperation Treaty (PCT) Gazette* has a reasonable search engine, and is enhanced by abstracts and drawings which are no longer present in the paper version. The UK has released a PDF version of its *Patents and Designs Journal*, available at http://www.patent.gov.uk/patent/notices/journals/, which is segmented into the same chapters as the paper product, making it a more user-friendly tool. In September 2002, the USPTO ceased production of its paper gazette entirely, in favour of an internet-only product.

The drawback of using patent gazettes is twofold. Firstly, they are really only suitable for a search by date or publication number. They are unwieldy tools for a general subject search over a long period of time – in either paper or electronic form. The second drawback is that, even if the user locates a record of a patent, the amount of detail provided is limited. To obtain the full picture, it is necessary to obtain a copy of the complete specification.

Just as with gazettes, the internet has revolutionized the means of delivering full texts of patent specifications. Whilst a few countries (e.g. USA) provide searchable full text, most patent documents delivered over the internet are in non-searchable image formats such as PDF or TIFF files. These preserve the original layout and provide the technical drawings which often accompany the written description. However, it is advisable to check the document size before attempting a download. Whilst the average patent specification may run from 50 to 100 pages, some highly technical documents may be considerably larger than this. In August 2000, the European Patent Office published one application of some 400,000 pages (160 boxes of A4, each containing 5 reams). This would pose a challenge for even the most broad-band of internet connections.

Bibliographic standards and layout

One particularly helpful aspect of working with patents is the degree to which their citation and layout has been standardized.

The correct method of citing a patent document is defined by an ISO standard.[12] One of the most critical parts is the two-letter code which indicates the country of origin of the patent publishing authority – this is itself based upon a general ISO standard,[13] which has been modified by WIPO as standard ST.3, available from the World Intellectual Property Organization website at http://www.wipo.org/scit/en/standards/pdf/st_3.pdf.

A patent front page provides much useful information. Each of the significant bibliographic items, such as the title, abstract, name of inventor, etc., is marked with a small Arabic numeral, usually in brackets or in a ring. These numbers are INID (Internationally agreed Numbers for the Identification of Data) codes; the full definitions are found in WIPO standard ST.9 on the website (see http://www.wipo.org/scit/en/standards/standards.htm) or in a CD-ROM version.[14] The vast majority of patent offices use these numbers, providing a consistent means to identify key bibliographic elements. Even if a patent is in an unfamiliar language, reference to ST.9 will show that the text at INID code (54) must be the title of the invention, whilst the name of the applicant is at INID code (71) and so on. This system can considerably speed up the work if any translation is required.

Beyond the front page, the main body of a patent usually follows a predictable pattern, which can also aid the unfamiliar user. A typical order of the elements in an unexamined specification is:

- *preamble* – a description of earlier attempts at the solution of a known problem and often a useful mini-review of the pertinent literature, with references
- *short description* – a summary of the present application, highlighting how it differs from (and is better than) previous attempts to solve the problem
- *detailed discussion* – an extensive description of the working of the present invention, often by reference to the drawings section
- *example(s)* – most often encountered in chemical patents, in which individual laboratory experiments are described
- *test result(s)* – the methodology and results of testing, e.g. for bio-active compounds (agrochemicals or drugs) against target pests or diseases
- *claim(s)* – a formalized recital of the exact subject matter which the applicant considers to be worthy of the grant of a patent, and which will form the boundaries of the applicant's rights if granted
- *drawing(s)* – in support of the written description, to enable a better understanding of the invention
- *search report* – not always present, but if so, consisting of a listing of the items of prior art (patent and/or non-patent) which the search examiner considers to be the most serious barriers to the grant of the patent.

The layout of US patents is slightly different, in that they place the drawings immediately after the front page and before the commencement of the text.

In recent years, several major patent offices, including the Japanese and the European Patent Office, have introduced a system of paragraph numbering, to assist the unambiguous citation of a section within a document.

Terminology and vocabulary

Most patent documents are written in a type of 'patentese' which can be very difficult to follow, even for someone who is skilled in the technical field. The complexity of the language is a result of the somewhat uneasy compromise function of the patent specification – as a legal document to define the scope of a monopoly and as a technical document to disclose the nature of an innovation. In drafting, the patent attorney aims to word the disclosure in a way which will secure the broadest possible rights for their client. As such, they avoid common terminology which might be later construed as unduly limiting, and use language which allows for a greater freedom of action, often at the expense of readability. Hence, a patent may not call a spade a 'spade', but a 'ground-penetrating implement' or a 'material-moving tool'. This has clear implications when attempting to use a full-text patent database for a subject search.

Patent drafting permits attorneys to be their own lexicographers. Provided that a given word or phrase is used consistently within a document, it can be defined in ways which deviate markedly from what would be expected in everyday language usage. Use of these specific words or phrases in the specification, and especially the claims, can be highly significant. 'Claim interpretation' is the process of deciding whether a proposed new invention (or an alleged infringing action) falls within the claims of an existing document, and is a job for the skilled patent attorney.

Nonetheless, if casual users are prepared to persevere, and if their usage of patents is primarily for information purposes rather than legal or commercial decision-making, a specification can yield valuable new teaching to stimulate research.

Patents as legal documents
Publication stages

In the section on the mechanism of patent granting, it was noted that most countries publish patent documents twice. The publication stage is indicated by adding a suffix to the publication number. Typically, an 'A' suffix indicates that the document is unexamined, whilst a 'B' or 'C' denotes the granted patent. The exact interpretation of these Kind of Document (KD) codes is complex, as they are database- and time-dependent. Some assistance can be found on the website of Derwent Information at http://www.derwent.com. Derwent has also produced a useful introductory book,[15] as has the British Library.[16]

Many of the free-of-charge internet databases only provide copies of the unexamined stage. The text and claims of these specifications may differ substantially from the eventual granted case. *Unexamined applications should never be used to determine a company's actual patent rights.*

Languages and translations

Patents are still largely granted by national agencies, in the official language(s) of that jurisdiction. In order to obtain patent protection, applicants must file their application in each country, translated as necessary in order for the patent office to process it.

Consequently, an invention which is protected in multiple countries will be described in a cluster of published patent documents, each describing essentially the same invention. The cluster is referred to as a 'patent family', and will issue in a variety of languages. For example, a family may comprise an English-language US patent, a French-language French patent and a German-language German patent. There may be subtle legal differences, but the three documents will be substantially similar in their technical content, at least at the unexamined stage.

This apparent duplication can be extremely useful. The patent family provides a ready-made translation service for disseminating technical information. For example, a researcher in Austria wishing to consult the US patent can use a patent family database to identify the German-language equivalent and request this instead.

Patent term

Apart from revocation, when a patent is completely withdrawn by the authorities, many patents lapse prematurely and a few may have additional life added to them.

Normal term and premature expiry

Patent laws around the world are slowly moving towards a recognized minimum term of 20 years, counting from the national application date. Much has been done in recent years to try to harmonize laws, but most patents in force today were granted under older laws and may enjoy other lengths of term. The answer to the question 'When will this patent expire?' is not a trivial issue, and depends upon many factors.

One of these factors is the payment of renewal (or 'annuity') fees. Standards for these differ around the world. In the UK, the primary legislation is section 25 of the Act, with the exact fees defined by Statutory Instrument. Many countries use a sliding scale, making it more expensive to maintain a patent in force the closer it gets to maximum term.

Information sources on renewal fees are available on the websites of some patent offices, but should be treated with care by anyone who is not familiar with the payment regime. Some countries have legislation on the restoration of lapsed patents, which may allow for fees to be paid late without jeopardizing the life of the patent.

Term extension

Patent term extension has been available in the UK since at least 1907,[17] but more systematic mechanisms have emerged in many countries over the last 10 to 15 years. In Europe, the system is based on a separate legal instrument, called a Supplementary Protection Certificate (SPC). This is granted under a separate procedure but remains dormant until the corresponding patent has expired, then enters into force to provide a restricted extension period for part of the subject matter of the patent.

The only industries which currently benefit from SPC rights are pharmaceuticals and agrochemicals. The European legislation is in the form of two regulations.[18, 19] The intention of the SPC is to recognize that these two industries must complete extensive government registration procedures on safety and efficacy before they are allowed to introduce a new product. These procedures can take eight to ten years, whereas most patents will be granted in less than four – this means that the patent is likely to be in force for several years before the patent holder can launch the product. Until market authorization is obtained, the company holds a patent which it is legally prevented from exploiting. The SPC system uses a formula which restores this 'lost' period to the life of the patent, allowing the same effective period of market advantage to the patentee as is enjoyed by other industries.

Geographical effect of patents

In discussing the origin of a patent family, it was stated that 'Patent documents are still largely issued by national agencies.' There have been developments over the last 25 years, particularly in the last ten, to modify the truth of that statement.

A range of countries have formed regional patent systems, consisting of devolved patent-granting authorities who grant patents on behalf of their member states. In most cases, these regional patent offices exist in parallel with continuing national offices. The patents granted by the regional office have an equal standing with national patents. Consequently, it is necessary to check two sources when trying to establish whether patent rights exist in certain countries – firstly their national patents and secondly any regional patent system to which that country may belong.

The most significant regional patent office is the European Patent Office (EPO). This body is entirely independent of the EU institutions, and its membership differs quite markedly from the EU. At the time of writing, there are 25 full members and five associate members (so-called 'extension states') of the EPO:

- full members: Austria, Belgium, Bulgaria, Cyprus, the Czech Republic, Denmark, Estonia, Finland, France, Germany, Greece, Ireland, Italy, Liechtenstein, Luxembourg, Monaco, the Netherlands, Portugal, Slovakia, Slovenia, Spain, Sweden, Switzerland, Turkey and the UK
- extension states: Albania, Latvia, Lithuania, Macedonia and Romania.

Three of the extension states (Latvia, Lithuania and Romania) are candidates to become full members during 2002–3, along with Hungary and Poland, which would bring the membership to a total of 30 plus two remaining extension states.

There have been various attempts since 1975 to reach agreement on a single patent for the EU states, to be called the Community Patent. The principal difference between this and a granted European Patent is in the question of legal proceedings after grant. With the European Patent, granting is centralized but litigation is handled in each state individually. The Community Patent foresees a situation where a single patent is both granted and litigated centrally. At the time of writing, the Commission is considering abandoning earlier agreements on the Community Patent,[20, 21] which have never entered into force, and introducing a Council Regulation. Even so, deadlines on this have been set and passed without clear evidence of forward movement.

In addition to the EPO, there are working regional offices or agreements covering states from parts of the former Soviet Union (Eurasian Patent Office), sub-Saharan Africa (OAPI for Francophone, ARIPO for Anglophone states), the Middle East (Gulf Cooperation Council) and South America (Andean Community).

One further prominent international system should be mentioned. The Patent Cooperation Treaty (PCT) has been signed by 118 members as of November 2002, and is administered by the International Bureau of the World Intellectual Property Organization (WIPO) in Geneva. The PCT system limits its activities to the early stages of patent application, by providing a streamlined administrative procedure for applying for a patent in the member states. The International Bureau does not grant patents – it provides for publication of the unexamined application at 18 months and, in some cases, a preliminary opinion on patentability. It then forwards the application to the appropriate member states, and all the formal processes of substantive examination are carried out under national law. At the end of the day, a PCT international application matures into a bundle of one or more national patents, whereas a true regional system produces a single grant having effect in several states.

Copyright in patent documents

Information workers may be faced with questions about the copyright in patent documents. Paper document suppliers are well-established, and newer sources on the internet can supply entire documents in electronic form free-of-charge. This can raise policy questions about downloading, retention, printing out and re-distribution.

The Copyright, Designs and Patents Act 1988[22] provides at Section 47(3) that:

> Where material which is open to public inspection pursuant to a statutory require-ment, or which is on a statutory register, contains information about matters of general scientific, technical, commercial or economic interest, copyright is not infringed by the copying or issuing to the public of copies of the material, by or with the authority of the appropriate person, for the purpose of disseminating that information.

In 1990, the Comptroller-General of Patents, Designs and Trade Marks issued a notice[23] which explicitly applied this section of the Act to certain patent specifi-cations, namely UK patent applications and patent specifications, and transla-tions into English of granted European Patents designating the UK. This notice allows a person obtaining a copy of these documents from an authorized supplier to do certain acts which would otherwise constitute copyright infringe-ment (e.g. the making of further multiple copies in-house), *provided that* these acts are for the purposes of disseminating the information. It would not be per-missible, for example, to sell the second-generation copies.

This specific exemption applies to patent specifications published after the date on which the Copyright, Designs and Patents Act 1988 entered into force, that is 1 August 1989. For specifications published before this date, the same official notice refers back to a 1969 statement from the Controller of HMSO to the effect that Crown copyright in UK patent specifications would not normally be enforced.

There does not appear to have been any corresponding explicit statement issued concerning other patent documents (e.g. national patent applications from other countries, or PCT international applications). It is certainly widely accepted in the information community that 'there is no copyright in patent documents', but this is only based upon general exemptions in law equivalent to section 47(3). Document suppliers now provide paper or electronic copies of patents from many different countries on demand, without requiring signature on the normal copyright declaration forms.

Dealing with inventors
Confidentiality

It is of paramount importance that inventors maintain complete confidentiality over the details of their invention until a patent application is filed. This arises from the definition of novelty discussed at the beginning of the chapter – it should be noted that nothing is said about the provenance of a disclosure. The technical term for when an inventor fails to keep his own secret is 'shooting oneself in the foot'! In like manner, all librarians or information workers should be careful to ensure that they do not disclose any material which could jeopardize their client's patent application.

The situation in the USA is slightly different in that it allows a so-called 'grace period' between disclosure (including first offer for sale) and patent application without harming the chances of obtaining a patent, but this should not be used as an excuse for careless handling of proprietary information. In the same way, although the UK Patents Act 1977 does provide certain safeguards in cases where information becomes available through a breach of confidence (Section 2(4)(b)), these are minimal exceptions. By far the safest policy is to work to maintain complete secrecy until at least the time when the patent is applied for, and preferably up until the 18-month publication stage.

Librarians or information workers should bear in mind that an inventor may wish to have the reassurance of an explicit confidentiality agreement before they engage their assistance. For larger libraries, or those normally handling patentable material, this may be written into their standard operating procedures.

Library users may seek advice over choosing and using a so-called 'invention promotion' firm. These companies generally offer to handle some or all of the administrative procedures towards obtaining a patent and/or marketing a patented product, in return for a royalty payment. Some years ago, there was concern that a number of these firms were exploiting the market, demanding excessive fees or failing to fulfil their promises to inventors. The Patent Office has produced a booklet on this topic, in co-operation with the DTI and the Business Link scheme.[24] The US regulation is somewhat tougher – the appropriate part of the codified intellectual property legislation[25] now requires invention promotion firms to disclose substantial details to prospective clients, including data on the number of cases which they have handled over the last five years and their success rates.

Public information sources

There are many information sources which a small library or information unit can use to help a prospective inventor or patent user. Typically, users fall into one of two groups: either they wish to establish whether their own invention is amenable to patenting, perhaps as a hobby or as an innovative small business; or they are researching historical aspects of science and technology, for which patents form a very valuable resource.

Applying for a patent today

A guide book from the British Library's patent staff[26] is particularly useful in that its approach encompasses the role of the information department as well as the legal requirements and the role of the agent. It includes discussion of free-of-charge search resources for the end-user, as does a more recent book from the same team,[27] although as with all books about the internet, the latter is dating rapidly.

There is no doubt that one of the key aspects of successfully defending a patent is being able to prove that you have originated the idea. As mentioned above on the subject of software, it is important that even small inventors or innovators maintain adequate documentary evidence of their efforts before, during and after the patent application process. The UK government has recently launched an internet site to promote *The Innovation Logbook*, which is a combined notebook for storing ideas and guidebook to the services available for the inventor (available at http://www.innovationlogbook.gov.uk).

The UK Patent Office and the Department of Trade and Industry are key centres for advice on patenting in the UK, and both organizations have set up advice points on the internet. The Patent Office has created a separate *Intellectual Property* portal (available at http://www.intellectual-property.gov.uk), whilst the DTI has its own *Innovation Unit* site (available at http://www.innovation.gov.uk). A further very useful source of inventor-friendly information can be found from the *Institute of Patentees and Inventors* (available at http://www.invent.org.uk), which organizes the annual British Invention Show. For information biased towards the legal requirements, and for assistance in finding a qualified agent to assist with filing patent applications, users should be referred to the UK professional body, *The Chartered Institute of Patent Agents* (CIPA, available at http://www.cipa.org.uk/).

Enquirers who are unable to visit London should consider a local branch of the UK Patent Information Network (PIN). These are libraries which have a certain amount of UK (and in some cases, foreign) patent material available for their users, and with specialist staff for consultation. Some organize local inventor workshops, often in collaboration with local chambers of commerce or Business Link organizations. At the time of writing, there are 13 libraries in the network, excluding the main London library. These are located in Aberdeen, Belfast, Birmingham, Bristol, Coventry, Glasgow, Leeds, Liverpool, Manchester, Newcastle, Plymouth, Portsmouth and Sheffield. Further details about the PIN network can be obtained from the British Library at St Pancras, or via their website at http://www.bl.uk/services/information/patents/patentsnetork.html (*sic* – not /patentsnetwork.html). Individual libraries in the network also have dedicated websites describing their services.

Information about old patents

As noted above, the team at the British Library have a great deal of experience in handling public enquiries about patents information. The appropriate section of the *British Library* website at http://www.bl.uk/services/information/patents.html contains copious amounts of free advice and many useful links to other internet sites. Their section on 'historical searching' is particularly useful, providing glossaries of number formats for old patents (separate English, Scottish and Irish ones being required before 1852, for example) and clues to how to interpret antique markings. One of the principal curators at St Pancras, Stephen van Dulken, has also written a book[28] covering all aspects of historical patent searching in the UK back to 1617, and other books on famous 19th- and 20th-century inventions.

Specialist advice

The main areas where a library customer or information worker will need to seek specialist advice are identifying a legally qualified patent agent and possibly locating a specialist searcher. Many large law firms and smaller intellectual property practices in the UK have long-established links with firms of patent searchers, or in some cases they have dedicated in-house staff. Consequently, if an enquirer engages a qualified UK patent agent from the CIPA register, it is quite likely that their agent will be able to recommend a searcher as well. The register is available in paper form from the Institute at Staple Inn Buildings, High Holborn, London WC1V 7PZ, or via the CIPA website at http://www.cipa.org.uk/.

However, it is no longer mandatory for an inventor to use a patent agent when filing a UK patent application (although it is clearly advisable, in order to stand the best chance of obtaining good-quality patent protection). Under these circumstances, or for general background, an inventor may wish to identify a searcher independently. Unfortunately, there is no comprehensive directory of patent search professionals in the UK. A small number of private firms are listed in an annex to the CIPA members' directory, but this is by no means exhaustive. There are many UK broker firms comprising only one or two people, frequently former searchers from industry with specialist subject skills and experience. Not all of these smaller firms are willing to take on work for casual clients, preferring to maintain a select clientele of established applicants, but some will handle a wider range of work. It is worth consulting local business directories or Yellow Pages under section headings such as 'patent agents' or 'information services' and enquiring with any listed firms. There is no formal certification or registration process to become a patent searcher, and the customer is well advised to ask for information about the experience of the firm's principals before engaging them. However, on account of confidentiality agreements with clients, it is quite possible that even a well established firm will be unable to supply specific references to other customers.

Future developments
Potential law changes

Over the past year, the UK Patent Office has launched several significant consultations, although at the time of writing none has proceeded beyond this stage. Most of the changes, if passed, will impact primarily the operation of patent agents, and are unlikely to affect information workers directly. Two such exercises have addressed the possibility of outsourcing UK search or examination work to other national patent offices, and the means to provide a UK legal basis for applicants to file their applications electronically.

However, information staff should be aware of ongoing developments in the software field. Both the European Commission and the UK government have been consulting in this area. The Commission has also issued a proposal for a draft directive.[29] At present, the European Patent Office and the UK Patent Office hold somewhat different views. Some attorneys maintain that it is possible to get a grant of a software patent under either authority, provided that it is carefully framed, but the EPO Boards of Appeal and the UK Patents Court have taken different approaches on questions of validity when these patents have been challenged in court. Specific professional advice should be taken in this field; the CIPA may be able to assist in identifying patent practices with experience in software inventions.

The most significant change, if it happens, will be on the question of grace periods (see above). The consultation is now closed and the supporting documentation has been posted on the UK Patent Office website at http://www.patent.gov. uk/about/consultations/grace/index.htm. One of the bodies which submitted a viewpoint was the Patent and Trade Mark special-interest

Group of CILIP. A UK grace period, if adopted, might be advantageous for certain inventors (e.g. academics who wish to discuss their invention in a public forum before patent filing), but it is important to emphasize that the situation with respect to filing patents outside the UK would not be changed. Inventors need to be aware that a pre-filing disclosure in the UK, even during a national grace period, might still lose them their rights overseas. If in doubt, by far the best policy is to maintain complete confidentiality.

The impact of the World Trade Organization

The World Trade Organization (WTO) was founded in 1995, and currently has some 140 member states, many of them from the developing world. Member states are required to ratify the Agreement on Trade-Related Aspects of Intellectual Property Rights (TRIPS). This agreement outlines certain minimum standards of patent protection. Member states must offer protection for all inventions, in all fields of technology, provided that they fulfil the normal patentability criteria. Patent protection must also be available for a minimum term of 20 years. A substantial number of developing countries had non-compliant legislation at the time they were admitted to WTO membership, and efforts to ratify TRIPS have resulted in many countries amending their patent laws in recent years. Particularly complex transitional provisions are found in those countries which have hitherto not allowed protection for certain inventions, notably new chemical products or new pharmaceutical drugs *per se*. It was originally intended that most states would have completed this harmonization by 2005, but the Fourth Ministerial Conference of the WTO, held in Doha, Qatar, in November 2001, extended the deadline for least-developed countries to apply provisions on pharmaceutical patenting up to 1 January 2016.

The effect for the information specialist is that the last decade of the 20th century, and probably most of the first decade of the 21st, will have produced patent documents under a wide range of transitional laws and regulations, which makes the task of determining patent term and legal effect more than normally complex.

Towards a world patent?

As noted above, we are still a long way from a 'world patent'. However, major patent offices foresee a crisis looming in terms of workload. Patent application rates (notably for the so-called trilateral offices – the USA, EPO and Japan) are continuing to rise rapidly, and it is proving ever more difficult to attain the balance between adequate technical examination and timely patent issuance. To this end, there have been proposals to harmonize, and ultimately unify, more aspects of national patent systems. At the present time, the PCT is the main international mechanism which is actually operating, but as noted above, this only streamlines initial filing and publication procedures. At a diplomatic conference in Geneva in 2000, around 40 states signed a new Patent Law Treaty, but this has yet to enter into force. Even when it does, it will only impact upon procedural aspects of patent filing, not on substantive law such as search and examination. A follow-up Substantive Patent Law Treaty is still in its very early stages.

A 'Conference on the International Patent System' held in Geneva in March 2002 launched the WIPO Patent Agenda, with the aim of starting 'worldwide discussions for the purpose of preparing a strategic blueprint for the future evolution of the international patent system'. One of the aspects discussed at this conference was the possibility of patent offices sharing the results of prior art searches and/or substantive examination. This is seen as a way of reducing or eliminating duplication of effort. As noted in the course of this chapter, patents are both technical and legal documents, and if the technical (prior art, inventive step) and legal (claim interpretation, grounds for rejection, post-grant litigation) criteria are harmonized, it seems possible in theory that the entire effort of granting patents could be handled centrally. However, as the experience of the Community Patent shows, intellectual property is also a political arena, and it remains to be seen whether there will be substantial progress in the foreseeable future. Certain countries have pressed for reform of the PCT, to turn it into a genuine patent granting process, but even these developments will be a long time in coming.

In the meantime, there is likely to be smaller-scale reform. Co-operation in trade and intellectual property makes it probable that further regional systems will emerge in due course. The most likely candidates seem to be South-East Asia (under the auspices of ASEAN or possibly wider membership), the remaining parts of South America (Mercosur), and North Africa and parts of the Middle East (the Arab League). Other possibilities are agreements under the trading blocs for the Caribbean states (Caricom) and the Free Trade Area of the Americas (FTAA).

References

1   Patents Act 1977.

2   Reports of Patent, Design and Trade Mark Cases (1894) *Edison Bell Phonograph Corporation v. Smith and Young* [1894] RPC 389 at 398.

3   Department of Trade and Industry (2000) *The Patents Regulations 2000*, SI 2000 No. 2037 (implementing Directive 98/44/EC on the Legal Protection of Biotechnological Inventions).

4 Rivette, K. G. and Kline, D. (2000) *Rembrandts in the Attic: unlocking the hidden value of patents*, Harvard Business School Press.

5 Schmiemann, M. (1999) Exhaustion of patent rights and the European Union, *World Patent Information,* **20** (3–4), 193–5.

6 US Court of Appeals for the Federal Circuit (1998) *State Street Bank & Trust Co. v. Signature Financial Group Inc.,* 149 F.3d 1368.

7 UK Patent Office (2001) *Your Software and how to Protect it: a guide for small businesses.*

8 Liebesny, F. (1973) *The Scientific and Technical Information Contained in Patent Specifications: the extent and time factor of its publication in other forms of literature.* OSTI Report No. 5177, Department of Education and Science, Office of Scientific and Technical Information.

9 Liebesny, F. *et al.* (1974) Scientific and Technical Information Contained in Patent Specifications: extent and time factors of its publication in other forms of literature, *Journal of the American Society for Information Science,* **25** (5), 339.

10 US Patent Office/Department of Commerce (1977) *The uniqueness of patents as a technological resource,* Eighth Report of the Office of Technology Assessment and Forecast, US Government Printing Office.

11 Oppenheim, C. and Sutherland, E. A. (1978). Studies on the Metallurgical Patent Literature, II: case study on GALVALUME, *Journal of Chemical Information and Computer Sciences,* **18** (3), 126–9.

12 ISO 690:1987 *Documentation – Bibliographic References – Content, Form and Structure,* International Organization for Standardization.

13 ISO 3166-1:1997 *Codes for the Representation of Names of Countries and their Subdivisions – Part 1: country codes,* International Organization for Standardization.

14 World Intellectual Property Organization (2001) *Handbook of Patent Documentation and Information,* Part 3, WIPO Publication No. 208(E).

15 Derwent Information Ltd (2002) *Derwent Global Patent Sources.*

16 van Dulken, S. (ed.) (1998) *Introduction to Patents Information,* 3rd edn, The British Library.

17 Patents and Designs Act 1907, 7 Edw. 7, chapter 29, s. 18(1).

18 Council of the European Union (1992) Regulation (EEC) No. 1768/92 of the European Council of 18 June 1992 concerning the creation of a supplementary protection certificate for medicinal products, *Official Journal of the European Communities,* **35** (L182), 1–5.

19 Council of the European Union (1996) Regulation (EC) No. 1610/96 of the European Parliament and of the Council of 23 July 1996 concerning the creation of a supplementary protection certificate for plant protection products, *Official Journal of the European Communities,* **39** (L198), 30–5.

20 *The Convention for the European Patent for the Common Market, done at Luxembourg, 15 December 1975* (1976) Cmnd 6553, HMSO.

21 Council of the European Union (1989) Council Agreement (89/695/EEC) of 15 December 1989 relating to the Community Patent, *Official Journal of the European Communities*, (L401), 1–27.

22 Copyright, Designs and Patents Act 1988, 36 & 37 Eliz. 2, chapter 48.

23 UK Patent Office (1990) *Official Journal (Patents)*, **49**, (5 December), 5131.

24 Department of Trade and Industry (1999) *Step-by-step Guide to Using Invention Promoters*, Innovation Unit. Document reference no. DTI/Pub. 4522/3k/10/99/NP.URN 99/173. Also available at http://www.innovation.gov.uk/inventors/promotion_fr.html.

25 United States Code (n.d.) *Improper and Deceptive Invention Promotion*, Title 35 USC § 297.

26 Newton, D. C. (ed.) (1997) *The Inventor's Guide: how to protect and profit from your idea*, The British Library/Gower.

27 Newton, D. C. (2000) *How to Find Information: patents on the internet*. The British Library.

28 van Dulken, S. (1999) *British Patents of Invention 1617–1977: a guide for researchers*, The British Library.

29 Commission of the European Communities (2002) *Proposal for a Directive of the European Parliament and of the Council on the patentability of computer-related inventions*, COM 2002(92) FINAL, CEC, Brussels, 20 February 2002.

6

Some fundamentals of contracts and some applications in information work

Laurence W. Bebbington

Contracts are a fixed feature of everyday life – the purchase of a train or concert ticket, buying a meal in a restaurant, or a pair of shoes, are all examples of contracts entered into freely every single day without any obvious major formalities. We become more aware of contracts when we actually have to sign them – such as our contracts of employment. Contracts are diverse. They may involve small or large sums of money, small or large items, last for short or long periods, be of different types – employment, sale, hire purchase, etc. Contracts are now a profoundly important feature of information work. They extend to such key areas as buying IT hardware and systems, commissioning software, consultancy services, outsourcing IT functions, web-hosting agreements and ownership of intellectual property – such as copyright works. A major area of contracts in information work – licensing agreements – is dealt with separately in Chapter 7. This chapter looks at one or two areas of recent or increasing importance in the use of contracts in information work, namely IT contracts for hardware and software, outsourcing contracts, and aspects of intellectual property ownership and assignment in academic institutions.

The basics of contract law

Descriptions of what constitutes a contract abound in legal texts. Sir Frederick Pollock described a contract as 'a promise or set of promises that the law will enforce'.[1] Or a contract 'is a legally enforceable agreement giving rise to obligations for the parties involved'.[2] Or it 'is an agreement giving rise to obligations which are enforced or recognized by law'.[3]

In general the formation of a contract requires four elements:

1   An *offer*: this involves communicating a willingness to enter into a contract. It indicates the terms upon which the offeror is prepared to be bound (e.g. the price of goods, delivery date) as long as the offeree also agrees to the terms on offer.

2   An *acceptance*: this is a final and unconditional agreement to the terms offered by the offeror.

3   An *intention to create legal relations*: if two parties arrive at an agreement without intending to be legally bound by it then no contract exists. Commercial agreements are strongly presumed by the courts to be legally binding unless there is clear evidence or intention to the contrary.

4   *Consideration*: this involves an exchange or transfer between the two parties. If I say, 'I will give you my 1543 edition of Vesalius' *De Humani Corporis Fabrica*', it is rather different from saying, 'I will sell you my 1543 edition of Vesalius' *De Humani Corporis Fabrica* for £20,000.' The former is a promise not supported by consideration. It asks for nothing in return. It is a gratuitous promise not normally enforceable by law.

Once an acceptance takes place, a contract normally becomes binding. In disputes, various rules relating to offer and acceptance are used to identify the point of acceptance. These are important. Once acceptance occurs, the parties are legally obliged to fulfil their respective obligations.

Offer and acceptance may involve a preliminary stage – the invitation to treat. This is an invitation by one party inviting the other to make an offer. It is 'simply an expression of willingness to enter into negotiations which, it is hoped, will lead to the conclusion of a contract at a later date'.4

Certainty and completeness are also important in the formation of a contract – an agreement must be reasonably clear and complete. For example, where two parties have had dealings in the past, then their previous dealings may be used to clarify any uncertain terms in an existing contract. A contract needs to be sufficiently certain and complete for it to be enforceable by a court, and in various circumstances the courts will use certain approaches to impart certainty into a contract. If it is impossible to give clear meaning to the parties' intentions, then no contract exists. Capacity is also important. Some individuals' capacity to enter into a contract is limited by law. Organizations also often seek to limit those who can enter into contracts on their behalf by prescribing which employees have authority to do so. In some instances certain formalities must be observed. A general rule of the law of contract is that a contract does not have to take a specific form – in writing, for instance. An oral agreement can be binding, or oral statements can vary an existing written contract. The obvious reason why most important contracts are reduced to writing is to achieve certainty – it may be difficult to enforce a contract where two parties disagree over what was said. An assignment of copyright is an example of a contract which must be in writing and signed by or on behalf of the assignor.

The contents of a contract

The contents of a contract are expressed in the terms of the agreement. These are the obligations entered into by each party. These terms may be either express or implied:

1 *Express terms* are laid down by the contracting parties themselves. In a written agreement, most statements will normally be considered a term of the contract. Oral statements made before the contract may become a term or a representation. The distinction is important – a *term* is an obligation imposed by the contract. Failure to comply with it leads to the remedies associated with breach of contract. A *representation* is a statement which may encourage a party to enter into the contract but it is not a term of the contract. A representation which turns out to be untrue may allow the innocent party to take action for misrepresentation. A misrepresentation makes the contract voidable by the innocent party and may give rise to a right to damages depending on the nature of the misrepresentation. In disputes, this classification of terms and representations can be complex and depends eventually on the intentions of the parties. If the intentions of the parties are unclear, then a court will look at such factors as the importance of the statement, the timing of the statement, requests for verification of the statement, special knowledge or skill possessed by one party, etc. For example, if one party possess special knowledge or skill over the other, then a statement made by the more expert party is more likely to be held to be a term rather than a representation.

2 *Implied terms*: further terms may be implied into contracts by the courts in addition to the written ones. This can happen when a difficulty arises with a contract which is not dealt with by the written express terms. It may then be that a term is implied into the contract. These include:

- terms implied by fact (things which have not been included owing to mistake, or oversight, because they seemed so obvious, etc.)
- terms implied by custom (in a particular locality, for instance)
- terms implied on the basis that they are commonly part of contracts in a particular trade (publishing contracts, for example).

A further group is terms implied by law. These are extremely important. Certain statutes, for example, may imply terms into certain types of contract. Section 14 of the Sale of Goods Act 1979 implies terms into a consumer contract that goods, when sold by someone 'in the course of a business', must be of satisfactory quality and reasonably fit for the buyer's purpose.

Contractual terms are classified further depending on their importance. If I contract to buy 15 PCs to build a local area office network for a new business, then the prompt delivery of machines according to the correct specification and price is almost certainly more important to me that the colour of their casing. Contractual terms are distinguished according to the legal consequences that follow from their breach:

1   *Conditions*: a condition is crucial to the agreement. It is an essential term of the contract. Breach of a condition will have very important consequences for the innocent party. Statute law, case law and the contract itself give guidance on what terms are likely to be conditions. If the make and specification of the PCs for my office LAN are not as agreed, and are entirely inadequate for my business, then this is fundamental to me, particularly if I am working to a tight schedule to get my new business up and running. Or if the machines are not delivered by the agreed due date, then normally this would be a breach of a condition. I could repudiate the contract and claim damages.

2   *Warranties* are less important terms of the contract. Breach of these is not likely to have major consequences. Again, the wrong colour of the casing of my office LAN PCs will be less important to me in getting my business running as long as the specifications, price and installation schedule are all as agreed.

    The distinction is of vital importance in the event of a breach of the contract. Breach of a condition allows the innocent party either to terminate the contract or to sue for damages. Breach of a warranty allows the innocent party to claim damages but not to terminate the contract. The innocent party must continue to perform his or her own contractual obligations – such as an agreed schedule of payments. Failure to do so may place that party in breach of contract.

3   *Innominate terms* can be conditions or warranties. The difficulty with them lies in the fact that it is impossible to know in advance how serious the consequences will be of a breach of an innominate term. It is only once a breach has occurred that the effects become clear. Thus, innominate terms may be classified as conditions or warranties depending on the consequences of a breach. This introduces uncertainty, since a party to the agreement can never be sure if he or she is entitled to terminate the contract. Thus, if a party terminates the contract when in fact he was not entitled to do so, then

he will have repudiated his contractual obligations, leaving himself open to a claim for damages.

A contract is described as breached when one party 'without lawful excuse fails or refuses to perform what is due from him under the contract, or performs defectively or incapacitates himself from performing.'[5] In every breach of contract the innocent party can sue for damages. The general purpose of damages is to place the aggrieved party in the position it would have been in had the contract been performed according to its terms. A breach of contract does not automatically entitle the innocent party to terminate the contract. Only breach of a condition, or of an innominate term where the breach is sufficiently serious, gives the innocent party the right to terminate. Whatever the circumstances, great care must always be taken in terminating a contract.

Parties to contracts know that things can go wrong – this does seem to be especially true of IT contracts. Exemption clauses are used to attempt to exclude or limit liability for breach of contract or liability in tort. Exemption clauses must be incorporated into the contract at the time the contract is made. They are of two kinds:

1 An *exclusion clause* seeks to exclude all liability for breach of contract. The supplier of my office LAN, for example, may seek to exclude all liability for late delivery of my PCs and peripherals in any circumstances which are beyond his control.
2 A *limitation clause* seeks to limit liability for breach of contract, for example, to a specified sum of money in damages.

Exemption clauses are often contained in standard form contracts. The benefits claimed for exemption clauses are that they help the contracting parties to allocate risks (e.g. insurance risks), they clarify the division of responsibilities between the parties, thereby reducing potential litigation, and they allow the mass production and use of standard form contracts.[6] They can, however, be abused – they can be imposed by a party that has superior bargaining power on a 'take it or leave it basis'.[7] Exemption clauses are subject to major controls developed by the common law and statute, for example:

1 *Incorporation*: the clause must be validly incorporated into the contract. This can be done by signature of the contract, by giving reasonable notice of separate written terms, or by incorporation based on previous dealings between the parties.
2 *Interpretation*: if properly incorporated into the contract, the exemption clause must also be shown to be drafted so as to exclude or limit liability for

the actual breach. This means that the wording of the clause will be very carefully looked at to ensure that it does indeed exclude or limit the liability. This is done according to the *contra preferentem* rule, which means that the clause will be interpreted in a fashion that is least favourable to the party seeking to rely on it. This is because the party relying on the clause might deliberately use ambiguous language to escape liability unfairly. Two circumstances in which exemption clauses will be subject to even stricter construction are where a party seeks to exclude liability for his own negligence and where a party seeks to protect himself from liability for a very fundamental breach of contract. A party to a contract cannot rely on an exclusion clause where the effect of that clause has been misrepresented to the other party.

3   *Statutory controls*: exemption clauses are also subject to major statutory regulation under the Unfair Contract Terms Act 1977 (UCTA 1977) and the Unfair Terms in Consumer Contracts Regulations 1999 (SI 1999/2083). UCTA 1977 does not apply to all contracts. One type of contract to which it does not apply is contracts which create or transfer most forms of intellectual property. This whole area is a complex one. The basic intention is to control the use of exemption clauses excluding or limiting liability for breach of contract, or negligence, by protecting consumers and customers who agree to contracts based on a supplier's standard terms and conditions. This is particularly important in the IT field, where dealings are often conducted on the basis of standard terms. Interpretation and application of the Act, however, raises many issues – for example, how much of a variation in 'standard terms' is required before such terms cease to be standard? Each situation must be looked at individually. UCTA 1977 limits the degree to which liability can be excluded or limited for breach of contract, or for negligence in tort, and where contracts for the supply of systems and/or software will have terms implied into them by the Sale of Goods Act 1979 (SGA 1979) and the Supply of Goods and Services Act 1984 (SGSA 1984). For example, when goods are being sold in the course of a business, the implied terms are that the goods should conform to their description, should be of satisfactory quality and fit for their purpose(s), should be free from minor defects, should be of reasonable appearance and finish, and should be safe and durable. Under the UCTA 1977, if one is dealing in the course of business on written standard terms, then liability for these cannot be excluded or limited by a supplier unless it is reasonable to do so. Similar restrictions apply to attempts to limit or exclude liability for pre-contractual misrepresentations. The reasonableness test includes a number of factors such as the relative bargaining strength of the parties, knowledge of the existence of the term, whether there was any inducement to accept the term (such as a

reduction in price), availability of insurance, etc. It is not possible to exclude or limit liability for death or personal injury if it is as a result of the tort of negligence or negligence in the performance of a contract.

IT contracts

In recent years a string of IT cases have come before the courts relating to IT hardware and software contracts, for example. These prominent cases have often featured suppliers' liabilities in the provision of failed or defective IT systems, or systems that have been delivered well beyond the agreed delivery date.

It has been argued that contracts for the supply of IT equipment and software present special problems stemming from the unique characteristics of information technology and software.[8] These include the intangibility of software and its effects, which can lead to misunderstandings between parties in a contractual relationship for the supply of hardware and software. Such contracts also often take IT managers, consultants and suppliers either to the limits of their expertise and experience, or even beyond it. Often the parties to IT contracts fail to fully understand each other's products or requirements. IT contracts also normally involve input from many sources such as IT managers, consultants, users, suppliers, customers and legal advisers. This provides adequate scope for the definition and supply of inadequate or unsuitable systems. Also bespoke software is frequently supplied with defects as a matter of course, and extensive testing and live use are often required before the new software truly functions effectively. Sometimes, however, effective functioning is heavily delayed or never achieved, with the consequence that the disappointed buyer seeks to offset any losses incurred by damages or other appropriate means of redress. Constant developments in hardware and software can also mean that minor upgrades or changes can have major practical implications. Again this is not always taken full account of. Finally, new operating modules supplied, or hardware and software, often do not integrate properly with existing systems and applications. All of these factors tend to make the successful definition, negotiation and implementation of IT projects difficult. The courts will recognize this, and make suitable allowance for these problems. The case of *The Salvage Association v. CAP Financial Services Ltd* [1995] FSR 654 illustrates what can go wrong – and how expensive it can be. The defendant had been engaged to supply accounting software for a marine salvage company. Upon delivery of the software it was obvious that it was not complete and contained numerous errors. CAP were allowed further time to revise the software but eventually the claimant terminated the contract and claimed damages. CAP was caught by a clause in the contract by a term that stated that 'it would assign competent staff exercising appropriate skills' to complete the task – a term very similar to an implied term under Section 13 of the SGSA 1982. CAP was unable to rely on a limitation clause limiting its liability to £25,000. Damages of £663,000 were awarded.

Hardware contracts involve 'goods' and will be subject to the SGA 1979, while contracts for writing software will be subject to the SGSA 1982. The latter implies terms into a contract for services that where the supplier is acting in the course of a business, there is an implied term that the supplier will carry out the service with reasonable care and skill, within a reasonable time and for a reasonable payment.

Some actual cases

In recent years a spate of further cases have reached the courts illustrating the problems associated with contracts for hardware and/or software and failed, defective or late IT systems. They chart the changing fortunes of users and suppliers in IT disputes. In 1995, in *St Alban's District Council v. International Computers Ltd* [1996] All ER 481, the council contracted with ICL for the supply of a computer system to administer the community charge. Software was to be delivered and installed in stages from late 1988 to February 1990. The contract was concluded on ICL's standard business terms. An error in the software overestimated the number of community charge payers, resulting in a loss of over £1.3 million to the Council. ICL conceded that the software had been defective but argued that, since the wrong calculation had been undertaken in December 1989 (before the final completion date for installation of all of the software), the system was still in the course of development. It argued that it was only contractually obliged to supply a fully operational system for February 1990. This view was rejected. The court found that the supplier should have been able to supply software that functioned properly at each stage of the agreed development. The system should have been able to calculate the right number of community charge payers in December 1989. The software had to be reasonably fit for its purpose. ICL also sought to rely on an exclusion clause limiting its liability to £100,000. The limitation clause was held unenforceable for several reasons: the parties to the contract were regarded as being in unequal bargaining positions; the Council had been under pressure to conclude the contract to meet government deadlines; the limitation of liability (£100,000) was small in relation to the potential risk and actual loss; and ICL were insured up to an aggregate of £50 million worldwide. It was better for the loss to be shouldered by a large international company than by a local council. The original award of damages of over £1.3 million was reduced on appeal to £685,000.

A few years later, in *South West Water Services v. ICL* [2001] Lloyd's Rep. PN 353, a £3.5-million contract, which included the supply of a new customer information system, went badly wrong. This was a complex contract, in which ICL was to supply hardware and enter into a subcontract for the software. They failed to enter into the subcontract. Deadlines for the supply of the new customer information system were revised. The system was further delayed. After looking at remedial strategies, South West Water (SWW) terminated the contract when it became plain that ICL could not meet the delivery deadline, and sued for breach of contract and misrepresentation. ICL's statement about subcontracting part of the work was argued to be a misrepresentation upon which SWW had relied. An entire agreement clause was held by the court to be unreasonable. Other exclusion clauses which limited ICL's liability to £250,000 or a refund of the sums already paid were also unenforceable. ICL had attempted to exclude all sorts of liabilities which, it had argued, had been incorporated into the contract by relying on its standard terms and conditions. The rest of the contract, however, had been subject to extensive negotiation. Since to all intents and purposes ICL was dealing on its standard terms they were subject to the test of reasonableness. Damages of £3 million were awarded and repayment of all other sums that SWW had paid under the contract.

In *Pegler v. Wang* [2000], 70 Con. LR 68, Wang failed to supply the greater part of a £2-million system. The judgment catalogued a series of failures to provide system modules, delivery of modules that did not work, etc. Pegler sued for over £23 million in damages for breach of contract and misrepresentation. In this case Wang had sought to rely on limitation clauses that were heavily modelled on its standard terms, and which limited direct, special or consequential loss resulting from the 'supply, functioning or use' of the system. However, in this case Wang had failed to supply the system at all. The court found that, if Wang had wanted to exclude or limit liability for delays in supply or total failure to supply, then it needed explicitly worded clauses in the contract to that precise effect. Wang was liable. Over 500 separate instances where the contract had been breached were identified by the court, and Wang's performance was described as 'disastrous'. An aspect of this case was that Wang had 'talked up' their system and had promised to deliver a system which they had good reason to believe would not match the customer's requirements, if it could be delivered at all. This was a serious misrepresentation and Wang would not have been allowed to benefit from an exclusion clause in their standard terms had it been necessary to determine this. So £9 million in damages were awarded. Wang went into voluntary liquidation shortly after this case.

Other cases, however, point to relief for suppliers. In *Anglo Group plc v. Winther Browne & Co. Ltd* [2000] 72 Con. LR 118, the court found that the purchaser of a standard, rather than a bespoke, software package was under a duty to co-operate with a supplier to secure as good a fit as possible between user needs and the IT solution. In this case Winther Browne entered into a contract with

BML, a software supplier, in a deal financed by Anglo Group plc. Winther Browne stopped making payments to Anglo Group and sued BML for breach of contract, alleging that the software was defective. The case is important since a large number of standard packages are extensively used in business. A precise match, therefore, between customer needs and expectations and standard products is unlikely to be possible. In this case the court found that only an 80% fit between needs and the package was possible. 'The design and installation of a computer system requires the active co-operation of both parties', said the judge. It is inevitable that in buying such packages the customer might need to adapt some of its practices and procedures and the customer had a duty to co-operate with the supplier in finding reasonable solutions to problems. The judge criticized Winther Browne for failing to obtain the services of a consultant in defining its requirements and procuring the system. He found the software supplier's standard terms (which placed responsibility for system selection firmly on the user) to be fair and reasonable. Importantly, he found that in an agreement to supply a package system there is an implied contractual term on the user to clearly communicate any special needs to the supplier, and for the supplier to specify whether or not these can be met. In this case Winther Browne could not terminate the contract since the software company had largely met its obligations. By stopping its payments to Anglo Group, Winther Brown had itself committed an actionable breach of contract.

One of the most important cases in recent years that appears to offer substantial relief for IT suppliers is *Watford Electronics v. Sanderson CFL Ltd* [2002] FSR 19, in which the Court of Appeal upheld the reasonableness of an exclusion clause in a contract excluding liability for indirect or consequential loss arising from negligence or otherwise, and limiting liability to the amount paid under the contract. Watford had sought damages of over £5.5 million for breach of contract. The case is very important since the Court of Appeal made it clear that judges should be reluctant to intervene in cases where the parties are clearly experienced businessmen and can be deemed to be of equal bargaining power and skill. Watford Electronics was also well aware of the commercial considerations which would lead a supplier to include limitation of liability clauses. This was directly relevant to determining whether such clauses were fair and reasonable having regard to the circumstances which were, or ought to have been, known to or in the contemplation of the parties when the contract was made. Only if one party has been taken unfair advantage of, or had agreed to something so unreasonable as plainly not to have understood or appreciated what was being accepted, should the court interfere.

Consequences for IT contracts

These and other cases dealing with similar issues provide important guidance to suppliers and users in negotiating contracts for hardware and software provision. They illustrate the need for expert legal advice especially in drafting large-scale IT contracts. Dealing on the supplier's standard terms will subject exclusion or limitation clauses relating to breach of contract to the relevant provisions of UCTA 1977. Attempts to exclude or restrict other implied terms such as satisfactory quality and fitness for the purpose will be subject to a reasonableness test. In addition, the case of *Anglo Group plc v. Winther Browne & Co. Ltd* now suggests further implied terms that may be implied in contracts for the supply of a standard IT system – for example:

- both supplier and customer are under obligation to co-operate with each other in devising and accepting reasonable solutions to problems
- the customer must articulate clearly any special requirements to the supplier
- the supplier needs to advise the customer clearly if those needs can be met and if so, how, etc.

The case of *Pegler v. Wang* demonstrates that all possible scenarios may need to be explicitly covered by suppliers. Suppliers must not oversell their systems – if they do, it could lead to claims for misrepresentation or breach of contract. Standard terms cannot be uncritically incorporated into a contract, and careful negotiation and drafting of situation-specific exemption clauses is essential. Where clauses have not been subject to some negotiation, it is more likely that they will be found to be unreasonable. But where a contract has been subject to extensive negotiation between parties of equal bargaining power and experience, then it is less likely that the contract will be regarded as standard. Suppliers need to be attuned to situations of inequality of bargaining power with their customers and how this might come out against them in the event of any dispute.

Suppliers also need to review their insurance situations. Since it can be difficult to assess direct and indirect losses to a customer when things go wrong, both the supplier and the customer may wish to enumerate the types of losses that a customer can recover or which the supplier wishes to exclude in the event of a breach of contract. Users or customers need to be fully aware of their responsibilities and roles in active and informed co-operation with their suppliers. In some circumstances this may extend to engaging a consultant to assist with the procurement. In such circumstances a consultant may assist in defining the user's requirements, and in determining whether a specification of requirements meets the user's needs, whether the projected system as built is fit for its intended purpose, etc. This, of course, is a further relationship that the user needs to manage via a suitably drafted contract.

Clearly, IT contracts are potentially very complex creatures. Large contracts are in evidence in many aspects of information work, from the type of systems procurement described above to the purchase by libraries of library management systems with many modules (circulation, acquisitions, cataloguing, serials, inter-library loans, management, etc.). Situations are relative, however, and the basic principles of system specification and contract negotiation apply to all purchases of hardware and software. The more that information professionals understand about the issues involved, the greater the likelihood that effective systems can be successfully specified and procured. Such contracts tend to go through discrete phases. These include:

- investigation and specification of user requirements
- issue of an invitation to tender (ITT)
- responses to the ITT from interested suppliers
- evaluation of responses to the ITT and selection of a supplier
- negotiation of a contract
- detailed system design
- system development
- system delivery and installation
- system acceptance testing
- system changeover and operation by the user.

Purely in relation to the contract, many issues need thorough ongoing attention. For example, everything done needs to be matched against the contractual commitments (specifications, timetables, schedules, costs, etc.). Any changes should be properly recorded and documented. Systems development and installation may need to be flexible and requires a willingness by both parties to adapt as required. Performance of key contractual tasks also needs to be monitored against costings and budgets. Problems should be identified at an early stage and their potential legal implications assessed – for example, failure to perform a crucial task that may constitute a breach of contract needs to be immediately identifiable. Supplier and customer need to work closely together in a properly constituted project management group.

Conflict resolution

Where serious problems appear to be developing, then resorts to litigation are rarely advisable without proper legal advice. Other avenues are possible – especially if the contract itself provides for dispute resolution procedures. Simple negotiation between the parties at senior management levels may be an appropriate first step. After all, both parties may have previous dealings and may wish to preserve the possibility of dealing further with each other in the future. This may involve 'without prejudice' negotiations. 'Without prejudice' discussions are normally privileged from disclosure in the event of court action.

The contract may provide for other procedures to be adopted such as mediation or arbitration. Mediation is basically a process of negotiation facilitated by an independent mediator, normally an expert with suitable experience of the IT industry or IT law. Various techniques and approaches will be used by a skilled mediator in order to try and bring the parties to an agreement. If an agreement is reached it will become part of the contract. If not, other dispute resolution techniques may be pursued. Expert determination may be suitable for very technical issues and is a procedure which leads to a binding result, or arbitration may be an option.

Arbitration is a judicial procedure but is generally less formal and restrictive than court litigation, with the parties having more freedom over agreeing the tribunal and procedure for the dispute. The results of an arbitration are binding and enforceable in a court of law.

Litigation is always complex and potentially very expensive. It is also potentially very public and may damage a company's standing and reputation. It is also dangerous – the result can never be taken for granted. Thus, any other ways of settling disputes always need to be explored.

Outsourcing

Although it cannot yet be described as a mature market, outsourcing of IT functions or business processes is a rapidly expanding aspect of the information industry. Although large outsourcing contracts often tend to hit the headlines of the specialist computing press, outsourcing is an option which is increasingly being examined and adopted by smaller organizations. As a service or option it is certainly not unknown in a number of areas of the traditional information industry.

Publishers, for instance, have used outsourcing in various ways – copy-editing, indexing, printing and commissioning content are tasks which have been outsourced by publishers for many years. As aspects of publishing have become increasingly computerized, more publishing functions can be outsourced or contracted out. Libraries have outsourced various functions, one of the most frequent candidates being the traditional technical services such as acquisitions, cataloguing, serials management, etc. Sometimes simple functions can be outsourced as part of a larger process – for example, the purchase of bibliographic records, spine labelling of classmarks on books, lyfguarding of books, transportation of inter-library loan materials, and library cleaning and maintenance services.

The outsourcing of technical services in libraries has occurred in the USA for some time but has often been a controversial subject in the UK. From time to time it resurfaces on the agenda of various institutions. Technical services activities illustrate precisely why outsourcing is potentially an attractive option – staff who catalogue and classify library materials are often positioned high on professional salary grades and so are expensive in costs. They also have very specialized skills that the library could redeploy elsewhere, such as reference and enquiry work. Repetitive and time-consuming tasks are often ideal candidates for efficiency savings and the economies of scale that characterize certain outsourced activities. Many companies outsource general business activities such as accounting functions, payroll administration, human resource management, equipment procurement functions, security, building and equipment maintenance, facilities management, etc. Information and communications technology (ICT) management is an obvious candidate for outsourcing by many organizations and there is a developing trend to outsource in this field. These functions are dynamic, increasingly complex and often need strategic and operational management skills which, given the current pace of developments in ICT, are moving beyond the competence of the in-house expertise of many small, medium-sized and even some large companies and organizations.

Several factors are commonly advanced to justify outsourcing:

1   It can free a company to concentrate on, and improve, its core competencies or business activities and processes by outsourcing some or all of its non-core activities.
2   It can provide access to very specialized skills that an internal workforce may not have.
3   It can provide access to a far wider range of services than many companies or organizations can normally afford by employing their own staff.
4   It can free staff to concentrate on more specific aspects of, for example, a company's information systems management activities.
5   It can reduce costs and help organizations understand and manage their costs more clearly.
6   It can lead to increased operational improvement and quality of service provision.
7   It allows the redeployment of resources – including human, financial and space resources.

Outsourcing should be concerned with maximizing the quality of operations. An organization contemplating outsourcing any aspect of its activities needs to have an intimate understanding of its own business before it contracts out any of its functions. Outsourcing should not be seen as a cost-cutting panacea. A clear view as to the most suitable type of outsourcing needs to be developed – for instance, are one or two specific functions to be selectively outsourced or is outsourcing to be undertaken on a broader front? A strategic approach to outsourcing is essential.

Outsourcing can be considered broadly as 'a conscious business decision to move internal work to an external supplier'.[9] IT outsourcing has been defined by the Computing Services and Software Association as the 'delegation to a third party of the continuous management responsibility for the provision of an IT service under a contract that includes a service level agreement.' When one considers the potential complexity of modern ICT systems and services, then outsourcing can be viewed as a potentially attractive option. Larger organizations may have complex ICT requirements, including the management of data and computing services, desktop computers, workstations, mainframe or mini-computers, communications services (including data, voice, mobile and other network services), security services, specialized application systems, video and audio conferencing, etc.

Nevertheless, there can be serious problems and dangers in outsourcing. The relationship between the company outsourcing its operations and the company supplying the service does not always last its full agreed term. Companies that outsource operations can end up dissatisfied with the service that they receive. Sometimes the anticipated benefits do not materialize. For these reasons, outsourcing needs to be carefully investigated, thought out, costed and planned. Outsourcing provides opportunities to re-examine what is currently happening in the organization and how it is being done; existing processes can be looked at and costed; unique or critical procedures can be reviewed and important or new longer term activities identified. It involves close collaboration and working with one or more external partners and is, therefore, an important relationship that needs to be properly managed for the longer term. Poor choice of an outsourcing partner can be costly.

Outsourcing thus involves important legal requirements. As with any major contractual relationship, it should be preceded by a diligent, clear and realistic specification of the customer's requirements – such as the services to be outsourced and the service standards required. Key staff who understand the applications, services, etc. to be outsourced need to be closely involved in this. Specifications will be put out to tender and a short-list of potential suppliers drawn up. At an early stage the outsourcing company must vet responses carefully to ensure that all of its key needs, terms and conditions are being properly met. All of this means that prior to outsourcing a company must appoint a suitable project team to manage the outsourcing activity.

Key aspects of an outsourcing contract

Outsourcing contracts themselves may take some time to negotiate. They are of crucial importance, since the contract must match the customer's needs with the services to be provided. Contracts are in effect the means by which the customer retains control. They tend to cover a range of key areas, some of which are:

1 *Staff issues*: where the outsourcing involves the transfer of staff to the outsourcing company, then very major personnel issues are raised. For example, some staff from the customer organization may be transferred to the outsourcing supplier, while a small number remain with the customer. These issues need careful handling. Some staff may be made redundant and it is necessary to handle this situation in accordance with redundancy procedures. Important legal requirements also operate in the form of the Transfer of Undertakings (Protection of Employment) Regulations 1981 (TUPE 1981). These are designed to protect the right of employees and recognized trade unions to be consulted in good time, and to ensure that transferred employees are employed on their existing terms and conditions and salaries with the outsourcing company. Where outsourcing affects existing IT or other staff, it cannot be conducted in secret. Trade unions and affected staff must be involved at an appropriate stage in order not to fall foul of employment law requirements. The TUPE 1981 Regulations can also apply if an outsourced function is taken back in-house. This is a complicated area and requires specialist legal advice in order to work out the full implications.

2 *IT*: where appropriate, or essential, the contract needs to specify how and when the customer will have key hardware upgraded and replaced during the lifetime of the contract. Failure to specify upgrade conditions may mean that the company is saddled with the same hardware for the whole of the contract period. If one of the benefits to outsourcing is to capitalize on new industry hardware developments as they happen, then the customer should ensure that this is explicitly written in to the contract.

3 *Existing assets*: some of the customer's existing hardware and software assets may need to be disposed of in the contract. For example, existing hardware and software may be moved to the outsourcing supplier, or the supplier may need to enter the customer's premises to carry out the service. These things need to be considered and catered for in the contract – in fact, sometimes they are catered for in an entirely separate contract. Also, any licensing and

intellectual property issues will need to be reviewed in order to ensure that the outsourcing supplier is entitled to use these assets. Additional licensing charges may be incurred here.

4 *Services and levels of service*: the contract must include or incorporate the services to be supplied and the agreed service levels. A detailed service level agreement covering all aspects of the service is essential. Other issues such as maintenance, backup and disaster recovery, security, etc. must be carefully dealt with. Exactly how service levels are to be tested or measured needs to be specified.

5 *Monitoring processes*: the contract needs to include a formal monitoring requirement. The customer can use this to assess the supplier's activities and performance against the agreed standards.

6 *Performance remedies*: where the supplier is not performing to agreed levels, the contract can specify the ways in which this can be remedied. Service credits, for example, are an increasingly common remedy, although these need to be set at appropriate levels. These can be set at different thresholds that reflect the seriousness of failure to perform as agreed. Liquidated damages (a contractually agreed amount of money representing a genuine estimate of financial loss) are another possibility. Where there is a serious breach of the agreement, then the contract needs to make provision for the types of losses that can be recovered and whether or not there is a limit on the losses recoverable.

7 *Change management*: as suggested above, IT requirements may change during the course of an outsourcing contract. But other aspects of the customer's operation may change as well. Any contract will be based on the situation between customer and supplier at a specific point in time. Although the trend is for shorter outsourcing contracts, the customer needs to ensure that any other key factors of the business that may change in the lifetime of the contract are properly catered for. This can be a difficult negotiating area. It can be precisely in the areas of unanticipated change that the outsourcing company makes its profits by charging for new, additional or unanticipated services. In those areas where the customer can identify likely changes, these should be catered for in the original contract, if possible.

8 *Dispute settlement*: although outsourcing relationships need to be based on trust and require close working relationships, things can go wrong. Any contract may need to make provision for the settlement of disputes using such services as mediation, arbitration, etc.

9 *Charges*: the contract needs to provide for charging mechanisms and schedules.

10 *Termination*: the duration of the agreement and grounds of termination by either party need to be clearly set out.

11 *Miscellaneous issues*: other issues may need to be addressed. In some instances the supplier will have to comply with the requirements of the Data Protection Act 1998, since it is likely that personal data relating to the customer's employees will be processed in certain outsourcing arrangements. There may be sectoral specific requirements that have to be complied with, such as specific arrangements in the financial services sector, to ensure compliance with financial services legal requirements. The contract may also need to make provision for confidentiality issues.

This is a broad survey of an area of increasing popularity. Outsourcing, or the contracting out of services or facilities, can bring considerable benefits if planned and managed carefully, and conducted with a partner with whom a good working relationship can be established.

Ownership and assignment of copyright in academic institutions

An entirely different area where contractual issues are beginning to have an impact is the ownership and exploitation of copyright works created in academic institutions. Interest in the first ownership, and subsequent assignment, of copyright in university research, teaching and learning materials has been generated by the so-called 'journals crisis' or 'serials crisis'. Initially this debate has arisen from the inability of universities to maintain purchasing power for scholarly material published in academic journals. As publishers have relentlessly increased journal prices over a period of years, and with a burgeoning number of specialist journals being published, universities have found it impossible to maintain subscriptions to existing titles and afford new publications:

> Most people – including members of the research community – are entirely unaware of how expensive commercial journals have become. Faculty members are often shocked when confronted with the prices of the most expensive scientific journals. [10]

The irony is that much of this material which universities find it increasingly difficult to afford and make available to their staff and students was, and is, being created by their own scholars and academics. These scholars and academics have been giving their research output away by assigning copyright in scholarly journal articles to publishers, in return for publication. Publication, of course, is the life blood of the respected academic and is vital to securing advancement.

Having seen this precious intellectual property generated by their employees given away, universities have then been forced to buy back the material either in print or electronic form, or both, at what might be thought to be inflated and excessive prices. In addition, consolidation in the publishing industry has meant less competition. This in turn has the potential to further increase subscription costs. The universities have consequently been trapped in a vicious circle. Thus, there has been a search for new channels of scholarly dissemination and publication. Increasingly, the internet has been seen as offering opportunities to create a freer and stronger market for scholarly publishing, through new publishing ventures or models which maintain publishing quality but at more reasonable costs than the commercial model appears to be offering. Initiatives such as SPARC (the Scholarly Publishing and Academic Resources Coalition) and various open access initiatives are examples of this.

In effect, however, the debate over who should own the copyright in scholarly articles has led to a rather wider debate over the ownership of copyright in a much broader range of copyright materials produced by academics. These include lectures, course handouts, printed and electronic learning materials, etc. This debate has been running in both the legal and librarianship literature for some time[11–15] and has attracted the interest of various other affected parties such as the Authors' Licensing and Collecting Society.[16] The wider interest of universities in clarifying ownership of copyright in materials other than scholarly articles has been fanned by some universities scenting opportunities to commercialize learning materials – for instance, by developing electronic course materials and franchising them, possibly even on a global basis. Increasingly fundamental to these issues, however, is the issue of who owns the intellectual property rights to the materials produced by academics in the first place.

Who owns what?

In the UK, the normal rule is that the author or creator of a literary, dramatic, musical or artistic work made after 1 August 1988 is the first owner of the copyright in it. However, there are several exceptions to this rule, the most important exception being contained in Section 11(2) of the Copyright, Designs and Patents Act 1988. This establishes that, where a copyright work is produced by an employee in the course of his or her employment, then the employer becomes the first owner of the copyright unless the employee and employer have made an agreement to the contrary. Such an agreement could be secured, for example, by an author – such as an academic – insisting on a clause in the employment contract specifying that he or she is the first owner of the copyright in everything produced, or in specific types of works, prior to taking up employment. Such a contrary agreement, however, need not be subject to any formalities. A clear oral agreement is also sufficient. Such an approach leaves little room for doubt if indeed it can be negotiated into the contract. It is unlikely, however, that a new academic taking his or her first step on the academic ladder would have sufficient bargaining power to secure such a clause, although an established professor with a clear research and publications track record would obviously be in a much stronger position.

It is also possible for an agreement to the contrary to be implied as a term into the employment contract in a number of ways – for example, by custom and practice in a particular trade or profession, or by the conduct of a particular employer over a period of time. Thus, where a particular university over a period of time has allowed individual academics to deal directly with publishers and assign copyright in their journal articles to a publisher in return for publication, then a case can certainly be made that a contrary agreement may exist in such circumstances.

There is good reason for the existence of the basic rule for the employer being the first owner of copyright in works created by the employee. The employer pays the employee to perform certain agreed contractual tasks and part of these may involve the creation of copyright works. The author has received consideration for his work. There must also be some certainty for an employer to expect to be able to utilize and exploit such copyright works made in the course of employment. Also, employers invest considerable resources to enable employees to undertake their duties. Universities, for example, provide academics with office, laboratory and other expensive working environments; they invest in training, conferences and other professional development activities for their staff; they provide expensive resources such as PCs, workstations or mainframes, and many general and specialized software applications; they provide library and computing facilities; and library, computing and administrative staff often have important input into the creation of certain materials that are likely to be protected by copyright.

There are two important dimensions to the rule: the author must be an employee, and the work must be made 'in the course of employment'.

The various tests that employment law has evolved to determine whether or not someone is an employee (employed under a contract of service) can be applied in cases where the status of the creator may be unclear. It is clear, however, that academics are employees for the purposes of Section 11(2) of the Act. Although full-time and even part-time academics retain some flexibility over the ways in which they engage in their professional duties, after looking at the whole of the relationship between the university and the academic, many factors strongly support the view that academics are employed under a contract of service. These factors include such things as the employer's right to allocate teaching hours, precise timetabling of teaching activities, requirements to perform research, teaching and administrative duties, payment of a monthly salary, pension entitlements, the provision of working facilities, secretarial support, etc. It is also increasingly common for academic positions to be advertised in well defined subject areas within a discipline or field in which the appointed person will be obliged to teach, research and publish. All of these factors support the view that academics are employees for the purposes of the Act. Wherever there is ambiguity, however, the exact position as to who owns the rights in intellectual property created by the 'employee' is best spelled out clearly in a contractual fashion.

But for copyright in the work to be first owned by the employer, the employee must also create the work in the course of employment. This is taken to mean 'within the scope of his duties'.[17] Again, there can be little doubt that the position of the academic has changed over time. Academics are usually employed to undertake research, teaching and administrative duties. However, as outlined above, even though the basic rule that the employer is the first owner of copyright in works produced within the scope of this triad of duties, an implied term in the employment relationship or custom and practice can alter this position and vest first ownership of copyright in the author. So a number of these ownership issues are unclear in many institutions.

An unresolved situation

There is resistance in many (although not all) universities to altering the current vague situation in relation to ownership of copyright in journal articles, in particular. Some universities appear to be prepared to approach this problem very directly and assert the university's ownership rights in all copyright works produced by their staff. This has the potential to disturb certain traditional freedoms that academics have enjoyed. For example, if a university fully asserts its purported ownership rights over all materials, this is not far removed from the university being able to decide where the item should be submitted for publication, when it should be submitted and on what terms it should be submitted, or even to stop publication of the item altogether. Also, universities who take an aggressive stance on this matter have other issues to think through – with ownership come other responsibilities and burdens. Permissions to use copyright works need to be administered, for example, licences for their use need to be drafted, and copyright works need to be defended against infringement. It is not clear that universities have either the expertise or the resources to do this, nor are they necessarily in a position to develop them easily. Possibly more sensibly, many more universities are continuing with their traditional practice of waiving their ownership rights and leaving the author to continue to negotiate with publishers. At the same time, however, an increasing number of universities are also asking their academic authors to think more carefully before assigning copyright entirely to a publisher. Some universities are encouraging authors to negotiate with publishers to retain or reserve certain rights in relation to their works. These include either one or more of the following rights:

- the right to mount the work on an academic's personal website
- the right to mount the work on a departmental intranet
- the right to mount the work on an institutional e-print server
- the right to mount the work on a non-commercial subject-related e-print server.

The reservation of these rights is often achieved by amending the publisher's copyright assignment form (a contract) and returning it to the publisher. It must be noted here that in contractual terms such an alteration is a rejection of the publisher's offer. Under the law of contract, acceptance of an offer must be unconditional. By amending the assignment a counter-offer is being made. It is then up to the publisher to accept or reject the counter-offer. If institutions seek to rely on their academics to reserve certain rights that allow the institution (and indeed the wider scholarly community) to exploit a copy of the work, then any wording that seeks to do so must be extremely carefully drafted. A precise and effective form of words must be used in order to reserve the rights properly and reserve them in perpetuity. A failure in drafting, therefore, may not reserve the desired rights or may render them subject to revocation. This situation appears to be somewhat 'messy' and universities might consider if there are better ways of approaching this problem.

Universities certainly have very strong grounds for asserting ownership rights over teaching materials produced by their academics. This again reflects the changed circumstances of the needs, requirements and expectations placed on university teachers in the way that teaching is now undertaken in educational institutions. The joint report in 2003 by the HEFCE/SCOP Working Group on Intellectual Property Rights (IPRs) in E-learning Programmes confirms this.[18] It contains useful information and model contract clauses on a range of issues relevant to the development, and where applicable the commercialization, of e-learning materials. The report, however, perhaps takes a particular view of what might be classed as 'e-learning' materials and a comparatively managerialist approach to some issues. Given its origins this is perhaps understandable.

Clearly the first ownership of copyright materials produced in universities is of significant concern to many players in the information chain – creators, employers, publishers and users. Each needs to know exactly where they stand. Where possible, therefore, it is highly desirable for all of the ownership and exploitation issues to be clear at each appropriate and relevant stage through suitable contractual arrangements. The ownership of this material is of fundamental concern to the information industry. Exactly how this particular issue develops in the next few years will be interesting to see.

Conclusion

Contracts and licences are having a profound impact in the information profession and beyond. The ownership and exploitation of content is predicated on the law of contract and licensing. The creators of that content, and their employers, are increasingly interested in asserting greater control over the use of their creative output. Any such increased interest is of crucial concern to others in the information chain – publishers, aggregators and consumers. The next few years may witness important conflicts and disputes in this area. The cost and expense of hardware, software and peripherals is a major outlay for all organizations, from the smallest to the largest, and the contractual framework in which this activity needs to be conducted now needs to be understood by a much wider range of individuals – including IT managers, consultants, suppliers and users. Many other areas are witnessing an expanding and more complex use of contracts and licences – areas such as outsourcing, web design and hosting, electronic publishing and licensing agreements, etc. A basic familiarity with aspects of the law of contract is becoming yet another requisite in the job specification of information professionals.

References

1 Winfield, P. H. (1950) *Pollock's Principles of Contract Law,* 13th edn, London, Stevens, 1.
2 Koffman, L. and Macdonald, E. (2001) *The Law of Contract,* 4th edn, London, Tolley, 1.
3 Treitel, G. H. (1999) *The Law of Contract,* London, Sweet and Maxwell, 1.
4 McKendrick, E. (2000) *Contract Law,* 4th edn, Basingstoke, Macmillan, 32.
5 Treitel, G. H. (1999) *The Law of Contract*, London, Sweet and Maxwell, 772.
6 McKendrick, E. (2000) *Contract Law*, 4th edn, Basingstoke, Macmillan, 222.
7 Koffman, L. and Macdonald, E. (2001) *The Law of Contract*, 4th edn, London, Tolley, 137.
8 Bainbridge, D. (2000) *Introduction to Computer Law*, 4th edn, London, Longman.
9 Elliott, T. L. and Torkko, D. E. (1996) World Class Outsourcing Strategies, *Telecommunications*, **30**, 37–9.
10 Frazier, K. (2000) SPARC: encouraging new models of disseminating knowledge, *Collection Building*, **19** (3), 117–23.

11   Cornish, W. R. (1992) Rights in University Inventions: the Herchel Smith Lecture for 1991, *European Intellectual Property Review*, **19**, 13–20.

12   Gorman, R. A. (2000) Copyright Conflicts on the University Campus: the first annual Christopher A. Meyer Memorial Lecture, *Journal of the Copyright Society of the USA,* **47**, 291–316.

13   Monotti, A. L. (1994) Ownership of Copyright in Traditional Literary Works in Universities, *Federal Law Review,* **22**, 340ff.

14   Monotti, A. L. (1997) Who Owns my Research and Teaching Materials – my University or me?, *Sydney Law Review,* **19**, 425–71.

15   Monotti, A. L. and Richardson, S. (2003) *Universities and Intellectual Property: ownership and exploitation,* Oxford, Oxford University Press.

16   Authors' Licensing and Collecting Society (1998) *Publishing – Academic Authors and Their Rights.* Available at http://http://www.alcs.org.uk.

17   Laddie, H. et al. (2000*) The Modern Law of Copyright and Designs,* London, Butterworths, 2000, 823.

18   HEFCE/SCOP (2003) *Working Group on Intellectual Property Rights in E-Learning Programmes*. Available at http://www.hefce.ac.uk/pubs/hefce/2003/03_08/03_08.pdf.

7

Agreements, user licences and codes of practice

Richard McCracken

Introduction

Digital or electronic networks, products and archiving bring libraries increasingly into sophisticated and complex areas of copyright and related rights management and licensing that have traditionally been the territory of the publishing and broadcasting industries. When physical books are replaced by works presented in soft copy and delivered by digital readers or via digital networks, then access to such works is determined by rights licensing and trading.

The commercial models for licensing digital library content are still emerging. Some publishers and other rights owners push towards subscription-based digital rights management licences that treat individual works in much the same way as databases. Some librarians prefer a model based on the acquisition and ownership of content as though the library were still a collection of physical objects. Other mixed-economy models may emerge.

In all models, librarians will be called upon to exercise skills in negotiating licensing terms and conditions as well as price if they are to acquire content effectively and efficiently. This is intellectual property in a pure form. If books as physical objects helped define the libraries of the past, then the current negotiation of licences attached to electronic works defines the libraries of the future. That is why the business of licensing electronic rights is so difficult. If the licence itself defines the product, then what we are doing by negotiating and licensing electronic rights is trying to define an answer to the question, 'What is a library?'. This chapter will help librarians and information workers to develop a practical approach to defining and negotiating licences tailored to meet current needs and yet make provision for future developments.

The nature of licensing

Buying licensing rights is different from buying a physical object in a very important and fundamental way. The first sale doctrine does not apply. Under the first sale doctrine, ownership of a physical copy of a copyright work brings with it rights such as the right to sell a used book, hold it in an archive or swap it, and so on. This means, for example, that if a library buys a copy of a book or subscribes to a print magazine or learned journal then, under the first sale doctrine, it may retain old copies as part of its archive or grant access to readers who are not members of the library. This applies even if the subscription lapses or the journal is discontinued or the publisher is taken over or goes out of business.

However, if the library instead subscribes to an electronic journal, it does not buy a physical copy of the work and the doctrine does not apply. Depending on the terms of the subscription licence, access to archived editions of the journal may evaporate along with a lapsed subscription, and casual readers may be excluded from reading the journal. This places a responsibility on licensees to analyse and be clear about their needs before negotiating a licence. In buying or subscribing to printed works the main (often the only) concern is agreeing a price. In negotiating a licence, understanding and negotiating the terms of the licence is a crucial additional factor.

Trains and boats and planes

Negotiating a digital or electronic licence is complicated because of the sheer number of options available. It makes no more sense to talk about a digital/electronic licence than about a paper licence. The point is, *a digital licence to do what?*

This can be likened to the idea of booking travel through a travel agent as opposed to buying a bus ticket. In buying hard-copy print works, one buys a licence that allows the work to be read. This is rather like buying a bus ticket that allows one to travel by a single means of transport (bus) along a set route. The transaction is very simple. The passenger states the destination and the driver sets the price.

However, the digital media are, theoretically at least, seamless in the sense that a digital product made available in one format may be delivered to, or accessed by, users via a number of other digital formats. For example, a CD-ROM may be mounted on a server, accessed by web or internet delivery, transmitted by digital broadcasts or downloaded onto other machines. The transport system suddenly becomes global and much more complex. It becomes less like buying a bus ticket and much more like booking travel through a travel agent.

In using a travel agent, the transaction becomes much more complex because the range of options increases greatly. One might travel to the same destination by a variety of transport: bus, taxi, hire car, rail, boat or plane, singly or in combination. Stating the destination or even the means of travel is not enough. The travel agent has to narrow the options by asking a whole range of questions relating to destination, transport, accommodation, dates and duration, how much the traveller can afford, the categories of passenger (adult, child, group) and so on. And the passenger will have answers to these questions prepared, or at least sketched out, before starting to book the travel.

The travel agent model applies equally well to decisions that have to be made in the effective licensing of intellectual property. Budgetary constraints, the preferred or essential means of distribution, convenience and breadth of access must be taken into account in defining the core purpose of the licence, just as one might define the 'destination and purpose of travel' when booking a travel ticket.

This means that is essential to define the library's requirements before licensing negotiations start. While such an analysis (balancing a cold assessment of real needs against the temptation to meet every wish) is often just as difficult as reaching agreement in the negotiations themselves, it can't be avoided if the licence is to meet needs. Defining need defines the licence, and the licence limits the library's boundaries. A proper analysis saves money, achieves a satisfactory licence and guides the negotiation. It acts in a way similar to a project specification or template.

The work invested in clearly defining the core, target audience or user group before entering negotiation may then be captured in a range of standard contract conditions. Standard contracts, either agreed between a single library and a rights owner or owners, or recommended nationally as a result of consensus reached between libraries and rights owners, are extremely beneficial. They can be used to capture core requirements consistently across a range of acquisitions licensed from a number of rights holders – publishers, authors and societies. The differing licences offered by publishers, societies and authors may then be matched against a standard contracts template to see if they meet the licensee's requirements. Some libraries make use of a standard template set out as a tick box table, against which licences are measured for usability.

Standard licences are an extremely effective way of handling the repetitive licensing of a large number of small and broadly similar transactions. They introduce clarity, consistency and speed to the licensing process by making it possible to handle large numbers of individual licences without having to explain or negotiate terms and conditions. They allow licensees and licensor alike to be confident that they understand the level of rights granted across a range of material and can encourage the growth of a long-term, sustainable relationship between the parties. They are an essential element if the management of rights clearance is to be handled digitally.

Recognizing the importance of both licensor and licensee groups reaching agreement on a common set of licensing objectives, publishing and library associations in many countries have set up working groups with a brief to develop a consensual approach towards generating standard, recommended licences for electronic libraries. Tilburg Library, Denmark, was one of the first to develop electronic licensing principles for use by librarians in negotiating with publishers and other rights owners. The European Copyright Users Platform (ECUP) and the European Bureau of Library, Information and Documentation Associations (EBLIDA) have provided pan-European forums as representative interest groups acting on behalf of libraries and other copyright user groups. In the USA, similar representative bodies and user coalitions have worked to lobby on behalf of users, to provide a focus for debate, offer advice and draft model licences.

In the UK, the Joint Information Systems Committee (JISC) of the Further and Higher Education Funding Councils and the Publishers Association (PA) set up a joint working group to discuss areas of agreement and conflict between their two constituencies. An original model licence was produced and was followed up by further meetings, resulting in a toolkit designed for use by libraries and publishers engaged in licensing electronic products. The toolkit has three elements:

- a standardized licensing framework used to structure agreements
- a range of exemplar licences covering common situations such as licensing access to a CD-ROM, or the right to access a publisher's server or to digitize a text original
- an agreed set of definitions that can be used in licences as a reference standard.

The final, refined version of the original standard licence was then produced to take account of feedback supplied by both users and rights owners.

Similarly, the Copyright Licensing Agency in the UK, a collecting society representing the interests of both publishers and authors, is seeking a mandate from its members for a digital rights licence. As well as representing its members' interests, the CLA has engaged in extensive talks with representatives from user groups.

One of the most productive current forums for discussion between educational institutions, libraries, publishers and authors is hosted by the SURF Foundation (broadly equivalent in the Netherlands to the JISC in the UK). SURF held conferences in 2001 and 2002 on the subject of 'Copyright Management for Scholarship', in which delegates moved towards establishing a set of frameworks or guidelines to best practice in licensing for educational use. The SURF website contains a number of licensing principles and guidelines (see the section at the end of this chapter).

These moves and many others world wide often express a common view that consensus between owners and users is a more workable way forward than one much-lobbied alternative – legislative change incorporating a widening of users' rights in the digital media.

Open source licences

The view that copyright can be manipulated, worked and licensed in conditions counter to commercial licensing models is also growing. Open source or open access licences, allowing for free and unrestricted use of copyright materials, are used by many authors and, increasingly, by a number of institutions. Such licences, far from being the end of copyright, depend upon copyright to enforce the shared values of the groups and collectives that make use of them. Open source model licences typically allow users to adapt and make use of content for non-commercial purposes, providing that their adaptations are fed back into the community for re-use and re-licensing, also under open source licensing. The question of validation and academic citation is handled by a requirement that the original authors of the work should always be cited and that any changes to the work should not interfere with the moral rights or academic reputations of the authors. These models, sometimes in hybrid forms combining the characteristic spirit of the open source movement with the commercial demands of academic publishing, are increasingly part of mainstream intellectual property management.

While there has been much progress towards reaching a shared view of what such standard licensing may achieve, achieving a single standard licence is still some long way off and may never be attained. It is difficult to imagine a single licence with terms wide enough to encompass every possibility while at the same time being concise enough to be manageable. It is more likely that a range of standard licensing conditions will evolve, each designed to meet a particular range of common circumstances. As a more defined and consistent view of what constitutes a digital library emerges, and as publishers begin to find new and better ways of defining (and widening?) the rights they are able to offer, so licences evolve. We continue to be in a period of evolution.

Some general principles

This chapter is not intended to provide a single model licence. National negotiations between library associations and publishers will develop licensing outcomes better suited to wider library needs, while any licence committed to print will rapidly become outdated. The intention here is rather to set out a range of general principles by which licensees may take a realistic approach to negotiating a licence and to assess the real value of the licences they are offered.

Standard licences come with limitations. They must be drafted with care. Small-scale, multiple negotiations, while cumbersome in volume, at least have the advantage of allowing licensees to develop new skills in the process of undertaking the work. Faults in one licence may be corrected easily in another. Faults in a standard or blanket licence may have long-lasting consequences.

Inevitably, standardization fails to cover every eventuality. It addresses the most common circumstances with some variation for the more common exceptions, and relies, therefore, on an accurate analysis of activity. A useful model is to target the following areas in order of priority:

(a) those essential core activities without which the project (the library) will fail
(b) those surrounding activities that are attractive but not absolutely essential to the core
(c) peripheral (fringe) activities which, however attractive, are unlikely either to arise or to be used in any meaningful way.

The preparatory analysis should be used to define the terms and conditions of the licence, but a well structured analysis is also a useful negotiating tool. It can be used to approach the negotiations as follows. The core activities (a) are essential. They must be obtainable within budget (if not, then the material should be dropped) and cannot be bargained away in the course of negotiation. The surrounding activities (b) may be secured under option (secure now, pay later). The fringe activities (c) may be used as bargaining or negotiating points in the course of arriving at an agreed licensing arrangement.

This chapter will now take a little time to analyse the structure of the relationship between licensor and licensee. Just what does the licence deliver? There must be a grant of rights from the licensor (the publisher) to the licensee (the library). This has implications for both parties. Firstly, publishers can only grant or license the rights that they control. If electronic rights have been retained by the author, or imbedded third-party materials have not been cleared for use in electronic formats, or the publication dates from a time when electronic rights were not anticipated and so were not acquired, then the publisher will simply not be able to license electronic use. This has had an impact, for example, in delaying the CLA's attempts to put in place a standard digital licence for UK education. Where digital rights are not held consistently throughout a work, publishers may make material available for limited electronic use by licensing those parts of the work in which they do have electronic rights, excluding those in which they do not. This option, which is sometimes employed by picture archives, for example, should be avoided wherever possible. Such licences place the responsibility of clearing all copyright content upon licensees, who then assume liability for failing to clear properly.

The licence

Copyright licensing is determined by the conjunction of three elements: copyright law, contract law and the capabilities of the relevant technology. Publishers licensing copyright use the acts restricted by copyright as tools in order to define the extent of any licence. It is necessary to become familiar with the restricted acts in order to help in the analysis of intended use of materials (and, therefore, licensing requirements). In UK Copyright law the restricted acts are, in lay terms:

* copying
* issuing copies to the public
* performing, showing or playing to the public
* broadcasting
* adapting
* storing in any electronic medium
* rental and lending
* importing infringing copies
* dealing in infringing copies
* providing means for making infringing copies
* provision of premises or apparatus for making infringing copies
* provision of premises or apparatus for infringing performances
* authorizing infringement.

UK legislation is about to be changed to incorporate the EC Directive on copyright in the information age. The most significant changes for readers of this chapter are:

* levels of protection offered to security devices and rights management information
* research fair use defence limited to non-commercial research only
* confirmation that negotiated licences override fair use exceptions.

The changes, implemented in February 2003, remain open to interpretation. Some commentators take the view that the level of protection offered to security measures may make it an offence to be in possession of a means of evading or circumventing security devices, such as encryption, watermarking and other technological measures designed to prevent unlicensed access to works. This will make it impossible to access encrypted or otherwise protected work for the purposes of exercising fair use provisions without the rights owner's co-operation. Some collecting societies have proposed that blanket licensing schemes could take account of this by offering a percentage reduction in the fee equivalent to an agreed estimate of the amount of copying made annually under fair use provisions.

In assessing licensing requirements, one analyses the delivery process from supplier to end-user, asking which of the restricted acts may be committed along the way. In the case of digital libraries, securing the right to copy, store in an electronic medium (both to deliver content and to archive), issue copies to the public, perform, show or play to the public, adapt, rent and lend is an obvious and essential component of any licence, though circumstances may change from library to library.

There are other restricted acts, however, which are less obviously related to libraries, but which libraries may commit inadvertently and which cannot be catered for in a licence. These derive from library staff or library user guidelines encouraging users to commit restricted acts. Libraries should be careful to avoid *authorizing* any activity that could be construed as infringing and to give users sufficient guidance on their responsibilities under copyright law so as to avoid any suggestion that library equipment or facilities are being used for the purposes of infringement. Authorization may also be implied by acts of omission. Failing to display guidelines by photocopiers, for example, or to have well written user and staff guides to good practice, have been interpreted by some courts as implying authorization.

Copyright legislation seeks to balance the copyright owner's monopoly right in controlling the use and exploitation of the work with fair dealing provisions or defences covering the free use of material for the purposes of criticism or review, research and private study, and so on. To these must be added the fact that is possible to use an insubstantial portion of a work without charge. (If infringement depends upon using a *substantial* part of a work, then use of an *insubstantial* part does not infringe.) Libraries will be familiar with those provisions that apply to them and it is not intended to go into the provisions in detail here. However, access to fair dealing exceptions and defences is threatened by the implementation of the EC Directive and the increasing use of digital rights management systems by rights holders, making it increasingly difficult for users to make full use of the provisions without falling foul of legislation outlawing the circumvention of security devices. The proposed legislation may provide for redress by allowing for appeal to the Secretary of State responsible, but the process is likely to be long-winded and more trouble than it is worth – though class actions on behalf of the sector may be effective.

The fact is that the technical characteristics of digital media, and the use of contractual (licensing) conditions, both restrict easy access to the provisions of fair dealing.

The technology cannot think. It cannot anticipate or interpret a user's intent in accessing content. So it cannot interpret or apply fair use provisions. This has an effect on the licensing culture that might develop. In the early days of broadcast television, the absence of playback facilities meant that, in order to repeat the screening of a play, the entire cast had to re-assemble and perform the work again. They were paid repeat fees. Even following the introduction of recording technology, the practice was retained because by then the additional payments had become a recognized part of the culture. So the limitations of the technology had a direct impact upon the licensing and payment for rights in performances. In a similar way, the impossibility of developing digital technology that will identify and recognize the intent behind access to a digitized work (because intention is what determines the degree to which the fair dealing provision may apply) is a driver behind the argument that fair dealing provision does not apply in a digital environment. The fact that this argument coincides with the commercial interests of rights owners makes it more potent. It should be resisted. It is important for libraries (and other users) to retain provisions for fair dealing.

For the sake of clarity, and in the interests of preventing the erosion of their statutory rights, licensees are advised to insist upon the inclusion of a clause stating that nothing in the licence shall be deemed to affect any statutory rights that may be granted under copyright law. A simple clause such as the following may be used:

> Nothing in this licence shall in any way exclude, alter or affect any statutory provision relating to acts permitted in relation to copyright works under the applicable national copyright legislation.

Licence structure

All licences follow the same basic structure: an introductory section setting out the aims of the agreement and describing or defining the parties, and including a series of definitions of terms; a central section setting out the terms of the agreement (licence) itself; and a final, nuts-and-bolts section dealing with issues of termination, applicable law, etc.

The introductory section

The licence will often commence with a brief introduction (or *recitals*) giving an outline of what the contract is intended to achieve. While it could be easy to see this introductory section as somehow separate from the body of the contract, it gives the context in which the rest of the contract will be interpreted in case of dispute. So it should be treated with respect.

Two other sections also address the interpretation of the contract: the *definitions* and the choice of *applicable law*. Of these, the selection of applicable law (the jurisdiction to which the parties agree to submit in interpreting the contract) is perhaps the most straightforward as the jurisdiction of choice should always be that of the library – primarily, though not exclusively, for reasons of cost.

The definitions are much more contentious and should be approached with care. This chapter discussed previously the way in which the digital library is defined by the licence rather than by its capacity to store and display physical objects. In agreeing the definitions by which the licence operates, the parties to a large extent reach an agreed definition of a library.

The definitions are an agreed, short, clearly defined interpretation of the larger concepts underlying the licence. What, for instance, is meant by the phrase 'the library' in an agreement between a publisher and a library? Is it the physical construction, the library building or the user community? Definitions will define the parties to the licence and the licensing terms. As a general rule, the licensor will attempt to define the rights granted under licence as narrowly as possible, while licensee will attempt to negotiate definitions that broaden the grant of rights. As a brief but useful example, consider how the body of users who will have access to a digital library might be defined. A definition that specifies a body of users simply as students of a university excludes use by any other category of user (including staff of the university). Other, less obvious user groups include walk-in users, students accessing other campus libraries during vacations, local schools, reciprocal use or access by other libraries, and so on. Libraries with a strong commercial research bias should consider how to deal with the restriction of fair use to instances of non-commercial research. Is this something that could be protected under negotiated licences?

The physical location of the library may also be addressed. In arriving at a site licence, how should one best define the 'site'? Is it enough to limit the licence to a physical location (library premises located at the campus of a particular university) or should the site be defined in terms of the institution? Is remote access from halls of residence or departmental centres or other remote users intended or required?

The answers to these questions will vary enormously according to individual conditions appropriate to each licence. The task of defining the licence must be approached carefully. While the rights granted under the licence will be subject to separate definition in the central section of the licence, the definitions of the key players and the wider concepts underlying the licence are crucial to the licensee's acquisition and performance of rights granted under licence and to its ability to function as a library.

Some licences attempt to subdivide users into two (or more) categories in an attempt to mirror current or traditional library models. Of these, the two most common categories are 'authorized users' (members of the institution) and 'walk-in users' (casual or drop-in users). The two groups may be granted different levels of access under licence, and may be further subdivided by differentiating between ad-hoc users who are members of the public and those who are, for example, users from another licensed institution simply making temporary use of the library – for example, students using another university's library during vacations.

It is important that whatever definition is agreed is sufficient to cover any identifiable user group. The four most common categories are based around permutations of the following:

- members of the institution of which the licensed library is a part – staff and students of a university, for example
- users who are not members of the institution but who have access rights under a registration or access agreement
- users who are not registered – casual, ad-hoc or drop-in members of the public
- users who are registered with the library under an access agreement, but who access the materials remotely, not by using on-site work stations.

The site itself may also be defined in this section. Site definitions should not be limited to the physical site of the library itself but should be extended to cover other possible access points such as halls of residence, regional offices, lodgings and homes of members, etc.

The central section

The central section of the licence will be taken up by the agreement itself. Although the licence is the sum of its parts and the central section cannot be interpreted in isolation, this is often seen as the core of the contract. It sets out the rights that are being bought or licensed. It differs from the recitals section in that, whereas the recitals may deal in wishes, desires, intentions and objectives, the agreement must be stated in terms that can be clearly defined and are grounded in the practicalities of buying or licensing services or goods. In the case of a licence covering access to, or use of, the digitized works, this will take the form of defining the rights being licensed, the price being paid, and the scheduling and calculation of payment. It is an inclusive listing of the rights being acquired. If it subsequently emerges that rights that need to be exercised have not been covered, there are only two possible outcomes: living with a licence that does not meet the requirements fully, or having to re-negotiate an extended licence, probably at cost.

The central section, therefore, focuses on the grant of rights. This defines what the licensee, and hence their users, are able to do with the materials licensed under the agreement. The needs of users are key. One cannot encourage or authorize users to perform activities that are not covered by the acquisition of rights. There is a need to make sure that the analysis of institutional and user requirements carried out as a preliminary to the negotiation of the licence is fully reflected in the rights acquired. It is essential that this list should be a comprehensive and realistic reflection of the analysis. Any activities not covered by the listing will limit ability to meet the objectives identified in the analysis. The listing must also be realistic. The more that is purchased, the higher the cost (although one would expect to see a reduction in the unit costs). The wider the range of rights sought under licence, the less able, and the more reluctant, the rights owners will be to negotiate a licence. This is a game in which the desire of licensees to license as widely as possible at the lowest cost plays against the licensor's desire to retain control over their material. By this, rights owners seek to derive maximum benefit from the digital market by using licences to slice the rights available more thinly at maximum revenue. A similar game will also be played between primary and secondary rights owners for control over the use of the material and the revenue accruing from it. For example, publishers may not be in a position to license their entire catalogue. Authors may control the electronic rights in some work(s) and may not have licensed them to their publisher. Should this be so, the publisher may be unable to license the required rights. (The outcome of this, of course, is that the publishers should warrant that they own or control the rights being acquired under licence. Unless they do so, the library may discover that it is subject to subsequent claims from other rights owners (authors, for instance) claiming licensing payments in respect of their own work. The library might even be forced to withdraw the work from use. The licensor's warranties would be detailed in the latter stages of the contract.)

Readers may be familiar with the subscription packages available from satellite or digital broadcasters. Typically, in order to access the few premium channels in which they are interested, subscribers are forced to take a package in which less valuable channels are 'bundled' together with premium channels so as to increase the monthly subscription. Rights holders licensing the digital markets will make use of the same marketing strategies.

While the rights sought under licence will vary from library to library, some of the more common requirements are:

- the right to access the rights owner's server/or to digitize hard-copy originals
- the right to store the licensed materials electronically
- the right to make the materials available on the library's infrastructure and information services
- the right to index the materials
- the right to make the materials accessible to users (as defined in the definitions section of the licence) for the purposes of commercial and/or noncommercial research, teaching and (private) study
- the right to permit users to print materials and/or to download materials for the fair dealing purposes specified above
- the right to permit the reproduction and inclusion of the materials in hard or soft copy in course packs.

The rights listed are, typically, those that the majority of rights owners are comfortable in licensing. They will as a rule be comfortable with the digitization and use of materials in ways that maintain the integrity of the original documents, that is the right to manipulate content will not generally be licensed, though open source licensing models do allow for manipulation under licence. In some current licences this restriction may take the form of specifying the electronic format in which the digitized works are licensed. For example, use in PDF format only may be specified. There are disadvantages associated with specifying use in terms of format as opposed to specifying a form of use or function. By specifying PDF as the licensed format, the licensor and licensee are attempting to ensure that the integrity of the materials will be respected by means of a format that does not allow manipulation. They run the risk that PDF may become outdated over time and the licence may date alongside it. It would be better to specify that the licensee warrants that the integrity of the work will be maintained by only using formats that prevent manipulation. In that way the user is not tied into using a single, specified format that may become outdated over time as the technologies of the new media develop.

The question of outdated formats is particularly problematic for licences managing long-term archives. Some materials released within the last 20 years or less are already proving difficult to access as their formats become redundant. Some archives strip away the formatting from work immediately following acquisition and archive in a pure, stripped form. If this is a concern, then the institution's acquisitions policy should be reflected in negotiating licences.

The specification of format is associated with other restrictions that are placed upon licensees. These are stated alongside the rights granted in the licence. The most common restrictions are:

- use by means of a network that is not secure
- use by users who are not registered and issued with a password or other, similarly secure means of identification
- systematic reproduction
- distribution, loan or sale outside the defined library user group
- sub-licensing to third parties (is this something that might affect partner institutions or sub-licensed course-users?)
- interlibrary loan (although still referred to as interlibrary loan by some publishers, the term suggests a limited understanding of library activity as a paper collection; interlibrary resource sharing or interlibrary use are more applicable to electronic use if access is limited to sharing information between libraries).

It may also be found that it is here that licensors will attempt to impose restrictions on the licensee's ability to make use of national fair dealing provisions.

Other restrictions

Other restrictions on the limit of the licence may not be expressed in terms of rights limitations but will have an equal effect on the use of the material.

The licence will have a *term*: start and finish dates. The commencement of the licence and the termination of the licence should be agreed and specified. The question of what happens as the termination date approaches also needs to be addressed and agreed. What are the exit options? While the termination date will be fixed, earlier cancellation will be possible if there is a fundamental breach of the licence, if a partner becomes insolvent, or if either party is capable of terminating the agreement by giving the other an agreed period of notice of cancellation.

It is important to avoid becoming tied to a contract that has no termination date or termination facility. A contract that does not specify an agreed means of termination may oblige the library to continue paying for rights and services that it no longer requires.

The issue of continuing access or right to use the materials after termination must also be considered. Remember that a fundamental difference between subscribing to a hard-copy journal and an electronic journal is that if a hard-copy subscription ends, the library may continue to keep and make use of its archive copies. When a licence to use electronic material ends, there is a possibility the right to access and use the materials ends with it. The right to continuing access and user rights is not automatic and, unless provision is made in the licence, it may be discovered that the ability to use the material is limited to the duration of the licence. You should therefore negotiate the right to continued access and use of materials. Licensors will insist on a reciprocal commitment from the licensees regarding limitations on use, manipulation and respect for the integrity of the material and continuing compliance with security conditions. You should not agree to something that cannot be guaranteed. Warranties can be expensive if breached. If it really is not possible to guarantee (and who could, in their right mind?) that users won't infringe or breach the terms of the licence, then restrict any warranty to what is reasonably under the library's control.

Delivery and payment

What is the licensor undertaking to provide the licensee? Before agreeing to a licence, the licensee must be sure that the licensor undertakes to supply them with the services they are expecting and that are required. Will the licensor provide materials in the form of electronic files – if so, in what form and by what date? Will the materials not be supplied but rather be made available under a licensee's right to access the licensor's server – if so, how and by what date? Or are the materials to be digitized by the licensee from hard copies already owned by the licensee? A licence may well cover all three possibilities, and we have already examined the necessity of having a warranty from the licensor, setting out the breadth and the nature of the rights they control and grant, so as to avoid the possibility of licensees being hit twice by claims or counterclaims from several rights owners claiming to hold rights in the same material.

It is also important to understand the requirements of the licensor. Licensees, too, have responsibilities under any licence. We have seen how limitations imposed on licensees centre around rights owners' legitimate concerns that the integrity of material should be respected. As well as limiting the rights granted, this is reflected in a desire for licensees to warrant that they will respect the licence terms and will do so on behalf of the institution, its employees and licensed users. This often takes the form of the licensee undertaking to co-operate with rights owners in informing them of actual or potential breaches of their rights and in being responsible and liable for the actions of their own staff and licensed users. While licensees may be able to commit themselves to this warranty in respect of staff, they will be vulnerable to the actions of licensed users, where there will be data protection issues as well as technical difficulties in identifying individuals. Here, it is reasonable for licensees to be responsible for the actions of users only insofar as the licensee has been negligent in failing to make users aware of licence restrictions, and to set in place codes of practice, including disciplinary codes, to handle instances of rights infringement. Licensees must be diligent to avoid authorizing users to perform infringing acts. Once a possible breach has been identified, licensees must be speedy in keeping licensors informed and in bringing the infringement to a close. They must not collude, either openly or by omission, in any continuing breach of the licence.

Payment, of course, is an undertaking performed by the licensee. But what form will the payment take? As well as the total cost (and it is important to make certain that the total fee quoted really is the total – that there are no hidden extras), how the fee is calculated must also be considered. Is it an annual licensing fee, for instance? If so, will it be based on user numbers or on sampled usage? Who will pay? Are any of the costs for individual transactions met by users or is the entire licence fee met centrally? In addition to specifying the licence fee, the licence will make provision for how the fee will be paid, by whom, when the fee is due (either in full or by instalments) and how it will be calculated.

Standard conditions

The final part of the licence will include standard licensing clauses specifying under which legislation the contract will operate, how disputes may be settled, a reference to what happens if the contract is damaged by uncontrollable or unavoidable circumstances (*force majeure*), and a commitment by the parties to perform their responsibilities. The library's own national courts should be chosen in preference to any other. The possibility should be discussed of submitting to agreed arbitration – for example, by representatives from the national library and publishers associations. It is important to avoid non-specific phraseology in describing how undertakings will be performed. Contracts should minimize dispute, not generate room for further argument, and the use of broad, descriptive phrases such as 'best endeavours' that are difficult to assess objectively may provoke further argument in the case of dispute. Courts in common law jurisdictions, such as the UK, are notoriously loath to rule on guesswork about terms such as 'quality', 'reasonable', 'best' and so on, while those in civil codes may derive interpretations from loose phrasing that were not strictly intended.

Achieving a clearly defined contract is only possible if the parties themselves are clear about their intentions. Difficult though it may be to define requirements dispassionately and clearly, if the exercise helps to bring about a clear understanding within and between the parties, then it is even more worthwhile and should be embraced fully.

Further information

This chapter provides a commentary on standard licensing agreements in order to help users approach the business of negotiating a licence with confidence. It is not intended to replace the need for proper legal advice in drafting the licence itself. There are many sources of advice readily available. Of these, the most useful may come from the national library associations and the standard licence formats that many national associations have agreed with publishers' representatives and with collective licensing bodies representing publishers, authors, music rights owners and so on. The principles of the approach outlined in this chapter are not intended to replace the use of standard, agreed licences recommended by national or other representative bodies. For advice tailored to the needs of particular circumstances, it is best to speak to a national association. For further background advice and shared experience, the list of web resources below will be useful.

Model licensing clauses

UK National Electronic Site Licence Initiative (NESLI) Site Licence, available at http://http://www.nesli.ac.uk.
UKOLN, available at http://www.ukoln.ac.uk.
Copyright Licensing Agency, available at http://www.cla.co.uk.
European Copyright Users Platform (ECUP) Heads of Agreements, available at http://www.kaapeli.fi/eblida/ecup.
European Bureau of Library, Information and Documentation Associations (EBLIDA), available at http://www.eblida.org.
Definitions of common words and phrases, available at http://www.library.yale. edu/~llicense/definiti.shtml.
JSTOR Library License Agreement, available at http://www.jstor.org/about/license. html.

Licensing principles

SURF, available at http://www.surf.nl/copyright.
International Coalition of Library Consortia, available at http://www.library.yale.edu/ consortia/statement.html.
American Association of Law Libraries; American Library Association; Association of Academic Health Science Libraries; Association of Research Lib-

raries; Medical Library Association; Special Libraries Association: Principles for Licensing Electronic Resources – available at http://www.arl.org/scomm/ licensing/principles.html.

Intellectual property

UK Patent Office IP portal, available at http://www.patent.gov.uk.
European IPR help desk, available at http://www.ipr-helpdesk.org/index.htm.
Australian Copyright Council, available at http://www.copyright.org.au.
SCONUL, available at http://www.sconul.ac.uk.

Examples of commercial contracts

Emerald, available at http://www.mcb.co.uk.
American Institute of Physics Journal, available at http://www.aip.org/ojs/service.html.

8

Data protection: an overview

Laurence W. Bebbington

Introduction

Since the Statute of Anne in 1709, copyright has become the first pillar of the information industry. Data protection in a period of only 20 years shows every indication of becoming its second. The collection of personal information about individuals is a significant feature of information work. Libraries, publishers, website owners, non-profit organizations, employers and others all process personal information about individuals. A list of collectors and users of personal information would be endless. The marriage of computer and communications technologies to deliver content and communicate with end users or consumers, not merely for professional or educational purposes but increasingly for leisure and recreational use as well, necessarily means that information and service providers collect, obtain and use personal data about identifiable, living individuals. One thing is certain – a very great deal of personal information about any living individual is available on a scale hitherto unknown.

Data protection

Data protection is concerned with protecting personal information concerning living individuals. More specifically, it seeks to protect individuals from harm, distress or adverse consequences resulting from the collection, use or sharing of inaccurate, out-of-date or unlawful personal information about them. It concerns itself with transparency, fairness, lawfulness and accountability. It encompasses any information that can be used to identify a living individual, including businesses trading as sole traders or partnerships or nominated individuals who may act as human contacts for organizations and businesses. Data protection law needs to strike a difficult balance between the rights of individuals to privacy and protection from harm and the needs of organizations to use personal data for the legitimate purposes of their businesses.

The Data Protection Act 1998

The main legislation in the UK is now the Data Protection Act 1998 (DPA 1998). This implemented EC Directive 95/46/EC on the Protection of Individuals with Regard to the Processing of Personal Data and on the Free Movement of Such Data (1995). Article 1 of the Directive highlights two main aims – which arguably are likely to be in tension in many ways:

Object of the Directive

1   Member States shall protect the fundamental rights and freedoms of natural persons, and in particular their right to privacy with respect to the processing of personal data.

2   Member States shall neither restrict nor prohibit the free flow of personal data between Member States for reasons connected with the protection afforded under paragraph 1.

The Directive crowns a long period of interest in privacy and data protection at both a general and a sectoral level by several international organizations, including the Council of Europe,[1-3] the Organization for Economic Co-operation and Development[4,5] and, more belatedly, the European Community itself.[6] The DPA 1998 repealed its predecessor the Data Protection Act 1984. It has already been amended by subsequent legislation such as the Freedom of Information Act 2000. It is longer and more detailed than the 1984 Act and has spawned numerous Statutory Instruments providing much more detail concerning its operation. In certain areas it interacts closely with other legislation such as the Regulation of Investigatory Powers Act 2000 (RIPA) and the Human Rights Act 1998 (HRA). This chapter seeks to provide an overview of the main features of the 1998 Act.

Key aspects of the Data Protection Act 1998
Important terms defined

Certain important terms and phrases are used throughout the Act. A list of defined terms is to be found in Section 20. Data protection law applies whenever personal data are 'processed' – including every conceivable kind of personal data. Processing is very broadly construed. It means obtaining, recording or holding data, and carrying out any operations on the data, including organizing, adapting, retrieving, consulting or using, disclosing, disseminating, aligning, combining, etc.

'Data' include both data processed automatically by equipment and manual data recorded in a 'relevant filing system'. For manual information to be subject to the Act three conditions apply:

1   There must be a set of information about individuals (e.g. employees, customers).
2   The set of information must be structured either by reference to the individual (e.g. name, payroll number) or by criteria relating to them (e.g. age, job, medical history).
3   The structure must permit specific information relating to the individual to be readily accessible.

If these conditions are met, the manual data are subject to the Act.

'Personal data' are data that can identify, either directly or indirectly with other information, a living individual. They include expressions of opinion and indications of intent in respect of the individual. Sensitive personal data can relate to certain types of information about an individual (e.g. his or her religion). These are subject to more rigorous processing requirements.

A 'data controller' is someone who, alone or jointly with other persons, determines the purpose(s) for which and the manner in which any personal data are processed.

A 'data processor' is anyone (other than an employee of the data controller) who processes data on behalf of the data controller. Data controllers are directly subject to the Act. Where a data processor is used to process data, then the data controller must have a written contract with the data processor covering all aspects of the relationship, including compliance with security obligations imposed by the seventh data protection principle (see below).

A 'data subject' is an individual who is the subject of personal data. A 'recipient' is any person to whom personal data are disclosed. 'Third party' in relation to personal data means any person other than the data subject, the data controller (or his or her employees) or a data processor.

The data protection principles

Eight data protection principles are at the heart of the statute. They are enumerated in Part 1 of Schedule 1:

1 Personal data shall be processed fairly and lawfully.
2 Personal data shall be obtained only for one or more specified and lawful purposes.
3 Personal data shall be adequate, relevant and not excessive in relation to the purpose(s) of processing.
4 Personal data shall be accurate and, where necessary, kept up to date.
5 Personal data shall be kept for no longer than is necessary.
6 Personal data shall be processed in accordance with a data subject's rights.
7 Personal data shall be kept secure.
8 Personal data shall not be transferred outside the EEA unless the destination country provides an adequate level of data protection.

The first data protection principle

In full, the first principle provides that:

> Personal data shall be processed fairly and lawfully and, in particular, shall not be processed unless –
> (a) at least one of the conditions in Schedule 2 is met, and
> (b) in the case of sensitive personal data, at least one of the conditions in Schedule 3 is also met.

The definition of processing is so extensive that it means that virtually anything done with personal data must be done in a fair and lawful manner. Interpretation provisions in Schedule 2 Part II of the Act provide advice and guidance on compliance with the principles, as does the legal and other guidance issued by the Information Commissioner, most of which is available at http://www.dataprotection.gov.uk/.

Fairness relates to the ways in which data are obtained. Are the data fairly obtained? Consideration will be given to:

• whether the person who supplied the data willingly was deceived or misled as to the purpose(s) of the intended processing
• whether the supplier of the data was authorized by or under any enactment or any international obligation entered into by the UK to supply it.

Where a data subject provides the data personally, the data controller must tell the data subject, so far as is reasonably practicable, or make available as soon as possible, the 'fair processing information', namely:

- the identity of the data controller
- the identity of any nominated representative of the data controller for the purposes of the Act
- the purpose(s) for which the data are to be processed
- where relevant, an opt-out for the purposes of direct marketing
- where relevant, a description of channels to be used for contacting individuals for marketing purposes (e.g. e-mail)
- any further necessary information given all of the circumstances in order to make the processing fair.

Personal information will not be obtained fairly if the data subject is not told of any non-obvious uses to which the information will be put. The fair processing information must be provided to a data subject where the data has been obtained from someone other than the data subject himself either before or as soon as possible after the time the data controller first processes the data, or within a reasonable period of disclosure of the data to a third party, or in any other circumstances, within a reasonable period. Where information has been obtained from someone other than the data subject, then the data controller does not have to provide the data subject with this information:

- if this would involve disproportionate effort
- where recording or disclosing the data is necessary for the data controller to comply with any legal obligation, other than a contract (certain appropriate safeguards must be adhered to in order to make this exception available).

For processing to be lawful, at least one of the conditions in Schedule 2 must be met in every case. Some of these are:

- where the data subject has given consent to the processing
- where the processing is necessary either for entering into, or for the performance of, a contract to which the data subject is a party
- for compliance by the data controller with any legal obligations upon him, other than a contract
- to protect the vital interests of the data subject
- for the administration of justice
- for legitimate interests pursued by the data controller provided processing does not harm the legitimate interests of the data subject.

Consent to processing must be informed and clearly given – it can never be implied, for example.

Sensitive personal data can only be processed if, in addition to the Schedule 2 condition, a further condition from Schedule 3 is also met. Sensitive personal data is defined as:

> . . . information as to –
> (a) the racial or ethnic origin of the data subject
> (b) his political opinions
> (c) his religious beliefs or beliefs of a similar nature
> (d) whether he is a member of a trade union
> (e) his physical or mental health or condition
> (f) his sexual life
> (g) the commission or alleged commission by him of an offence, or
> (h) any proceedings for any offence committed or alleged to have been committed by him, the disposal of such proceedings or the sentence of any court in such proceedings.

The Schedule 3 processing conditions include:

- explicit consent to the processing given by the data subject
- the need to meet any right or obligation imposed on the data controller as an employer
- the need to protect the vital interests of the data subject (i.e. a matter of life and death)
- where information contained in the personal data has been made public as a result of steps deliberately taken by the data subject
  etc.

Schedules 2 and 3 must be consulted for a full list of the processing conditions, as must appropriate Statutory Instruments under which the conditions have been expanded.

Processing conditions raise issues for data controllers. For example, exactly how is explicit consent given for the processing of sensitive personal information? Or what constitute the vital interests of the data subject for processing under the Schedule 2 condition? Guidance on these issues can be taken from the Commissioner's various publications or the increasing range of books dealing with the constantly evolving data protection regime.[7–9]

The second data protection principle

Under the second principle personal data 'shall be obtained for one or more specified and lawful purposes, and shall not be processed further in any manner incompatible with that purpose or purposes.' The Act indicates two main ways in which a data controller can specify the purpose(s) for which personal data may be obtained. The first is by a notice given to the data subject which itself satisfies the fair processing information requirements of the first principle. The second is in a notification given to the Commissioner under the Act's notification regime. Any subsequent disclosure of personal data for processing by a third party must conform to the original purposes, meaning that processing by that third party must be compatible with the original purposes for which the data were obtained. Existing data cannot be used for new purposes without renewed consent.

The third data protection principle

The third principle requires that personal data 'shall be adequate, relevant and not excessive in relation to the purpose or purposes for which they are processed.' Data controllers should solicit only the minimum amount of information that is required to undertake properly a task or provide a service. A website operator providing a free and openly accessible alerting service needs little more than an e-mail address, for example. To solicit fax numbers would be inappropriate. Information cannot be collected speculatively because it might be useful at some future point without any idea on how it might be used. The Commissioner has advised that that 'Data controllers should continually monitor compliance with this Principle, which has obvious links with the Fourth and Fifth Principles.' Information that is not reviewed and updated may become inadequate for its purpose, for instance.

The fourth data protection principle

According to the fourth principle, personal data 'shall be accurate and, where necessary, kept up to date.' Section 70(2) of the Act states that 'data are inaccurate if they are incorrect or misleading as to any matter of fact.' This principle is not contravened by the data controller where information is inaccurate but where it was supplied by the data subject or a third party and has been accurately recorded, as long as the data controller has taken reasonable steps to ensure the accuracy of the data. If the data subject has informed the data controller of the data subject's view that the data are inaccurate the data must record that fact. Note that data need only be kept up to date 'where necessary'. The 'reasonable steps' required to ensure accuracy depend on each individual case. It will depend on the nature of the data and the consequences or harm caused to the data subject by inaccurate data. Some factors for consideration here as suggested by the Commissioner are:

1   Is there a record of when the data were first recorded and last updated?
2   Are those who use the data aware that the data do not necessarily reflect the current position?
3   Are there procedures for updating the data that are followed at suitable intervals?
4   How effective are these procedures?
5   Is the fact that the personal data are out of date likely to cause damage or distress?

Obviously databases, especially if used for marketing purposes, should be 'cleaned' regularly.

The fifth data protection principle

According to the fifth principle, personal data 'processed for any purpose or purposes shall not be kept for longer than is necessary for that purpose or those purposes.' This requires effective and regular review, retention and destruction policies and procedures. Information that is no longer required for its purpose should be deleted or destroyed. The retention of certain data or information may be required by statute or for legal purposes. The Commissioner has also issued guidance on retention periods for personal data arising out of the employment relationship, in use of CCTV surveillance, etc. which provide benchmarks and guidance that data controllers can follow for these purposes.

The sixth data protection principle

The sixth principle demands that personal data 'shall be processed in accordance with the rights of data subjects under this Act.' The Act provides that a person will contravene this principle if, but only if, he or she fails:

* to provide information required under a subject access request under the Act
* to comply with notices dealing with a data subject's rights (1) to terminate or prevent the commencement of processing that is likely to cause substantial damage or distress; (2) to prevent processing for the purposes of direct marketing; (3) to exercise certain rights in relation to automated decision-taking
* to comply with a notice requiring rectification, blocking, erasure or destruction of inaccurate or incomplete data in respect of exempt manual data only during the transitional period up to and including 23 October 2007.

The seventh data protection principle

The seventh principle requires that 'appropriate technical and organizational measures shall be taken against unauthorized or unlawful processing of personal data and against accidental loss or destruction of, or damage to, personal data.' Part II of Schedule I provides guidance on determining the appropriateness of security measures to be adopted. Factors to be taken into account include:

- the state of technology
- the cost of security measures
- the harm that could result from unlawful processing, accidental loss of personal data, etc.
- the nature of the data to be protected
- the reliability of staff with access to the data
- the suitability of data processors and their security measures.

Security features should be considered at the systems design stage of a new system. The Commissioner has provided further guidance on security considerations, which include:

- the existence of an organizational security policy
- clear responsibility for security
- sufficient resources and facilities for security needs
- physical and technological access control procedures (e.g. building access; secure room access; authentication/password procedures and levels; backup procedures; procedures for effective destruction and deletion of data; secure disclosure controls; business continuity and disaster control; staff selection and training; detecting and dealing with security breaches; etc.).

Adoption and compliance with relevant published standards such as BS 7799 needs to be considered by some organizations.

The eighth data protection principle

The eighth data protection principle stipulates that personal data 'shall not be transferred to a country or territory outside the European Economic Area, unless that country or territory ensures an adequate level of protection of the rights and freedoms of data subjects in relation to the processing of personal data.' An 'adequate' level of protection will have regard to:

- the nature of the personal data
- the country of origin
- the country of final destination
- the purpose(s) of processing
- the length of period during which the data will be processed
- the law in force in the destination country
- the existence of relevant, enforceable codes or other rules in that country
- the security measures in respect of the data in that country.

The eighth principle does not apply in certain circumstances – for example, if the transfer:

- has the consent of the data subject
- is necessary for entering into, or performance of, a contract between the data subject and the data controller
- is necessary for reasons of substantial public interest
- is necessary to protect the vital subject interests of the data subject.

The European Commission may make findings on the adequacy of data protection regimes in countries outside the EEA. Data can be transferred to such countries, but there is a need to observe any restrictions that may be contained in any finding – a country might be designated as adequate only for transfers that do not contain sensitive personal data, for instance. Details of such countries can be obtained on the Commissioner's website or the website of the European Commission. Countries currently designated as adequate include Switzerland, Hungary and Canada.

The Commission has also developed model contractual clauses for data transfers that can be used between data controllers[10] or between data controllers and a data processor,[11] under which the recipient accepts binding conditions relating to the processing of the data. These are restrictive and may not suit all needs.

In the case of the USA, adequacy may be presumed if the recipient of the transfer is a member of the 'Safe Harbor' programme. The resistance in the USA to the introduction of a national data protection regime, and continuing lack of uptake of, and problems with, the Safe Harbor programme (it does not cover all business sectors, for example), in effect mean that in some circumstances data controllers might be better advised to legitimate their data transfers by one of the available derogations under the eighth principle.

Any transfer should conform to all of the principles – for example, a transfer should not send more than the minimum amount of data needed for the processing, should be fully secure, etc.

Notification

Notification is the process by which data controllers notify the Commissioner of certain details about their processing of personal data. These details form the data controller's entry in a Register of Data Controllers, which is available for public inspection. An entry in the Register must include the 'registrable particulars' for the data controller, which are:

- name and address
- name and address for any nominated representative
- a description of the personal data being or to be processed and of the category or categories of data subject to which they relate
- a description of the purpose(s) for which the data are being or are to be processed
- a description of any recipient(s) to whom the data controller intends or may wish to disclose the data
- the names, or a description of, any countries or territories outside the EEA to which the data controller directly or indirectly transfers, or intends or may wish to transfer data
- where appropriate, a statement of the fact that certain data being processed is of a type that does not require notification (where processing is of manual data only; personal data falling within the definition of 'relevant filing system' or personal data within non-automated accessible records, unless it is assessable processing; automated processing for core business purposes such as staff administration, accounts and customer and supplier records, membership records of non-profit organizations, etc.).

The Commissioner must consider whether any notification involves 'assessable processing' – processing that could cause substantial damage or distress to a data subject or otherwise significantly prejudice his rights and freedoms. If it is assessable processing, the Commissioner must inform the data controller of this finding within 28 days and whether or not it is likely to comply with the provisions of the Act.

Notification must be accompanied by a general description by the data controller of the security measures adopted to protect personal data. This statement will not appear on the Register. Notification costs £35 per year and is renewable annually. Section 20 of the Act requires a data controller to inform the Commissioner of changes in the registrable particulars or the security measures taken to comply with the seventh principle. To fail to do so is a criminal offence. Guidance on notification is available from the Commissioner's staff, which also publishes a guide on how to notify. Model templates for certain types of business or organization also assist data controllers who need to notify.

Individuals' rights under the Act

Part II of the Act confers rights on data subjects with regard to the personal data held about them by others. These rights are extremely important. They facilitate transparency and accountability. Through the provision and exercise of such rights, individuals can discover what information is held about them, how it is being used and whether it is accurate, and can question its use, prevent use or stop processing from commencing in certain circumstances, secure changes and alterations, and where necessary receive compensation for damage or distress suffered by the processing of inaccurate data. These rights are wider and stronger than under the 1984 Act.

A data subject's rights are:

1   Right of access to personal data (Sections 7–9).
2   Right to prevent processing likely to cause substantial damage or distress (Section 10).
3   Right to prevent processing for purposes of direct marketing (Section 11).
4   Rights in relation to the taking of decisions based solely on automated processing (Section 11).
5   Right to compensation for damage suffered, or distress caused in certain circumstances (Section 13).
6   Right to secure rectification, blocking, erasure and destruction of data which are inaccurate (Section 14).
7   Right to request an assessment by the Information Commissioner (Section 42).

Right of access to personal data

An individual may make a subject access request (SAR) under Section 7 of the Act and is entitled:

* to be told by the data controller if he, or someone else on his behalf, is processing personal data about him
* to be given a description of the personal data, the purpose(s) of the processing and the recipients or types of recipients to whom the data are or may be disclosed
* to have communicated to him, in an understandable format, the information constituting the personal data about the individual (this must be sup-

plied in permanent form unless this is impossible, requires disproportionate effort or the data subject agrees otherwise; the data controller must also supply information explaining the use of any codes or abbreviations required for the information to be properly understood; any information as to the source of the personal data must be disclosed if it is available)

- to be told by a data controller about the logic involved in any automated decision-taking about the individual where that decision is likely to constitute the sole basis for a decision significantly affecting him such as creditworthiness, work performance, reliability, conduct, etc. (provision of information as to the logic involved in such decision-taking is not required where that information constitutes a trade secret).

A data controller is not obliged to supply any information unless the access request is in writing (letter, facsimile, e-mail) but no data controller can compel use of its own SAR form if it uses one. Since there is no prescribed form for a subject access request, other than it must be in writing, organizations need to ensure that staff recognize and act upon such requests for information.

The data controller may charge a basic fee not exceeding the statutory maximum (currently £10) for providing the information. This must be paid before the data controller needs to start locating the information. Different fee structures apply to some accessible records.

In order to ensure that disclosure is only made to the right person, the data controller must be satisfied as to the identity of the requester. For this reason, although the Act does not prevent it, it may be inadvisable for a data controller to respond to oral requests for any personal information whatsoever. If accidental disclosure about an individual to someone other than the rightful data subject is likely to cause damage or distress, then the data controller might reasonably solicit a higher threshold of proof of identity. The data subject must supply enough information to facilitate the location of the information and may specify that his or her request is limited to personal data of any prescribed description.

The data controller must supply the information 'promptly' and always within 40 days of receipt of the written request, the information required to locate the data and the prescribed fee. A data controller need not comply with subsequent identical or similar requests unless a reasonable period has elapsed between them. What is reasonable will depend on the particular circumstances. Factors that will favour compliance with more frequent requests will include the nature of the data, where information is dynamic or frequently updated, the purposes for which the data are processed, etc.

During the period in which a SAR is being dealt with, the data controller may continue to make routine changes or deletions to the data as long as those changes would have been made anyway. This may mean that the eventual disclosed data are not exactly the same as those held at the time the request was received. However, the data controller must not make corrections or amendments that would not have been made, and must not target amendments or deletions to the information to make it more palatable to the data subject.

The copy of the information provided must be in 'intelligible form'. This may extend beyond written printouts or photocopies of materials. In the 'Information Society' after all, it could easily include video or audio extracts. A data controller does not have to supply a permanent copy of the data if it is impossible to do so, if the data subject agrees otherwise or if it involves 'disproportionate effort.' A data subject, however, still has the right to make arrangements to see the information if possible. Disproportionate effort is not defined in the Act. Once again it will depend on the circumstances of each case as to whether or not this qualification can be relied upon by the data controller. Factors which may influence this will include the cost of providing the copy of the information, the length of time taken to locate and provide it, the size of the organization, etc.

Where a data controller is a credit reference agency, a SAR under Section 7 of the Act will be taken to be limited to personal data relevant to the data subject's financial standing unless the request shows a contrary intention.

Possible exemptions

The Act makes provision for circumstances in which certain information does not have to be disclosed in response to a SAR. These exemptions are intended to accommodate the data subject's own interests or the interests of third parties, or to give priority to other claims. Subject access falls under the 'subject information provisions' described in Section 27 of the Act. These provisions essentially mean that where personal data or processing are exempt, then generally speaking the data protection principles do not apply. The main exemptions are for:

- national security
- crime and taxation
- health, education and social work
- regulatory activity
- journalism, literature and art
- research, history and statistics
- information available to the public by or under enactment
- disclosures required by law or made in connection with legal proceedings
- domestic purposes

- other miscellaneous exemptions as listed in Schedule 7, including: confidential references, management forecasts, corporate finance, negotiations, examination marks, examination scripts, legal professional privilege, self-incrimination, etc.

A data controller, for example, is not obliged to disclose personal data in response to a SAR if the disclosure would prejudice the ongoing investigation of a criminal offence or the detection of crime. Neither does a data controller who provides a confidential reference have to disclose the contents of that reference given for an employee to that employee. The recipient of the reference, however, may have to disclose a reference in response to a SAR.

In certain circumstances, responding to a SAR will result in the retrieval of records or information that contain personal data about other identifiable individuals. To comply with the SAR would involve disclosure of personal information about that third party. This includes the situation where the third party is the source of the information (e.g. a confidential reference). Here another balance needs to be struck – balancing the data subject's right to have all of the relevant information about him with the rights of a third party to have his own position, privacy and confidential relationship protected.

A data controller may be able to disclose the information without, for example, identifying the third party as the source of the data, or to provide as much information as possible without disclosing the identity of the third party – possibly by blocking out or omitting names. Where the identity of the third party can be effectively shielded, then this must be done and the data controller must provide the information in response to the SAR. A data controller must be careful in these circumstances. The Act provides that the data controller must take into account not only information that specifically identifies the third party, but also whether or not the third party could be identified from the information being disclosed 'and any other information which, in the reasonable belief of the data controller, is likely to be in, or to come into the possession of the data subject making the request.' Clearly this calls for a judgement about the state of knowledge or potential state of knowledge of the data subject. That may be a difficult judgement to make.

Where a third party is clearly identifiable in information related to the SAR, then the Act provides two scenarios in which the data controller must comply with the SAR, namely:

- where the third party has consented to the disclosure of the information
- where it is reasonable in all the circumstances to comply with the request without the consent of the third party.

In determining the latter point, the Act states that the following factors must be taken into consideration:

- any duty of confidentiality to the third party
- any steps taken by the data controller with a view to seeking the consent of the third party
- whether the third party is capable of giving consent
- any express refusal by the third party.

If a third party refuses permission to disclose, then a data controller needs to decide whether, given all of the circumstances known to him, the refusal is indeed reasonable. If not, then the data controller can proceed with disclosure.

If a court is satisfied that a data controller has failed to comply with a SAR, then it can grant an order requiring the data controller to comply with the request.

Right to prevent processing likely to cause damage or distress

An individual may require a data controller to cease, or not to begin, processing of personal data if that processing causes, or is likely to cause, unwarranted substantial damage or unwarranted substantial distress to him or to another. This 'data subject notice' as it is termed by the Act must be in writing. On receipt of such a notice, the data controller must reply in writing to the data subject within 21 days indicating either:

- that he or she has complied with the data subject notice, or intends to comply with it
- stating his or her reasons for regarding the notice as unjustified to any extent, and the extent (if any) to which he or she has complied or intends to comply.

This right cannot be exercised by the data subject if any of the first four conditions for processing in Schedule 2 apply, namely when:

- valid consent has been given to the processing
- the processing is necessary to comply with a contractual obligation entered into by the data subject
- the processing is necessary for any other legal obligation to which the data controller is subject
- the processing is necessary to protect the vital interests of the data subject, or

- any other conditions prescribed by the Secretary of State in delegated legislation.

If a data controller unjustifiably fails to comply with such a data subject notice to whatever extent then a court can grant an order requiring the data controller to comply with the notice in its entirety or to any extent that the court thinks fit.

Right to prevent processing for purposes of direct marketing

Section 11(3) of the Act defines direct marketing as 'the communication (by whatever means) of any advertising or marketing material which is directed to particular individuals.' At any time an individual can write to a data controller to require him to cease, or not to begin, processing for the purposes of direct marketing. The data controller must comply 'at the end of such period as is reasonable in the circumstances.' There are no exceptions to this right. It covers printed mail, e-mail, facsimile, telephone calls, inserts within publications, etc. The Commissioner has indicated that direct marketing covers 'a wide range of activities which will apply not just to the offer for sale of goods or services, but also the promotion of an organization's aims and ideals.' This brings an extremely wide range of activities of for-profit and not-for-profit organizations within this guidance – including, for instance, an organizational campaign designed to encourage individuals to write to their Member of Parliament on a particular subject. This means that data held on individuals for legitimate purposes needs to be marked, flagged or controlled in some way to stop direct marketing initiatives from any and all parts of an organization and for any purposes if a data subject has exercised this right.

A court can order compliance with a data subject notice under this section where it finds that a data controller has failed to comply with the notice.

Rights in relation to automated decision-taking

Increasingly, decisions are taken about individuals by entirely automated means without the need for human intervention or judgement. Section 12 of the Act allows an individual – again by written notice – to require that he or she should not be 'subject to a decision which produces legal effects concerning him or significantly affects him and which is based solely on automated processing or data intended to evaluate certain personal aspects relating to him, such as his performance at work, creditworthiness, reliability, conduct, etc.' This right can be exercised at any time. If such notice has not been given, and a decision significantly affecting the individual is taken purely on automated grounds, then the data controller must notify the individual that such a decision has been taken as soon as is reasonably practicable. Within 21 days of receiving this information, the data subject may write to request the data controller to reconsider the decision or to take the decision again on a different basis. Within 21 days, the data controller must inform the data subject in writing of what steps he or she intends to take to comply with the data subject notice.

The right does not apply to certain exempt decisions. Broadly, these are decisions leading up to, or needed for the performance of, a contract with the individual, where it is required under another enactment, where the effect of the decision must be to grant a request of the data subject or where steps have been taken to safeguard the legitimate interests of the data subject.

If a data subject feels that a person taking a decision in respect of him or her has failed to comply with a data subject notice, then a court can order the 'responsible person' (the person taking the decision) to comply.

Right to compensation

Any individual who suffers damage as a result of any contravention of the requirements of the Act by a data controller is entitled to compensation for that damage. An individual who suffers distress as a result of a contravention of the Act is entitled to compensation for that distress if the individual also suffers damage by reason of the contravention, or if the distress is as a result of a contravention relating to processing for the special purposes of journalism, or for literary or artistic purposes. Damage includes financial loss or physical injury. This remedy must be pursued through the courts. It is, however, a defence in any legal proceedings if the data controller can demonstrate that 'he had taken such care as in all the circumstances was reasonably required to comply with the requirements concerned.'

Right to secure rectification, blocking, erasure and destruction of inaccurate data

A court can order the rectification, blocking, erasure or destruction of personal data that the court is satisfied are inaccurate. Where the inaccurate data were supplied by the data subject or a third party, the court can order that the data be supplemented by a court-approved statement of the true facts. This can only be done where the data controller took reasonable steps to ensure that the data were correct, having regard to the purposes(s) for processing of the data, and if the data subject has already notified the data controller of his or her own view that the data are inaccurate and the data indicate that fact.

Following an order for rectification, a court can require a data controller to notify anyone to whom the data have been disclosed of the rectification, blocking, erasure or destruction where it is reasonably practicable to do so.

Right to request an assessment by the Information Commissioner

Any individual can request the Commissioner to assess whether any processing in relation to him is being carried out in conformity with the Act. The Commissioner has a wide discretion as to how to proceed but may make an assessment in a manner that is appropriate given all of the circumstances. The Commissioner must inform the data subject whether an assessment has been made and about any view or action taken as a result of the request. The Act equips the Commissioner with various powers to assess if processing is being carried out in accordance with the Act, namely:

1 *Information notices*: these can be served on a data controller requiring any information that will help the Commissioner ascertain if processing is being carried out in compliance with the Act.
2 *Special information notices*: these allow the Commissioner to ascertain that processing being carried out under the terms of the special purposes exemption is appropriate.
3 *Enforcement notices*: these can be served by the Commissioner in circumstances where a data controller has contravened or is contravening any of the data protection principles, and require the data controller to take specified steps to end the contravention or to refrain from processing specified data, in a specified way.
4 *Powers of entry and inspection*: if there are reasonable grounds for suspecting that an offence has or is being committed, the Commissioner may apply for a warrant to enter and search premises for evidence of the contravention.

This enforcement regime is subject to detailed requirements, including time limits, exemptions from compliance and appellate procedures against the exercise of these powers by the Commissioner. These are outlined in Part V of the Act.

Criminal offences

Significant criminal offences are created under the Act. The main offences are:

1 *Processing without notification*: under Section 21(1) it is a criminal offence to process personal data without proper notification in the Data Controllers Register unless, for example, the personal data are covered by exemptions

(for national security or domestic purposes); where the only personal data held fall into exempt categories (personal data within the definition of 'relevant filing system' or within non-automated 'accessible records'); or where the sole purpose of processing is the maintenance of a public register; or where the processing is exempted by any regulations.

2   *Failure to notify changes*: Section 21(2) makes it an offence to fail to notify the Commissioner of changes to the registrable particulars or to security measures taken to comply with the seventh principle. It is a defence to show that all due diligence was exercised to comply with this duty.

3   *Assessable processing*: where a data controller has notified the possibility of assessable processing to the Commissioner, it is a criminal offence (Section 22(6)) to carry out such processing before the expiry of the assessable processing time limit for a reply by the Commissioner or in advance of receipt of an assessable processing notice within the specified 28-day period.

4   *Failure to comply with a request for particulars*: where notification of processing is not required, it is an offence under Section 24 for a data controller to fail to make details of his registrable particulars available, in writing and free of charge, within 28 days of receiving a written request for them from any person. It is a defence to show that all due diligence was taken to comply with this duty.

5   *Failure to comply with a notice*: Section 41(1) makes it an offence to fail to comply with an information, special information or enforcement notice. It is a defence to show that all due diligence was taken to comply with the notice. It is an offence to knowingly or recklessly make a false statement in response to an information or special information notice (Section 47(2)).

6   *Unlawful obtaining or disclosing of personal data*: under Section 55(1) a person must not knowingly or recklessly, without the consent of the data controller, either obtain or disclose personal data or the information contained in personal data, or procure such a disclosure to another person. Defences are available, for example, if a person can show that the obtaining, disclosing or procuring was required or authorised by or under any enactment, by any rule of law or by a court, or where it is justified in the public interest.

7   *Unlawful selling of personal data*: where a person has obtained personal data in contravention of Section 55(1) above it is an offence to sell or offer to sell personal data. It is also an offence to offer to sell personal data which the person subsequently obtains in contravention of Section 55(1).

8   *Enforced subject access*: Section 56 seeks to end the practice of requiring data subjects to obtain copies of information held about them by someone else. It prohibits requiring individuals to produce certain records in connection with recruitment for employment, for the purposes of continued employment, or in relation to any contract for the provision of services by one per-

son to another. This practice has been used particularly to require job applicants to provide details of criminal records to prospective employers. This is now subject to much tighter restrictions.

Offences such as processing without notification, or before the expiry of the assessable processing time period, or enforced subject access, are offences of strict liability. Thus, a data controller will be criminally liable even though there was no intention to commit the offence or he or she did not know that he was committing an offence. If a corporate body commits a criminal offence under the Act, then any director, manager, secretary or similar officer will also be personally guilty of the offence if the offence was committed through his or her consent or connivance, or where the offence is attributable to any neglect on his or her part.

Codes of practice

In order to assist data controllers in implementing a compliant data protection regime, the Commissioner is in the process of publishing four codes of practice. Three of these have been published in draft. Their formal publication will not take place until all four are finalized. Although they are aimed at businesses where employment is a significant activity, any data controller will find them a valuable source of information and guidance on staying within the limits of the law in using personal data in many contexts. The four codes form the Employment Practices Data Protection Code and are:

1 *Part 1. Recruitment and Selection*: this part of the code provides detailed guidance on data protection issues involved in recruitment and selection. It includes general guidance on managing personal data in this context and detailed guidance on use of personal data in such activities as advertising positions, dealing with applications, verifications procedures, short-listing, interviews, pre-employment vetting and retention of recruitment records.
2 *Part 2. Records Management*: this part provides guidance on collecting, maintaining and using employment records in the workplace. Areas addressed are: collecting and keeping employment records, security issues, sickness and accident records, pension and insurance schemes, equal opportunities monitoring, marketing, fraud detection, workers' subject access rights to information held on them, employment references, requests for disclosure from outside the organization, publication and disclosure of information about employees, mergers and acquisitions, disciplinary and dismissal issues, outsourcing data processing and retention of records.

3   *Part 3. Monitoring at Work: an employer's guide*: this code addresses data
   protection issues associated with monitoring employees at work. It covers
   general monitoring issues and such areas as monitoring electronic communications, video and audio monitoring, in-vehicle monitoring, covert monitoring and monitoring private information.
4   *Part 4. Medical Information*: this will deal with issues relating to occupa-
   tional health, medical testing, drug and genetic screening, etc.

Purposes for interception

The area of monitoring at work is one of increasing concern, particularly in
relation to the interception, monitoring and recording of electronic communications (e-mail, telephone calls, faxes, etc.). This area of the law is complex and
is governed by three statutes. RIPA provides a framework for the lawful interception of communications on public and private telecommunications systems.
It prohibits the interception of electronic communications unless both sender
and recipient have consented to the interception, or where the interception is
connected with the operation of the communications service itself or, if the
interception is on a private system, it is for a purpose authorized by the
Telecommunications (Lawful Business Practice) (Interception of Communications) Regulations 2000. Such purposes include:

* to establish facts relevant to the business
* to ascertain compliance with regulatory practices or procedures
* to prevent or detect crime
* to investigate or detect unauthorized use of the telecommunications system
  etc.

Monitoring must only be undertaken where it is necessary and relevant to the
employer's business, and all reasonable efforts must be made to inform internal
and external users of the system that monitoring without consent may take
place. Any interception that cannot be brought within the Act or its Regulations
will be unlawful. Even if the interception is lawful, any personal data contained
in intercepted or recorded material will be subject to the provisions of the DPA
1998 if it is subject to any form of processing. This means, for example, that the
fair and lawful processing requirements of the Act must also be met in relation
to monitoring. Unless an exemption applies (e.g. processing necessary for the
detection of crime), data subjects have to be told that monitoring is taking place
and for what purposes. A condition from Schedule 2, and if necessary from
Schedule 3, needs to be met. The Commissioner clearly takes the view that

employee monitoring must be proportionate to the lawful objectives that the monitoring is intended to achieve.

Benchmarks

Part 3 of the Commissioner's Employment Practices Data Protection Code gives both general benchmarks for all monitoring activities and specific benchmarks for individual areas. Some of the general benchmarks are:

1   Identify specific individuals who can authorize monitoring.
2   Before monitoring, identify the specific business benefit to be gained and assess the impact of monitoring on such things as workers' privacy and trust. Limit the scope of monitoring to securing the identified benefits.
3   Consult trade unions or other representatives.
4   If monitoring is conducted to enforce organizational rules, then ensure that workers are aware of these rules.
5   Tell workers what monitoring is taking place and why, and periodically remind them of this.
6   Keep to a minimum those who have access to personal information collected through monitoring.
7   Do not monitor all workers if a particular risk is confined only to a section of the workforce.

Some of the specific benchmarks for communications monitoring are:

1   Establish a policy on electronic communications and communicate it to workers.
2   Analyse e-mail traffic data rather than the content of e-mails if this is possible.
3   Allow workers to mark personal e-mails as such.
4   Try to use monitoring to prevent misuse rather than to detect it.
5   Do not open e-mails that are clearly personal.
6   Provide workers with a separate e-mail account, or allow them to use web-based services for personal purposes.

Human rights aspects

The third dimension to monitoring is provided by the HRA which incorporated the European Convention on Human Rights into UK law and under which individuals are entitled to respect for their private life, family and correspondence. The rights are not directly enforceable against private-sector employers. Nevertheless, they may affect private employers, since courts and tribunals are obliged under Section 6 of the Act to interpret domestic laws as far as possible in a way that is compatible with the rights enshrined in the Act. This will have reference to the jurisprudence of the Convention which has established that an individual can have a right to privacy for communications made from his or her workplace and where that employee has a reasonable expectation of privacy for those communications.

However, it is simply not yet clear to what extent employees can rely on the HRA 1998 to limit or prevent monitoring at work under the RIPA 2000 and its regulations. The intricacy of this whole framework has merely been sketched here. Employers must approach the issue of monitoring extremely carefully given the complexity of the legislation and the ambiguities surrounding the limits on an employer's actions, and this summary is merely to raise awareness of the issues and not to be taken as a complete guide to action.

Personal data and the protection of privacy in the electronic communications sector

By 31 October 2003 the UK must implement a further privacy measure – Directive 2002/58/EC Concerning the Processing of Personal Data and the Protection of Privacy in the Electronic Communications Sector. This replaces an earlier directive, complements the data protection directive and further tightens the privacy obligations of organizations using digital communications technologies. It extends the privacy rules developed for telephone and fax services to all forms of electronic communications and is, therefore, relevant to telephone and internet users, communications network and service providers, online businesses, website operators, subscriber directory providers, and anyone who markets directly by telephone, fax, SMS or e-mail. The directive 'requires the confidentiality of communications to be protected, enables the provision of value added services with the consent of subscribers, and regulates the use of phone, fax, e-mail and mobile text messages for unsolicited direct marketing.' The main provisions are:

1 *Unsolicited commercial e-mail (UCE)*: an 'opt-in' approach is required for UCE. Direct marketing communications (fax, e-mail, mobile text messages, etc.) can only be sent to individuals who have given express and prior consent to receive them. An exception, however, applies to existing customer relationships where a recipient has bought *similar* services or products in the past. This is subject to several provisos, one of which is that the opportunity to opt out of further communications must be made available with every subsequent marketing communication. The existing Electronic Com-

merce (EC Directive) Regulations 2002 also contain requirements relating to UCE – for example, the requirement that UCE must be unambiguously identifiable as such immediately on receipt by the recipient.

2 *Software tracking devices*: to combat potential abuse of invisible tracking devices, website operators must provide users with 'clear and precise information' about devices such as cookies, spyware or web bugs used to collect personal information on them. Users must be given an opportunity to refuse installation of these devices on their computers. The methods for achieving this 'should be made as user-friendly as possible.'

3 *Subscriber directories*: subscribers will have stronger rights for deciding whether or not they want to be listed in subscriber directories. They must receive clear information about the directory in question, including any reverse search capability by which names and addresses can be identified by searching against numbers.

4 *Data retention*: once it is no longer needed for billing or other management purposes, the retention of electronic communications traffic data is permitted for national security and law enforcement purposes as long as measures adopted are proportionate and necessary and compliant with the European Convention for the Protection of Human Rights and Fundamental Freedoms. Location data can be processed if they are anonymized, or if prior consent of the subject has been obtained and the data are used only for a period necessary for the provision of a value added service.

5 *Security and confidentiality*: organizational and technical security measures must be taken to prevent unauthorized access to communications in order to protect their confidentiality. Appropriate measures will have regard to the available technology, the costs of implementation, appropriateness to the nature of the risk, etc.

In order to comply with these measures, businesses will have to take various steps. These will depend on existing practices but will include:

- ensuring that privacy policies and website warnings properly explain the use of software tracking technologies
- including opt-in marketing boxes on electronic forms and websites
- incorporating opt-out mechanisms in e-mails to customers
- reviewing and assessing security measures (e.g. encryption).

In addition, any business engaged in e-marketing activities will need to review its activities in this area in order to ensure compliance with the increasing range of legislation and sectoral codes that now affect online marketing.

Data protection in action

Data protection has teeth. The Information Commissioner's Annual Report for 2002 charts the increasing awareness among data subjects of their rights. It records that 859 visits were made by the Commissioner's staff to premises to investigate criminal data protection breaches; 106 offences were considered for prosecution, with action being taken in 66 instances, and 33 convictions. Offences included failure to notify, unlawful procurement and use of data for unregistered purposes.

Data controllers need to have in place a range of policies that will ensure compliance with the Act. Such policies can be developed, implemented and overseen by appointing a data protection officer. The Commissioner's *Guide to Data Protection Auditing* is available on the Commissioner's website and is a further important tool in ensuring compliance with the data protection standards. The guide assists data controllers in effective handling of personal information and respect for the interests of individual data subjects. It is also available free of charge on CD-ROM.

Effective policies need to address the many areas only summarized in this chapter, including notification requirements, data processing procedures, security policies, privacy policies, the management of subject access requests, disclosure rules and policies, overseas data transfers, staff awareness and training, etc. Although reviews of the data protection regime are being conducted at national and EC level, data protection is now very much a fixed feature on the information landscape. Commitment to it is no 'one-off' endeavour but rather a commitment to staying legal on a permanent basis in what has become one of the foremost responsibilities of the information profession.

References

1 Council of Europe (1981) *Convention for the Protection of Individuals with Regard to Automatic Processing of Personal Data*, ETS No. 108.

2 Council of Europe (1985) *Recommendation No. R (85) 20 of the Committee of Ministers to Member States on the Protection of Personal Data Used for the Purposes of Direct Marketing.*

3 Council of Europe (1999) *Recommendation No. R (99) 5 of the Committee of Ministers to Member States for the Protection of Privacy on the Internet.*

4 OECD (1980) *Recommendation of the Council Concerning Guide-Lines Governing the Protection of Privacy and Transborder Flows of Personal Data.*

5 OECD (1985) *Declaration on Transborder Data Flows.*

6 European Commission (1995) EC Directive 95/46/EC on the Protection of Individuals with Regard to the Processing of Personal Data and on the Free Move-

ment of Such Data, *Official Journal of the European Communities*, L 281, 23/11/95, 31–50.

7 Carey, P. (2000) *Data Protection in the UK*, London, Blackstone.

8 Jay, M. and Hamilton, A. (1999) *Data Protection Law and Practice 1998*, London, Sweet and Maxwell.

9 Rowe, H. (1999) *Data Protection Act 1998: a practical guide*, London, Tolley.

10 European Commission (2001) Commission Decision of 15 June 2001 on standard contractual clauses for the transfer of personal data to third countries, under Directive 95/46/EC, *Official Journal of the European Communities*, L 181 , 04/07/2001, 19–31.

11 European Commission (2001) Commission Decision of 27 December 2001 on standard contractual clauses for the transfer of personal data to processors established in third countries, under Directive 95/46/, *Official Journal of the European Communities*, L 006 , 10/01/2002, 52–62.

9

Criminal law and liability

Andrew Charlesworth

Introduction

When one examines the issue of crime and criminal liability in the context of the wider debate over the legal issues relating to publication and use of electronic information, it can be seen that it has thus far tended to play a fairly low-key role. While the media occasionally latches onto some aspect of criminal behaviour on the internet, such as computer hacking, or the distribution of pornographic and racist material, this has rarely had the galvanizing effect on lobbyists and legislators that has been demonstrated with issues such as copyright and data protection.

Many countries have continued to rely largely upon existing criminal legislation when dealing with internet-related crimes, with minor amendments to cover novel aspects of the new technologies. English law is a classical example of this process. The most recent criminal legislation to deal specifically with electronic information is the Computer Misuse Act 1990; obscene material is still dealt with by the Obscene Publications Act 1959, and child pornography by the Protection of Children Act 1978, as amended by the Criminal Justice and Public Order Act 1994. The Public Order Act 1986 and the Contempt of Court Act 1981 cover racial hatred and contempt of court respectively. Thus the majority of relevant legislation predates the explosion in the use of personal computers, which was in its early stages in the late 1980s, and virtually all of it predates the arrival of the world wide web in 1993. This state of affairs shows no immediate signs of radical change. Indeed, the main impetus for change has come, not from UK legislators, but rather from the European Union[1] and the

Council of Europe,[2] which have both taken an active interest in internet content regulation and the international control of 'cybercrime'.

At present, criminal offences on the internet can be fairly readily divided into four aspects:

- hacking (including unauthorized access to computer systems, unauthorized changes to electronic information, creation and distribution of viruses and similar destructive or disruptive software, and denial of service to legitimate users)
- the provision of illegal or illicit material for display or downloading
- the display or downloading of illegal or illicit material
- the provision of illegal or illicit services.

For the most part, those restrictions are, and will continue to be, enforced under national criminal law. This chapter will examine the issue of criminal liability for the provision, use or ownership of electronic information, with an overview of the relevant areas of English law. This overview will take in computer misuse, pornography, racial hatred, contempt of court and some other less well known offences.

Computer misuse

Key UK legislation:

- The Computer Misuse Act 1990[3]

Background

New computerized techniques, such as data mining, increasingly allow the extraction of potentially valuable commercial information from sources of data that were previously unavailable, or unusable.[4] The fact that digital information can be more valuable than its paper equivalent has created some major conceptual difficulties for the law. For example, the increasing commodification of digital information has, not unnaturally, led to the assertion of property rights in it. However, unlike most forms of property, electronic information has no tangible form, can be copied perfectly an infinite number of times, and can be created or destroyed with no obvious effect on the storage medium on which it is contained. This intangibility proved problematic when the UK legal system was faced with the challenge of providing a method of protecting property rights in electronic data via the criminal law.

In the 1980s the introduction of the personal computer led to a surge in the use of computer systems and computer networks. This in turn led to a rise in instances of unauthorized access to computer systems and their data. While the majority of these instances took place in the workplace, it was the stereotyped image of the teenage hacker that caught the attention of the media. The resultant media coverage raised serious concerns that unauthorized access to computer systems, and theft of, or damage to, electronic information, would prove to be disastrous for modern businesses.

When the first cases came to court, it soon became apparent that existing legislation such as the Theft Acts and the Criminal Damage Act were simply not suited to dealing with criminal offences against intangible objects.[5-6] Several high-profile cases involving computer hackers resulted either in acquittals or in convictions based on less than convincing judicial reasoning. The result of this lack of success, combined with pressure from business, and lobbying by some Members of Parliament, resulted in the passing of specific legislation in the form of the Computer Misuse Act 1990.

The Computer Misuse Act 1990

The Computer Misuse Act 1990 (CMA) remains the key UK legislation concerning the misuse of computer systems. It is designed to protect electronic information by criminalizing unauthorized entry to computer systems, and unauthorized amendment or deletion of computer data. The Act created three new criminal offences specific to computer misuse designed to avoid the type of problems that had arisen in previous computer misuse cases.

Those offences are provided for in Sections 1–3 of the Act. Section 1(1) makes intentional unauthorized access to any programs or data (hacking) an offence, and Section 1(2) states that there need be no intention to cause harm. However, a Section 1 offence is only a summary offence and thus on conviction the maximum imprisonment possible is no more than six months and the maximum fine £5000. The limited penalties available under this section may have been partially responsible for the problems in utilizing the Act. Section 2 and Section 3 contain the more serious offences. Section 2 applies to unauthorized access with intent to commit, or aid the commission of an offence, and Section 3 concerns the intentional unauthorized modification of the contents of any computer. The penalties for offences under Section 2 and Section 3 are considerably more severe. A conviction on indictment can lead to unlimited fines and up to five years' imprisonment. It is important, however, to note that under Section 3(1)(b) the degree of intent on the part of the defendant that the prosecution has to prove is stricter.

What is unauthorized use?

The CMA has caused the courts some difficulties, not least with the issue of what constitutes 'unauthorized use'. In *DPP v. Bignall*,[7] the court held that the CMA only covered unauthorized access to a computer or to data held on it, and not mere access by authorized users of the computer and data for an unauthorized purpose. This meant that, where an employer placed a restriction on access to data held on a computer to circumstances where such access was required for the purposes of an employee's work, if the employee wilfully disregarded the restriction as to purpose, there was no ground for action under the Act.

However, the House of Lords in the Allison case (see below) over-ruled this interpretation, holding instead that that access by a person to a computer was unauthorized for the purposes of Sections 1(1) and 2(1) of the CMA if that person was neither entitled to control, in the sense of authorizing or forbidding, access to the actual data involved, nor had the consent of a person entitled to exercise such control; and also that authority to access one piece of data could not be treated as authority to access other data of the same kind.

Other offences covered by the Act

Those who use the internet to gather and disseminate information should also be aware that the legislation covers more than the act of unauthorized access. In addition, the publishing of material that might be used in order to breach computer security, or to facilitate unauthorized entry into computer systems, may be caught by those provisions of the CMA that deal with the issue of conspiracy to commit an offence under the Act.

This was demonstrated by the prosecution and subsequent conviction in 1996 of the virus author Christopher Pile (a.k.a. 'The Black Baron'). Pile admitted 11 charges under the CMA with regard to writing and distributing computer viruses, and one charge of inciting others to spread computer viruses; he was jailed for 18 months.

The liability of an institution that carries hacker-related newsgroups such as alt.2600 on its Usenet newsfeed, thus potentially disseminating material which could allow others to access computer and telecommunications systems without authorization, remains untested. Similarly, providing equipment that incites a third party to commit an offence under Section 3 is also caught. In *R. v. Maxwell-King*,[8] the court held that supplying to a third party a device which, when fitted to a set-top box, allowed the upgrading of an analog cable television service to permit the subscriber to access all channels provided by the cable company regardless of the number of channels or the number of programmes for which the subscriber had paid, constituted incitement to cause an unauthorized modification of a computer under Section 3.

Offences abroad

It is interesting to note the extra-territorial element contained in the CMA. Normally, national legislation does not apply to individuals outside the immediate jurisdiction of the national courts. However, activities based on computer communications, such as computer misuse, can clearly have an extra-territorial effect. For example, a hacker in Germany working on a PC with an internet connection can access computers in the UK, perhaps via other computers in the USA. He or she is operating outside the UK, but his or her activities can clearly have a direct effect there. Section 4 and Section 5 of the CMA deal with this situation by stating that, if either the person committing the offence, or the computer against which it was committed, is in the UK, the British courts will have jurisdiction. In practice, this is more likely to be used against the UK-based hacker who is attacking computers outside the UK, primarily because the majority of crimes that fall under the Act would not meet the criteria required to trigger extradition proceedings against an overseas hacker.

Under Section 15 of the CMA, the UK courts may also commit individuals detained in the UK to prison under the Extradition Act 1989, prior to a decision on their extradition, where those individuals have committed offences involving computer misuse in another jurisdiction and those crimes would have been an offence if they had committed them in the UK. Extraditable offences must usually be punishable in both states by a minimum sentence of 12 months' imprisonment. This is demonstrated in the case of Allison.[9] Allison, while in the United States, had obtained account information from an employee of American Express who was authorized to access its computer records solely for the purposes of her employment, and he had used that information to encode forged credit cards and obtain fresh personal identification numbers, so as to draw large sums of money from automatic teller machines. Extradition procedures were initiated by the US government on the grounds of conspiracy to secure unauthorized access to the American Express computer system with intent to commit theft, to secure unauthorized access to the American Express computer system with intent to commit forgery, and to cause an unauthorized modification of the contents of the American Express computer system. These offences, if committed in the UK, would have breached the CMA Sections 1(1), 2(1) and 3 respectively.

Denial of service attacks

'Denial of service' attacks have received much recent publicity with high-profile attacks on commercial internet websites, such as Amazon and Ebay.[10] Often in such attacks, a hacker takes over a number of 'slave' computers, which are then controlled remotely to attack a target computer. Certain aspects of such 'distributed denial of service' attacks clearly fall under the provisions of the CMA, namely the taking over of third-party computers (often by use of 'trojan horse' software), but the actual attack itself would not appear to be a breach of the Act, as there is no attempt to gain unauthorized access to the target computer, merely to tie up its processing capacity with fake or flawed commands.

Interception of communications

Key UK legislation:

* The Regulation of Investigatory Powers Act 2000[11]

Background

Prior to the Regulation of Investigatory Powers Act 2000 (RIPA), interception of communications in the UK was governed by the Interception of Communications Act 1985 (IOCA). The IOCA put in place a statutory framework for interception of communications, in order to meet the criticisms levelled at the UK in 1984 by the European Court of Human Rights in the case *Malone v. UK*.[12] Under the 1985 Act, anyone who intentionally intercepted a communication in the course of its transmission by means of a public telecommunications system was guilty of a criminal offence. A public telecommunications system was defined as one run under a licence granted under the Telecommunications Act 1984 – for example, that of British Telecom. A person who engaged in the running of a public telecoms system was prohibited from interfering with the content of any message sent over the system or from disclosing the contents of an intercepted message. The 1985 Act set out a limited number of exemptions permitting legitimate interceptions, including when the Home Secretary issued a warrant permitting a telephone tap, or where the tapper had grounds for believing that the person being listened in to would consent to the tap.

However, the 1985 Act did not apply to telecommunications systems outside the public network, such as internal systems or networks within offices, and there was no other UK legislation to regulate the interception of communications on such systems. This meant that, for example, employers engaging in the interception of both telephone calls and e-mail within private networks were able to do so without legal sanction. This situation was challenged in 1997 by a further ruling of the European Court of Human Rights in the case *Halford v. UK*.[13] The ruling in that case, and the UK government's perception that the IOCA was outdated with regard to technological innovations in communications, resulted in new legislation to deal with both issues.

The Regulation of Investigatory Powers Act 2000

The Regulation of Investigatory Powers Act 2000 (RIPA) came into force in October 2000, and repealed the Interception of Communications Act 1985. It covers the interception of communications made via public postal systems, public telecommunications systems and private telecommunications systems. It applies to England, Wales, Scotland (with the exception of Part II: Surveillance and Covert Human Intelligence Sources) and Northern Ireland.

Public telecommunications systems are no longer just those systems for which a licence has been granted under the Telecommunications Act 1984, but any 'telecommunications service which is offered or provided to, or to a substantial section of, the public in any one or more parts of the United Kingdom'. This includes fixed line providers, mobile service providers and ISPs. 'Private telecommunication system' is defined as any telecommunication system that is not a public telecommunication system, but is attached to such a system. This would include office networks that are linked to a public telecommunication system by a private exchange, and local area networks connected to the internet.

The RIPA makes it a criminal offence to 'intentionally and without lawful authority' intercept any communication in the course of its transmission by public postal systems and public telecommunications systems. It is also a criminal offence to 'intentionally and without lawful authority' intercept any communication in the course of its transmission by private telecommunication system. This latter action, however, is not a criminal offence where the person intercepting the communication is a person with a right to control the relevant private telecommunication network, or a person who has the express or implied permission of such a person to intercept communications on that private network. In such circumstances, the interception may, if it is made 'without lawful authority', instead give rise to a civil action on the part of the sender or the recipient of the communication.

The RIPA does, however, allow for certain legitimate interceptions of communications by organizations on their private telecommunications networks – in other words, it provides 'lawful authority'. A general exception is made in the RIPA for interception where the interception is by or on behalf of a person running a telecommunications service for purposes connected with the provision or operation of that service – thus e-mail postmasters may examine mis-addressed messages in order to redirect them as necessary, or check e-mail subject lines for malicious code – for example to filter out the Kournikova virus.

The rules for legitimate interceptions are, however, mainly to be found in the Telecommunications (Lawful Business Practice) (Interception of Communications) Regulations 2000. To come within the Regulations, the interception has to be by or with the consent of a person carrying on a business, for purposes relevant to that person's business, and using that business's own telecommunication system.

Organizations may monitor and record communications:

- to establish the existence of facts to ascertain compliance with regulatory or self-regulatory practices or procedures, or to ascertain or demonstrate standards which are, or ought to be, achieved
- in the interests of national security
- to prevent or detect crime
- to investigate or detect unauthorized use of telecommunication systems
- to secure, or as an inherent part of, effective system operation.

Organizations may monitor but not record:

- received communications to determine whether they are business or personal communications
- communications made to anonymous telephone helplines.

It is worth noting that these interceptions will be legitimate only if the controller of the telecommunications system on which they occur has made all reasonable efforts to inform potential users that interceptions may be made. This may take the form of clauses in employment contracts and/or regular reminders in the form of notices in offices, and stickers on computers and phones. As yet, however, the courts have not had the chance to decide what exactly constitutes 'reasonable'.

Encryption

Under the RIPA, certain law enforcement agencies are provided with the power to serve a notice requiring the disclosure of an encryption key or disclosure of encrypted material where the agency has reasonable grounds to believe that disclosure would:

- safeguard national security
- prevent or detect crime
- be in the economic interests of the UK.

The notice has to be in writing and to contain certain specified information intended to safeguard the recipient, and the law enforcement agency must be able to provide reasonable proof that the recipient of a notice is in possession of either an encryption key or the protected information at the time the notice is served. A potential difficulty lies in the fact that disclosure of a private encryption key carries the risk that all communications encrypted with it can be read, even if the disclosure notice only referred to a specific communication.

Encryption notices are enforceable and a person who fails to make the disclosure required by a notice is guilty of a criminal offence if he or she knowingly fails to do so, and is liable to up to two years' imprisonment and/or an unlimited fine. The main defences available to recipients of such a notice are that they did not possess the relevant information or encryption key, or that they could not provide the necessary information within the required time period.

The RIPA also makes it a criminal offence for a person served with some encryption notices to 'tip off' others about their existence; such notices will contain a provision requiring the recipient to keep secret the giving of the notice, its contents and any response to it. Disclosure of such an encryption notice by the recipient may lead to an unlimited fine or imprisonment of up to five years.

Obscene materials and pornography

Key UK legislation:

- The Obscene Publications Act 1959 and 1964
- Unsolicited Goods and Services Act 1971
- The Protection of Children Act 1978 (amended by the Criminal Justice and Public Order Act 1994)
- The Telecommunications Act 1984 Section 43
- The Criminal Justice Act 1988 (amended by the Criminal Justice and Public Order Act 1994)

Background

If one is to believe the media, the most prevalent form of activity on the internet is the provision, distribution and downloading, of computer pornography. In the main, when this is discussed, the material in question is usually assumed to be photographic. However, pornography (and other forms of obscene material) on the internet may also take the form of movie clips, sound files and textual material. Whilst it is certainly possible to locate with relative ease material that most people would classify as pornography – by using an indexing site such as

Yahoo!, for example [14] – statements as to its prevalence often considerably over-state the role and status of pornography on the internet.

Examination of internet sites containing pornographic material appears to show that the majority of them fall into four main categories:

- those run by individuals which contain small personal collections of pornography, which are accessible at no charge, and which are rarely widely advertised
- commercial websites which contain relatively small amounts of pornography to advertise paper-based products such as magazines and books[15]
- commercial websites which contain links to large numbers of paysites that offer a small amount of material for free (these 'link websites' make their own money via referral fees and on-site advertising)
- commercial websites which contain large amounts of digital pornography, and which either charge for access to all but a very small amount of it, or require users to click on click-through advertising in order to access material.

Of these four categories, it is the latter two that appear to continue as major areas of growth, although the profitability of the link sites is debatable. Very few of the major sites offering links to, or actual, hard-core pornography appear to be hosted in the UK. In general, most bodies providing internet access, particularly academic institutions, are keen to avoid any problems with hard or soft-core pornography. This may be for legal reasons, or because it is thought that association with pornographic material would be damaging to the institution or business concerned, or simply because the high rate of accesses to sites containing pornography is disruptive to the operation of the computer on which the material is based. Thus a great deal of control on content is exercised by peer pressure on institutions without the aid of the law. This may even occur where the law of the country involved does not forbid the possession or distribution of such material. Indeed, many companies now expressly forbid employees to use company computer equipment to download or store pornographic material, whether illegal or not, on pain of dismissal.

The problem of defining 'pornography'

The question of the standard that one uses to establish whether material is, or is not, 'pornography' is a highly contentious one. It is also a debate that over the years has created some unusual alliances – for example, between radical feminists and Christian fundamentalists. An example of the type of definition that may be used is 'offensive, degrading and threatening material of an explicitly sexual or violent nature'. However, it is clear from the debates and the caselaw over the years that what to one person is 'offensive, degrading and threatening material' may well be to another a great work of literature or art, a protected social political or sexual statement, or just holiday snaps.

From the point of view of UK law, the debate over the meaning of pornography is one that has little relevance to the law itself. Despite the constant use of the word 'pornography' in much of the literature, the term is avoided in the relevant UK legislation, which concerns itself rather with whether the material in question is 'obscene' or 'indecent'. However, while this means that the courts are not caught up in an argument as to what is or is not 'pornographic', neither 'obscene' nor 'indecent' lend themselves easily to clear definitions either, and this difficulty of definition is reflected in both the legislation and the existing caselaw.

The problems that this definitional uncertainty may sometimes cause were demonstrated in June 1998 when British police seized a book, *Mapplethorpe,* from the stock of the library at the University of Central England in Birmingham. The book contained photographs of homosexual activity and bondage scenes taken by the internationally renowned photographer and artist Robert Mapplethorpe. Despite the fact that the book was widely acknowledged as a serious artistic work, the police told the University that its contents might contravene the Obscene Publications Act 1959. The book came to the attention of the police when a student at the University's Institute of Art and Design took photographs of prints contained in the book to a local chemist for developing and the chemist forwarded them to the police. Ironically, the student had taken the photographs to include them in a thesis entitled *Fine Art versus Pornography.* It seems that the police, at least, had little doubt as to their interpretation.

In UK law, different types of computer pornography can be caught by different legislation. The primary pieces of legislation are the Obscene Publications Acts of 1959 and 1964 (not applicable in Scotland) and the Protection of Children Act 1978 (as amended by Sections 84–87 of the Criminal Justice and Public Order Act 1994, see Section 172(8) for those parts of the Act applicable to Scotland), although the Telecommunications Act 1984 also contains relevant provisions.

The Obscene Publications Acts 1959 and 1964

The Obscene Publications Act 1959 (OPA 1959), section 1(1) states that 'an article shall be deemed to be obscene if its effect . . . is, if taken as a whole, such as to *tend to deprave and corrupt* persons who are likely . . . to read, see or hear the matter contained or embodied in it.' This test bears considerable similarity to that in an 1868 court decision, *R. v. Hicklin,*[16] where the judge stated that whether an article was obscene or not depended upon 'whether the tendency of the matter … is to deprave and corrupt those whose minds are open to such immoral influences and into whose hands a publication of this sort may fall.' [17]

It is clear that this legal definition of obscene has rather more specific meaning than would normally be attributed to the definition of obscene in non-legal usage. It is important also to remember that, while the depiction of sexual acts in pictorial or textual form is the most obvious form of potentially obscene material, the case law demonstrates that, for example, action may also be taken against aural presentations such as music albums,[18] pamphlets advocating the use of drugs,[19] and material showing scenes of violence.[20]

The key issues to consider when assessing particular material are:

1 *The possibility of the relevant material being seen as likely to deprave and corrupt.* Could an observer come to the conclusion that some of those who viewed the material might be depraved and corrupted by it?

2 *The likely audience for the material, as this will form part of the assessment of its tendency to deprave and corrupt.*
   When deciding whether material is obscene, an important determining factor is the consideration of who its likely audience is going to be. This is because some potential audiences are regarded as being more susceptible to being depraved and corrupted than others. Children are seen as an audience that is especially vulnerable in this respect. Thus, material made available in a forum or medium that is available to children will always be subject to stricter regulation than material that is not. Material on the internet is obtainable in relatively uncontrolled circumstances, and thus the definition of what is likely to deprave and corrupt those likely to have access to the internet will be accordingly low.

If an article is obscene, it is an offence to publish it or to have it for publication for gain. The OPA 1959, Section 1(3) as amended by the Criminal Justice and Public Order Act 1994 (CJPOA 1994),[21] defines a publisher as one who in relation to obscene material:

(a) distributes, circulates, sells, lets on hire, gives or lends it, or who offers for sale or for letting on hire, or

(b) in the case of an article containing or embodying matter to be looked at or a record, shows, plays or projects it, or, where the matter is data stored electronically, transmits that data.

Thus the transfer of obscene material, either manually by use of computer disks or other storage media, or electronically from one computer to another via a network or the internet, clearly falls under section 1(3). Thus, obscene material sent by e-mail, or posted to Usenet newsgroups, is going to be caught by the legislation. The OPA 1964, section 1(2) makes it an offence to have an obscene article in ownership, possession or control with a view to publishing it for gain.

Thus, obscene material placed on a web server will be caught even when an individual simply makes the data available to be transferred or downloaded electronically by others so that they can access the materials and copy them. This was demonstrated in the case of *R. v. Arnolds, R. v. Fellows.*[22] On appeal from their initial conviction, the defendants argued that the act of placing material on an internet site could not be regarded as a form of distribution or publication. The Court of Appeal, however, held that while the legislation required some activity on the part of the 'publisher', this seemed to be amply provided by the fact that one of the appellants had taken 'whatever steps were necessary not merely to store the data on his computer but also to make it available world wide to other computers via the internet. He corresponded by e-mail with those who sought to have access to it and he imposed certain conditions before they were permitted to do so.'

Transactions abroad

Some UK publishers of obscene material have sought to avoid the reach of UK obscenity law by uploading their material on webservers in other countries. In the case of *R. v. Waddon*,[23] the defendant had prepared the obscene material in England, and uploaded it from England to a website in the USA, from which it was then downloaded by a police officer in London. He argued at his trial that the material was not published in the UK for the purposes of the OPA 1959, and was thus outside the court's jurisdiction. However, the court held that Waddon was involved both in the transmission of material to the website and its transmission back again to this country, when the police officer gained access to the website – and there was, for the purposes of the OPA 1959, publication on the website abroad, when images were uploaded there, and then further publication when those images were downloaded elsewhere.

Defences against obscenity

The two main defences to obscenity charges contained in the OPA 1959 are innocent publication and publication in the public good. Innocent publication means that the person who published the material in question did not know that it was obscene and had no reasonable cause to believe that its publication would result in liability under the Act (Section 2(5)). In the internet context, it can be seen that while providers of facilities or internet service providers are unaware that obscene material is being put onto the internet via their system, they cannot be liable. However, if they are put on notice that this is occurring, they will have to take action to bring the activity to a halt. Failure to take such action would leave them at significant risk of prosecution.

An example of this has been the activities of the police in putting internet service providers on notice of Usenet newsgroups that contain potentially obscene material.[24] This provides great impetus to internet service providers to drop such newsgroups, as the notice would make it virtually impossible to run a successful defence of innocent publication. In contrast to providers who host web pages or newsgroups, those providers who simply provide a connection to the internet are unlikely to be able, even if they wanted to, to be in a position to accurately assess the nature of even a fraction of the data that their systems carry. They are thus unlikely to incur liability, even if some of their users use their systems as a conduit to access or distribute pornography, as there can be no actual knowledge of the material carried.

The defence of public good is found in Section 4 of the OPA 1959, which states:

> . . . publication of the article in question is justified as being for the public good on the ground that it is in the interests of science, literature, art or learning, or of other objects of general concern.

The defence does not mean that the article is not obscene, but rather that the obscene elements are outweighed by one of the interests listed. As may be gleaned from the discussion of the definition of pornography above, much may be read into the context in which the purportedly 'obscene' material is to be found. Indeed, the first case to arise under the legislation, in 1961, concerned D. H. Lawrence's book *Lady Chatterley's Lover.* Undoubtedly, some of the passages of the book were rather explicit for the period, but taken as a whole, the book's clear literary merits, which were defended by a number of experts, helped ensure its acquittal. It has been argued that, in some cases, the concept of literary merit has been rather liberally construed, for example, the book *Inside Linda Lovelace*, about the porn actress who starred in *Deep Throat,* was cleared on similar grounds in 1976.

A key problem with the Obscene Publications Acts is that the only certain way to test whether or not material is obscene, or if obscene serves the public good, is via the courts. The *Mapplethorpe* example cited above (see page 177) is a clear example of a work which in the eyes of a significant element in society (the police) is clearly obscene, and in the eyes of others (the University of Central England in Birmingham) a work of artistic merit. The uncertainty that this generates tends to have a 'chilling' effect on the nature and scope of material that is created, published and distributed in the UK, as publishers and other distributors are less willing to publish controversial material.

The Protection of Children Act 1978
The Criminal Justice Act 1988
The Criminal Justice and Public Order Act 1994

The relevant parts of the amended Protection of Children Act 1978 (PCA) deal with photographic representations of children under 16 (or persons who appear to be under 16). The Act makes it an offence to take, make, permit to be taken, distribute, show, possess intending to distribute or show, or publish, indecent photographs or pseudo-photographs of children. The Act defines 'distribution' very broadly. It is not necessary for actual possession of the material to pass from one person to another; the material merely has to be exposed or offered for acquisition. The PCA also criminalizes advertisements which suggest that the advertiser distributes or shows indecent photographs of children, or intends to do so. The legislative amendments made by the Criminal Justice Act 1988 further criminalize the mere possession of such photographs or pseudo-photographs.

The Criminal Justice and Public Order Act 1994 (CJPOA) Section 84(4) inserted a subsection (b) to Section 7(4) of the 1978 Act stating that 'photograph' shall include:

> . . . data stored on a computer disc or by other electronic means which is capable of conversion into a photograph.

While this definition of photograph covers digital representations of physical photographs (thus gif and jpeg image files, downloaded from FTP sites, embedded in web pages, or compiled from Usenet messages, will be treated as photographs), it was not considered sufficiently broad, and Section 84 of the CJPOA added the concept of the pseudo-photograph:

> 'Pseudo-photograph' means an image, whether made by computer-graphics or otherwise howsoever, which appears to be a photograph.

Thus a pseudo-photograph means any image which is capable of being resolved into an image which appears to be a photograph and, if the image appears to show a child, then the image is to be treated as that of a child. This means that there is no need for a child to have been used in the creation of the image. Indeed, the Act covers an indecent image which may not be based on any living subject.

The pseudo-photograph amendments deal with situations where, for instance, morphing software is used to create images which look as if they are of children from images of adults. Given the increasing difficulty of detecting faked photographs, and the tendency of defendants to argue that individuals in seized images were not in fact children, this change seems logical. Some have argued that the purpose of the PCA was to prevent harm coming to actual children, and that if no children are used in the making of pseudo-photographs, such photographs whether indecent or not should remain outside the law. Others counter that paedophiles have been known to use indecent photographs to persuade children that unlawful sexual activity is acceptable behaviour, and thus children may be harmed by the existence of such material.

What is 'indecency'?

Unlike obscenity, the term 'indecency' is not defined in either the PCA, or any other statute in which it occurs. When one examines statutes which refer to indecency, such as those which prohibit the import of indecent materials (see the Customs Consolidation Act 1876, the Customs and Excise Management Act 1979), or sending such materials through the post (the Post Office Act 1953), or their public display (the Indecent Displays (Control) Act 1981), it appears that 'indecency' relates to material that is considered 'shocking and disgusting', but less 'shocking and disgusting' than material which is considered obscene.

In practice, the test for indecency remains just as subjective, and thus just as difficult to pin down, as that for obscenity. In essence, the test would seem to be whether the item in question offends current standards of propriety or, to put it in the American phraseology, whether it offends contemporary community standards.[25] Given that community standards of adult behaviour tend to be rather higher where children are involved, an image involving a naked adult which might be perfectly acceptable could well be treated as indecent if a child or pseudo-child image were to be portrayed in a similar manner.

The provisions discussed above have clear relevance to activities on the internet. It would seem to follow from the *Arnolds* case mentioned above (see page 179), that placing of indecent pictures of children on a webserver will almost inevitably mean that they will be distributed; when such pictures are held on a computer, they can be plausibly said to be in someone's possession; a link to a website may be considered an advertisement; and a e-mail offering such pictures in digital or paper form certainly would.

Defences against indecency

A person or company charged under the PCA with distributing, showing, or possessing intending to show or distribute, has two potential defences, the first being that the person or company charged did not see the image and that they had no knowledge or suspicion that the image was indecent, and the second that there was a legitimate reason for possessing or distributing the image, for example for academic research.

It is also an offence to possess an indecent image of a child or indecent child-like image. The defences available are to be found in the amended version of Section 160 of the 1988 Act. These are similar to those contained in the PCA, but include what might be termed an 'unsolicited indecent material' defence:

(1)   It is an offence for a person to have any indecent photograph or pseudo-photograph of a child in his possession.

(2)   Where a person is charged with an offence under ss(1) above, it shall be a defence to prove –

(a) that there was a legitimate reason for having the photograph or pseudo-photograph in his possession; or

(b) that s/he had not seen the photograph or pseudo-photograph and did not know, nor had any cause to suspect, it to be indecent; or

(c) that the photograph or pseudo-photograph was sent without any prior request made by her or him or on her or his behalf and that s/he did not keep it for an unreasonable time.

With regard to the computerized making or possession of indecent photographs of children, the UK courts held in *R. v. Bowden* that the intentional downloading and/or printing out of computer data of indecent images of children from the internet constituted the 'making' of an indecent photograph and was thus an offence under Section 1(1)(a) of the Protection of Children Act 1978.[26] With regard to the unintentional storage of computer data of indecent images of children in a computer cache, the court in *Atkins v. DPP* held that this did not automatically constitute 'making', nor did their possession in a computer cache necessarily mean an offence had been committed under Section 160 of the Criminal Justice Act 1988, as the defendant, in such circumstances, must be shown to have known that he or she had the photographs in his possession, or to know that he or she once had them.[27]

In *R. v. Smith and Jayson*,[28] Smith had received an indecent photograph as an e-mail attachment, and Jayson had browsed an indecent pseudo-photograph on the internet. In both cases, their browser software automatically saved the images to a temporary internet cache on their computers. With regard to Smith, the court held that no offence of 'making' or 'being in possession' of an indecent pseudo-photograph was committed, simply by opening an e-mail attachment where the recipient was unaware that it contained, or was likely to contain, an indecent image, noting than in *Atkins* it was held that the Act did not create an absolute offence encompassing the unintentional making of copies. However, when Smith's opening of the e-mail attachment was considered in the light of the evidence relating to his other activities, the court did not believe him to be unaware of the nature of the attachment. In regard to Jayson, he argued that his act of viewing the indecent pseudo-photograph did not constitute the necessary intent to 'make' a photograph or pseudo-photograph. The court, however, held that the act of voluntarily downloading an indecent image from the internet to a computer screen was an act of making a photograph or pseudo-photograph, as the intent required was 'a deliberate and intentional act with the knowledge that the image was or was likely to be an indecent photograph or pseudo-photograph of a child.' Thus, Jayson did not have to intend to store the image with a view to future retrieval in order to meet the intent requirement for 'making'.

The Telecommunications Act 1984

Section 43 of the 1984 Act makes it an offence to send, 'by means of a public telecommunications system, a message or other matter that is grossly offensive or of an indecent, obscene or menacing character.'

While the Act deals in principle with indecent, obscene or offensive telephone calls, it is also capable of covering the transmission of obscene materials via public telecommunications systems in the form of electronic data. The meaning of a 'public telecommunication system' is 'any telecommunications system designated by the Secretary of State', and thus any of the British telecommunications companies so designated will be covered. Unlike the CMA 1990, which allows an element of extra-territorial jurisdiction, the Telecommunications Act 1984 does not give English courts jurisdiction in circumstances where a non-UK telecommunication system is used to send obscene materials into the UK. Neither does it apply in circumstances where the obscene material is transmitted via a local area network unless at some point in its passage via the local area network the material is routed through a public telecommunications system. It seems that the use of leased lines falls outside the scope of the Act. [29]

Unsolicited Goods and Services Act 1971

While the main focus of this Act was to put an end to the practice of sending people unsolicited goods, with a message that if the goods were not returned within a certain time, the recipients would have to pay for them (which is, in any case, legally unenforceable), Section 4 of the Act deals with unsolicited explicit sexual material. It is an offence under the Act to send an unsolicited book, magazine or leaflet that describes or depicts human sexual techniques. It is also an offence to send unsolicited advertising material for such a publication. The advertising material does not have to describe or depict human sexual techniques.

The definitions used in the Act seem to relate more obviously to books or magazines, and it has been claimed that this renders it inapplicable to material transmitted electronically.[30] Certainly, at present there have been no cases where the Act has been used against online materials. However, as junk e-mail (or spam), much of which advertises pornographic material, both digital and paper-based, becomes more of a problem, it may well be that either the courts will be asked to consider applying the Act to the online environment, or Parliament will be asked to consider extending the definitions.

Racial hatred

Key UK legislation:

* The Public Order Act 1986, Sections 17–19, Section 23

It has been suggested that certain sections of the Public Order Act 1986 (see Section 42 for those sections of the Act applicable to Scotland) may also be relevant to any discussion of criminal liability on the internet. Sections of that Act that are concerned with racial hatred state that an individual who publishes or distributes written material which is abusive, threatening or insulting to the public, or to a section of the public, or who has such material intending it to be displayed, published or distributed, will be guilty of an offence if that person intends to stir up racial hatred, or if in the circumstances racial hatred is likely to be stirred up (Section 17).

This may take the form of:

* the display of written material (Section 18)
* the publication or distribution of written material (Section 19)
* the distribution, showing, or playing, of a recording of visual images (Section 21)

where these are threatening, abusive, or insulting, and are intended to, or are likely to, stir up racial hatred.

It is a defence for an accused who is not shown to have intended to stir up racial hatred to prove that he or she was not aware of the content of the material and did not suspect, and had no reason to suspect, that it was threatening, abusive or insulting.

The provisions appear, on the face of it, to be applicable to web pages that are overtly racist. It is also possible that a web page which is not expressly racist, but which has links to other web pages that are, may be covered by the Act. In that case, as with libel, the important issue would be proving whether the owner of the linking web page knew that the material linked to was 'threatening, abusive or insulting'. However, the issue remains theoretical, as at present, relatively little use appears to have been made of this law in electronic, or indeed any other, forums. It is worth noting that some other countries – for example, Germany – have extremely stringent laws in this regard, such that online service providers such as CompuServe have fallen foul of laws relating to the prevention of pornography, Neo-Nazi propaganda and Holocaust denial.

Contempt of Court

Key UK legislation:

* Contempt of Court Act 1981

In England, but not in Scotland, a distinction is drawn between 'civil' and 'criminal' contempts. Civil contempt relates to circumstances where parties breach an order of court made in civil proceedings – for example, injunctions or undertakings – and as such are not relevant here. Criminal contempt deals with various types of conduct which, if allowed to go unchecked, would have the effect of interfering with the administration of justice, and is designed to have a punitive and deterrent effect.[31–32]

Criminal contempts essentially fall into five categories:

* publications prejudicial to a fair criminal trial
* publications prejudicial to fair civil proceedings
* publications interfering with the course of justice as a continuing process
* contempt in the face of the court
* acts which interfere with the course of justice.

While the law of contempt of court was developed by the judiciary through the common law, it has been modified to some extent by the Contempt of Court Act 1981. (The CCA 1981 does not codify or replace entirely the common law. It does, however, apply to Scotland (Section 15).)

The CCA 1981 makes it an offence of strict liability to publish a 'publication [which] includes any speech writing, broadcast, cable programme or other communication in whatever form, which is addressed to the public at large, or any section of the public' (Section 2 (1)) where such a publication 'creates a substantial risk that the course of justice in the proceedings in question will be seriously impeded or prejudiced.' (Section 2(2))

The fact that it is a 'strict liability' offence means that an offence occurs even where the person making the publication did not intend to interfere with the course of justice. The broad definition of 'publication' would cover Usenet messages, e-mail messages sent to mailing lists, and web pages. The publication of material relating to a case will only be an offence, where it occurs when the case is still *sub judice*. The statutory 'strict liability' rule is only applied during the period that the case is 'active' and the definition of 'active' is laid down in the Act. However, where an individual knows or has good reason to believe that proceedings are imminent, and publishes material which is likely or calculated to impede or prejudice the course of justice before the point laid down in the Act as the time when the case is 'active', this may be a common law contempt.

Actions which would commonly draw charges of contempt include:

- publication of material that prejudges the case, especially where it makes the express or tacit assumption that the accused in a criminal trial is guilty[33]
- publication of material which is emotive or disparaging, especially where there is an insinuation of complicity or guilt by association
- publication of material which is likely to be inadmissible at trial, such as previous convictions, or mention of evidence likely to be excluded as having been improperly obtained[34]
- publication of material such as a photograph of the defendant, where the issue of identification forms part of the trial proceedings
- publication of material hostile or abusive towards potential witnesses with the intention of coercing them into not testifying, or disclosure of witnesses' names following a court order that their names should not be disclosed if there was a danger that lack of anonymity would prevent them from coming forward[35]
- publication of jury deliberations
- publication of material breaching reporting restrictions in cases such where in open court there is identification of children, or identification of rape victims, involved in the proceedings[36]
- publication of material relating to court proceedings closed to the public, including where there is an issue of national security.

Defences to the 'strict liability' offence include:

1 A person is not guilty of contempt of court under the strict liability rule as the publisher of any matter to which that rule applies if at the time of publication (having taken all reasonable care) he or she does not know and has no reason to suspect that the relevant proceedings are active (Section 3(1)).

2 A person is not guilty of contempt of court under the strict liability rule as the distributor of a publication containing any such matter if at the time of publication (having taken all reasonable care) he or she does not know that it contains such matter and has no reason to suspect that it is likely to do so (Section 3(2)).

3 A person is not guilty of contempt of court under the strict liability rule in respect of a fair and accurate report of legal proceedings held in public, published contemporaneously and in good faith (Section 4 (1)).

The enforcement of the law of contempt has been rendered more difficult in modern times by the ability of individuals to publish material, in both traditional and digital media, in countries outside the court's jurisdiction. Consider, for instance, the *Spycatcher* saga, where the book in question was freely available outside the UK, but could not be published or excerpted in the UK. A Canadian example of this concerns the trials in Ontario, Canada, of Karla Homolka and Paul Bernado. During Homolka's trial for the murders of two teenaged girls, Kristen French and Leslie Muhaffy, the court ordered a publication ban on reports of the trial in Ontario, in order to ensure a fair trial for Homolka's husband Paul Bernado (a.k.a. Paul Teale), also charged with the murders. Despite the ban, information was widely available, due to coverage by US newspapers, cable and TV stations, and at least one website based at a US university. A Usenet newsgroup alt.fan.karla-homolka set up to disseminate and discuss information about the trial was censored by many Canadian universities.[37]

The internet has in many ways exacerbated this situation. It has been suggested with regard to the internet that, where the court cannot bring contempt proceedings against the original publisher, it may seek to do so against the internet service provider which distributed the material within the court's jurisdiction. Such an approach would, however, potentially create similar problems to those found in libel cases, where internet service providers have argued that the sheer volume of e-mail traffic, or the vast number of web pages on their systems, makes it impossible to check them all for possible libellous statements. As with libel, the courts are likely to treat rather more favourably (with regard to punitive measures) those ISPs and website owners who, once notified that material likely to constitute the basis for a contempt offence is held on their systems, do everything in their power to remove it as rapidly as possible.

Other criminal provisions
Blasphemy

The offence of blasphemy involves denial of the truth of Christian doctrine or the Bible, using words that are 'scurrilous, abusive or offensive to vilify the Christian religion.' It has been a common law offence since 1676. However, in the 20th century, the law of blasphemy fell into disuse, with no prosecutions between 1922 and 1978.

Despite the widely held view that the offence had become a historical anachronism, it resurfaced briefly in 1979, when the publishers of *Gay News* were successfully prosecuted for publishing a poem linking homosexual practices with the life and crucifixion of Christ.[38-39] More recently, in 1995, a UK website with a link to the banned poem on a server in Australia was investigated by the police after complaints from the public, but no prosecution was brought.

The common law offence can only be invoked in the case of blasphemy against Christianity and the Established Church, as was demonstrated in 1991, when a Muslim group unsuccessfully sought to invoke the offence against Salman Rushdie and the publishers of his book *The Satanic Verses*.[40] Given the decline in importance and influence of the Christian churches in the population as a whole, and the increasing importance attached to freedom of speech, it is unlikely that further successful blasphemy cases will be brought in the UK.

Gambling

Internet gambling is, by all accounts, a boom industry, with some estimates suggesting it will become a $40-billion-a-year industry by the year 2005. In the UK, betting, gaming and lotteries are currently covered by an array of regulatory laws, including the Betting Gaming and Lotteries Act 1963, the Gaming Act 1968, the Lotteries and Amusements Act 1976 and the Betting and Gaming Duties Act 1981.

However, in March 2002 the UK government released a White Paper suggesting wide-ranging reforms to UK gambling laws, including legalization of the provision of the full range of online gambling services by operators located in the UK, including gaming.[41] The White Paper states that online operators will need to meet the same entry standards as those in other gambling sectors, and that their operations will be subject to oversight by a Gambling Commission to ensure compliance with regulations. A kitemark or similar mechanism will be introduced to enable prospective customers to distinguish between those sites that are licensed and regulated by the Gambling Commission and those that are not. The government intends to consolidate all gambling legislation into a single Act of Parliament as part of the process.

While there do not appear to have been any prosecutions in the UK relating to online gambling, the rules surrounding the area are presently complicated enough[42] that those wishing to host a site for the purpose of gambling would be well advised to seek legal advice.

Regulation of trans-border flows of electronic information – international liability?

The growth of the internet, and in particular the expansion of the WWW, has led many countries to examine whether their existing law is able to cope with the potential problems that may arise. In the main, however, countries have refrained from rushing to create internet-specific laws. This is due in part to the volatility of the current situation, whereby it is impossible to predict either the speed of development or the direction of this medium. Many countries, even traditionally conservative states such as Singapore, are unwilling to pass legislation which might have the effect of damaging their ability to take advantage of the commercial opportunities which may arise from the changes. In the USA, several attempts have been made to impose criminal liability, or other sanctions, on the provision of access to pornographic material on the internet, including the Communications Decency Act 1996, the Child Online Protection Act 1998 and the Children's Internet Protection Act 2000. Thus far, none of these have withstood judicial scrutiny, in the main due to a failure to convince the judiciary that the way in which the laws have been drafted do not unduly interfere with First Amendment rights of free speech.

In the UK, most legal developments have arisen via the EU or Council of Europe. The EU published a Green Paper on the protection of minors and human dignity (COM (96) 483 final) in 1996. This opened a debate on the protection of minors and human dignity in audiovisual and information services, including internet services. An extensive consultation process led to the adoption of the Council Recommendation on the protection of minors and human dignity in audiovisual and information services.[43] Amongst its other provisions, online internet service providers are asked to develop codes of good conduct so as to better apply and clarify current legislation.

The Recommendation offers guidelines for the development of national self- regulation regarding the protection of minors and human dignity. Self-regulation is based on three key elements:

- the involvement of all the interested parties (government, industry, service and access providers, user associations) in the production of codes of conduct
- the implementation of codes of conduct by the industry
- the evaluation of measures taken.

The Recommendation is closely linked to the Action Plan on Promoting Safe Use on the Internet,[44] which in turn refers directly to the Communication on Illegal and Harmful Content on the Internet.[45]

Within the Member States themselves, there appears to have been a disinclination to engage in any wide-ranging legislative changes with regard to internet content regulation, and to rely on industry self-regulation. Where there has been legislative activity, it has more often had the aim of limiting the liability, if any, of internet service providers, than of penalizing website owners and end-users. However, there is a degree of consensus between the EU Member States that some regulation of internet content is both desirable and achievable, and that some changes in the laws of the Member States may well yet be necessary. How practical this will turn out to be is, of course, debatable, but it will add a further element to those issues which content providers should consider before placing material on the internet.

The Cybercrime Convention

In November 2001 the Council of Europe opened the Convention on Cybercrime for signature by Member States of the Council of Europe and by non-member states which had participated in its drafting. The Convention is the first international treaty on crimes committed via the internet and other computer networks. It will require parties to it to establish laws against cybercrime, to ensure that their law enforcement officials have the necessary procedural powers to investigate and prosecute cybercrime offences effectively, and to provide international cooperation to other parties in the investigation of cybercrime.

With regard to the substantive law issues, the Convention defines nine offences in four categories. These are:

- offences committed against the confidentiality, integrity and availability of computer data or systems (illegal access, illegal interception, data interference, system interference, misuse of devices)
- computer-related offences (computer-related forgery, computer-related fraud)
- content-related offences (offences related to child pornography)
- offences related to copyright and neighbouring rights.

It will be supplemented by an Additional Protocol making any publication of racist and xenophobic propaganda via computer networks a criminal offence.[46] The issue of racist websites was dropped from the Convention itself because a number of the states involved in the drafting, notably the USA, indicated that its inclusion would prevent them from signing.

The Convention has received significant criticism from privacy and human rights groups, which are concerned that it gives police overly broad powers and that its drafting excluded democratic controls. ISPs have also expressed concerns that the Convention's definitions are vague and could impose heavy burdens on providers who would not necessarily be reimbursed for expenses to meet law enforcement demands. The Convention will enter into force when ratified by five states, including at least three Member States of the Council of Europe. By May 2003, only Albania, Croatia and Estonia had ratified the Convention.

Conclusion

After a shaky start to legislatory, policing and prosecutorial approaches to cyber-crime in the UK, it would seem that major advances have been made over the last five years. Key changes to legislation have provided police and prosecutors with a range of new tools with which to pursue cybercriminals. In addition, the increased perception amongst politicians and the general public have led to greater support for police efforts to tackle problems. The National Criminal Intelligence Service, in a recommendation in 1999, called for the setting up of a national cybercrimes unit in the UK.[47] This was implemented in April 2001 with the creation of the 40-strong National Hi-Tech Crime Unit (NHTCU).

Increasingly, the police are also turning to international partnerships in order to tackle crimes – the recent crackdown on an international child pornography ring which called itself the Wonderland Club involved the co-ordination of raids across three continents. Indeed, the internet itself is being seen as a useful tool of law enforcement agencies in enforcement activities of internet crime, for example, a secure website, Net-Enforce, has been developed by the University of Glasgow to allow child protection and law enforcement agencies in different countries to exchange secure information; officers use tools such as the Whois database to track down people posting information by finding out who owns web addresses, and Neotrace, which allows police to trace the route of an e-mail.

The development of good working relations with UK ISPs has also been important, both in preventing the hosting of illicit material in the UK, and in tracking possible cybercriminals. Reducing the public perception that the internet is a 'lawless' or 'dangerous' environment is very much in the commercial interest of ISPs, as such a perception may limit the public take-up of internet access. ISPs are naturally wary, however, of measures that may impose significant costs upon them, given that their profit margins are often already fairly tight – hence significant opposition from ISPs to the interception capability sections of the Regulation of Investigatory Powers Act.

It is likely that, in the UK at least, primary attention will now turn to the issue of international co-operation to enhance the formal and informal law enforcement links that already exist. The Council of Europe's Cybercrime Convention looks like the most likely avenue for high-level agreement, although there have been significant concerns expressed, from a variety of interest groups, at the extent to which the Convention appears to subjugate civil rights issues to perceived law enforcement needs. In such a co-operative climate, web page owners may have to be prepared to deal sympathetically with the laws and values of countries other than their own, as the traditional print publishers have had to do, or consider restricting the accessibility of their material to specific internet domains.

Despite the attention paid in this chapter to the provisions of UK law, it is important never to forget the international nature of the WWW. A web page is usually accessible world-wide, and when putting either institutional or personal web pages on the WWW, it is worth considering who may view them. While there are jurisdictions more liberal than the UK with regard to freedom of speech, such as the USA, where even pornography may, under certain circumstances, attract First Amendment protection, there are many that are not. At present, thanks to a lack of international agreement over internet jurisdictional issues, it seems unlikely that a web page on a machine at an educational institution in the UK that is considered offensive or obscene by nationals of another country would result in a successful criminal prosecution (in terms of a penal sanction actually being applied) being brought there or in the UK. However, such a web page might prove costly with regard to other activities of the educational institution, such as overseas student recruitment and research ventures, because of the negative publicity.

Notes

1   European Commission Directorate-General Information Society web page 'Safer Internet Action Plan', available at http://europa.eu.int/information_society/ programmes/iap/index_en.htm and, http://www.saferinternet.org/ (gives details of recent developments – visited 15 August 2002).

2   The Council of Europe Convention on Cybercrime, available at http://conventions.coe.int/Treaty/EN/projets/FinalCybercrime.htm (visited 15 August 2002).

3   The Computer Misuse Act 1990, available at http://www.hmso.gov.uk/acts/acts1990/ Ukpga_19900018_en_1.htm (visited 15 August 2002).

4   Delmater, R. and Hancock, M. (2002) *Data Mining Explained*, Digital Press.

5   Charlesworth, A. (1993) Legislating against Computer Misuse: the trials and tribulations of the Computer Misuse Act 1990, *Journal of Law and Information Science*, **2**, 80–93.

6   Charlesworth, A. (1995) Between Flesh and Sand: rethinking the Computer Misuse Act 1990, *International Yearbook of Law, Computers and Technology*, **9**, 31–46.

7   [1998] 1 Cr App Rep 1.

8   *The Times*, 2 January 2001.

9   *R. v. Bow Street Metropolitan Stipendiary Magistrate ex p. Government of the United States* [1999] 4 All ER 1, (HL). Also *R. v. Governor of Brixton Prison, ex p. Levin* [1997] 3 All ER 289 (HL).

10 *Denial of Service Attacks*, available at http://www.cert.org/tech_tips/denial_of_service.html (visited 15 August 2002).

11 The Regulation of Investigatory Powers Act 2000, available at http://www.hmso.gov.uk/acts/acts2000/20000023.htm (visited 15 August 2002).

12 (1985) 7 EHRR 14.

13 Available at http://hudoc.echr.coe.int/Hudoc1doc/HEJUD/sift/626.txt (visited 15 August 2002).

14 Available at http://www.yahoo.com/Business_and_Economy/Companies/Sex/Directories/ (visited 15 August 2002).

15 For example: http://www.playboy.com and http://http://www.penthouse.com (visited 15 August 2002).

16 (1868) L.R. 3 Q.B. 360, 371.

17 Quoted in Heins, M. (n.d.) *Indecency: The Ongoing American Debate Over Sex, Children, Free Speech, and Dirty Words,* The Andy Warhol Foundation for the Visual Arts Paper Series on the Arts, Culture and Society Paper Number 7, available at http://www.warholfoundation.org/paperseries/article7.htm (visited 15 August 2002).

18 Singled out for abuse (1991) *The Independent*, (8 August), 17. Niggaz court win marks changing attitude (1991) *The Guardian*, (8 November).

19 *Calder v. Powell* [1965] 1 QB509, *R. v. Skirving* [1985] QB 819.

20 *DPP v. A & B Chewing Gum* [1968] 1 QB 119.

21 Section 168 and Schedule 9, para. 3.

22 [1997] 2 All ER 548.

23 6 April 2000 (CA).

24 *The Independent*, 20 December 1995.

25 See *United States v. Thomas* 74 F.3d 701 (6th Cir. 1996).

26 [2000] 2 All ER 418.

27 [2000] 2 All ER 425, 436.

28 7 March 2002 (CA).

29 Gibbons, T. (1995) Computer Generated Pornography, *International Yearbook of Law Computers and Technology*, **9**, 83–95.

30 Lloyd I. J. (1993) Shopping in Cyberspace, *International Journal of Law and Information Technology*, **1**, 335ff.

31   Bailey, S. H., Harris, D. J. and Jones B. L. (2001) Freedom of Expression: contempt of court. In *Civil Liberties: cases and materials,* 5th edn, Butterworths.

32   Smith, G. (ed.) (2001) Prohibited and Regulated Activities. In *Internet Law and Regulation*, 3rd edn, London, Sweet & Maxwell.

33   *A-G v. TVS Television* (1989) *The Times*, (7 July) (QBD).

34   *S-G v. Henry* [1990] COD 307 (QBD).

35   *R. v. Socialist Worker Printers and Publishers Ltd, Ex parte A-G* [1975] QB 637.

36   *Pickering v. Liverpool Daily Post and Echo Newspapers plc* [1991] 1 All ER 622 (HL).

37   Discussed in Froomkin, A. M. (n.d.) *The Internet As A Source Of Regulatory Arbitrage*, available at http://www.law.miami.edu/~froomkin/articles/arbitr.htm (visited 15 August 2002).

38   *R. v. Lemon* [1979] AC 617.

39   Cumper, P. (n.d.) *Religious Human Rights in the United Kingdom*, available at http://www.law.emory.edu/EILR/volumes/spring96/cumper.html (visited 15 August 2002).

40   *R. v. Chief Metropolitan Stipendary Magistrate ex parte Choudhury* [1991] 1 All ER 306.

41   UK Department of Culture, Media and Sport (n.d.) *A Safe Bet for Success: modernizing Britain's gambling laws*, available at http://www.culture.gov.uk/PDF/gambling_report_pgs.pdf (visited 15 August 2002).

42   See GamblingLicenses.com, available at http://www.gamblinglicenses.com/ (visited 15 August 2002).

43   See Council Recommendation 98/560/E, available at http://europa.eu.int/eur-lex/pri/en/oj/dat/1998/l_270/l_27019981007en00480055.pdf (visited 15 August 2002).

44   See Decision No 276/1999/EC, available at http://europa.eu.int/ISPO/iap/decision/IAP_Decision_en.pdf (visited 15 August 2002).

45   Communication on Illegal and Harmful Content on the Internet, available at http://europa.eu.int/ISPO/legal/en/internet/communic.html (visited 15 August 2002).

46   Draft First Additional Protocol to the Convention on Cybercrime on the criminalization of acts of a racist or xenophobic nature committed through computer systems and its Explanatory Report (26 March 2002), available at http://www.legal.coe.int/economiccrime/cybercrime/AP_Protocol(2002)5E.pdf (visited 15 August 2002).

47   National Criminal Intelligence Service (1999) *Project Trawler: crime on the information highways*, Central Office of Information.

10

Self-regulation and other issues

Heather Rowe and Mark Taylor

Introduction

One great attraction of the internet is its flexibility, its international reach and, some might say, its anarchic nature.

However, to say that such a delivery channel is unregulated is not true. This chapter focuses primarily on the self-regulation of multimedia and the internet, particularly in the area of advertising, although it also refers to certain relevant legislation. A number of specific examples are given relating to financial services, as excellent examples of how existing regulation is applied in the internet context – thus highlighting some of the problems.

This chapter touches on liability for content, discrimination and computer misuse, and some of the knotty jurisdictional issues surrounding advertising on the internet. The chapter is prepared from the perspective of English law and regulation, but mentions relevant initiatives of the European Commission which will affect doing business and advertising on the internet in EU Member States. It considers relevant voluntary codes of practice from bodies such as the International Chamber of Commerce (ICC).

New concerns and unique features arising from the internet

The internet is simply a medium of communication and, as such, is subject to many areas of general law. For example, a libel, an act of harassment, a breach of copyright or a fraudulent activity is just as actionable when perpetrated through the internet as when perpetrated through more conventional media. These areas are covered elsewhere in this book.

The internet also raises the issue of *where* a transaction takes place – relevant because it determines the regulatory and legal system(s) to which a party or transaction is subject. Problems in determining the location of a cross-border transaction and its governing law are not new but, given the global nature of the internet, come up increasingly with no absolute solutions. It has, for example, long been unclear exactly when an overseas firm is deemed to carry on business in the UK. Could it ever be said that, if you have a website hosted on a UK server and can deal with people in the UK from that website, you could (even with no physical presence) be carrying on business in the UK? The Data Protection Act 1998 certainly *would* apply in that situation.

There are complex contract law rules regarding international contracts with connections with more than one jurisdiction, such as when the contracting party controlling the website is in country A, while the server where the website is hosted is in country B and the proposed customer is in country C (the variables can be even more complex).

Even assuming a valid contract and a valid governing law clause, the country of the other contracting party may have consumer protection laws that it could apply to the transaction to protect its national consumers. For the EU, the Electronic Commerce Directive[1] (considered below) attempts to give EU companies doing business online some clarity as to the law that applies to electronic commerce dealings (usually, the laws of the 'country of origin' of the provider of 'information society services', but there are important exceptions).

The *primary* regulatory problems the internet faces are:

- the ease with which the internet can be used for cross-border transactions involving UK consumers having access to UK or *overseas* product or service providers
- the ease with which overseas product providers can set up a website and access prospective customers worldwide – advertising products aimed beyond their local market
- the increased use of 'electronic' documents to carry out investment transactions brings a particular new feature – the use of search engines and intelligent agents to help navigate and sift through the vast volumes of information available to find what is most relevant (taken together with hypertext links, search engines can bypass existing regulatory structures or safeguards (like consumer protection health warnings), particularly when a search engine summarizes a website in its own words)
- the use of electronic payment systems (raising issues of security of payments over the internet)

- concerns regarding the security of unencrypted messages sent over the internet
- whether 'health warnings' required or recommended by relevant laws, regulations and codes can be sidestepped, for example, because they appear only on a website's home page and a visitor can enter the website other than via the home page
- the proliferation of unsolicited commercial e-mail ('spam') that creates a major problem for the development of e-commerce.

The area of 'intelligent agents' is interesting. An intelligent agent is a small program that can be assigned to each customer to collate information about him or her. The agent performs these tasks while sitting on the technology-based distributor channel (be it an ATM, bank kiosk, mobile phone, PC or television) used by the customer. The agent appears on channel when the customer logs on. By switching on his PC the customer sends a signal for the agent to attend. When not at work, the agent sits on an agent server. The key feature is that you cannot *see* an agent and may be unaware of its presence. An intelligent agent can have a dual function – 'advice' and information collection. In handling customer enquiries and requests, the agent asks customers personalized questions about, say, the customer's life style – 'getting to know' the customer. Soon, software will be able to interrogate an individual, find out that individual's requirements from a financial product, his or her assets and inclination to risk. That software will then sift through the products advertised on the internet and produce recommendations – potentially making independent financial advisers or appointed representatives redundant.

Employees and premises are expensive. Websites are a relatively cheap and effective means of advertising. It is relatively inexpensive for investment firms to sell their products using intelligent agents. Software, whilst relatively expensive to develop, is subsequently cheap to replicate.

Professional investment advisers have to manifest their skills to the public – they take examinations. How will regulators judge a software package? Will action some day be brought by a disgruntled investor because an intelligent agent made a recommendation which caused loss? Who is responsible?

This is *not* just idle speculation. There has been a case on whether software can give advice, with judgment on 14 July 1998, in 'Re Market Wizard Systems (UK) Limited'.[2] The defendant, Market Wizard Systems (UK) Ltd, marketed and sold a computer software package known as the Market Wizard Equity Options Trading System. Mr Justice Carnworth held, in a reserved Chancery Division judgement, pursuant to a petition of the Secretary of State for Trade and Industry, that the computer package provided signals to users indicating the current positions to be held by selected traded stocks on that particular day, and which also provided guidance as to the course of action the user should take in relation to the buying or selling of the investment.

The brochure accompanying the software described the product as providing 'critical guidance when you need to make intelligent, disciplined trading decisions'. The judge held that the software package provided investment advice within the meaning of paragraph 15 in Part 11 of Schedule 1 to the Financial Services Act 1986. As such, the defendant was required to obtain authorization under the Act. Since no authorization had been obtained, the defendant's business was illegal.

In his judgment, His Lordship thought it necessary to identify *when* the advice was given. If it had been the defendant operating the software, in response to specific requests from customers, there would have been no doubt that it was providing investment advice. The fact, however, that the customer, not the defendant, actually operated the software, did not change the nature or source of the advice. The software therefore fell within the scope of what was then the Financial Services Act 1986.

It will be interesting to see if this point falls to be considered under the replacement to that Act, the Financial Services and Markets Act 2000 (FSMA). The Financial Services and Markets Act 2000 (Regulated Activities) Order 2001[3] defines regulated activities under the FSMA, and in conjunction with Section 19 of the FSMA, which makes it illegal to carry on a regulated activity unless authorized or exempt, it seems likely authorization would still be required.

General regulation of advertising in the UK

It is now clear (see below) that the rules applying to advertising generally apply equally to advertising on the internet, including advertising paid for by a third party on a website. What is less clear is the extent to which any commercial website might be treated as advertising. For instance, a website established in the name of a retail store might not of itself be considered to be advertising. However, such sites sometimes include journalistic style material in an effort to flesh out the retailer's marketing. That could be advertising. Once the site starts describing products, it probably would be regarded as advertising those products.

Another example of uncertainty is the electronic version of a product such as a newspaper: is the electronic version a product itself, or simply an advertisement for the 'real product'? In essence, commercial websites are blurring the sharp line in other forms of advertising between the advertisers and a journal's editors. Thus, in practice, if a website is clearly there to sell something, rather than simply consisting of access to the site itself (and perhaps basic factual information), it will probably be seen as advertising and the following regulations apply.

An overview of UK advertising regulation

Advertising in the UK has a system of self-regulation. The Committee of Advertising Practice (CAP) writes and enforces the British Code of Advertising, Sales Promotion and Direct Marketing.[4] It is through the CAP that all parts of the advertising industry agree to support the Code. The Advertising Standards Authority (ASA) supervises the Code and the self-regulation system. The idea behind this system is that, unless consumers can trust the advertisements they see, advertising would not be regarded as credible. The system relies on consensus and persuasion, backed by a series of sanctions, which have successfully overseen the various forms of advertising (*without* legislation) for over 30 years.

In 1995 CAP expressly included within its scope non-broadcast electronic media, including advertisements on CD-ROM and the internet. This brings self-regulation of such media into line with that for press, poster and screen advertising. The ASA's view is that they have jurisdiction over UK websites and will apply the same rules to the content of advertisements on a UK website as they do to other types of traditional advertising. Therefore, the Code applies to UK websites and multimedia products.

The ASA acts independently of the Government and aims to operate in the public interest. If an advertisement or promotion breaks the Code, advertisers are asked to amend or withdraw it. If they do not, even though the Code does not have the force of law, there are sanctions available:

1 *Adverse publicity*: the ASA publishes a weekly report on http://http://www.asa.org.uk detailing complaint adjudications, including the advertiser's name, agency and the medium involved. These reports are circulated to the media, government agencies, the advertising industry, consumer bodies and the public, and can result in wide (and probably unwelcome) media coverage.
2 *Refusal of advertising space*: newspapers can be asked to enforce their standard advertising terms of business which require compliance with the Code. They could refuse further space to advertisers which breach the Code and do not comply with the ASA's request for a withdrawal.
3 *Legal proceedings*: the ASA can refer repeatedly misleading advertisements to the Office of Fair Trading (OFT). The Director General of the OFT can apply to the court under the Control of Misleading Advertisements Regulations 1988 and obtain an injunction to prevent advertisers using the same or similar claims in future advertisements (see below).

The British Code of Advertising, Sales Promotion and Direct Marketing

The eleventh edition of the Code merged the Advertising Code, the Sales Promotion Code and the Cigarette Code into one publication. The Code applies to advertisements in newspapers, magazines, cinema, video commercials, e-mails, mailings, sales and advertisement promotions. Fly-posting, classified private advertisements, private correspondence and communications, health-related claims in advertisements, website content and television commercials are not covered. The Code provides specific rules for financial services and products, medicines and advertising to children.

The Code establishes principles to be followed by all marketers, such as general requirements that advertisements and sales promotions must:

- be legal, decent, honest and truthful
- be prepared with a sense of responsibility to consumers and society
- respect the principles of fair competition
- not bring advertising or sales promotion into disrepute.

The Code states that marketers have primary responsibility for ensuring that their advertisements are legal (Clause 4), and must hold documentary evidence to prove all claims (Clause 3). Marketers must not exploit the 'credulity, lack of knowledge or inexperience of consumers' (Clause 6) nor mislead consumers through inaccuracy and ambiguity, exaggeration, omission or otherwise (Clause 7). The Code must be 'applied in the spirit as well as in the letter.'

The Code covers issues such as depicting violence and anti-social behaviour, political advertising, causing fear and distress, matters of opinion, protection of privacy, advertising prices, comparisons and denigration.

The Code also contains provisions regarding distance selling (Clause 42). These were substantially amended to reflect the Data Protection Act 1998 and the Consumer Protection Regulations 2000. In distance selling, marketing communications are the final written advertised stage in the process that allows consumers to buy products without the buyer and seller meeting face-to-face. This includes internet and multimedia-based advertising and promotions. It is worth noting that advertisers, promoters and all others involved in handling responses must observe the Code. The Code provides the following:

1   Advertisements should state the full name and geographical address of the advertisers outside the coupon or other response mechanism so that it can be retained by consumers. Advertisements should include, unless obvious from the context, the main characteristics of the products or service; the

amount and number of any transport charges; the price, including any VAT payable, unless the advertisement is addressed exclusively to a trade; a statement that goods can be returned; any limitation on the offer and any conditions affecting its validity; the estimated delivery time, etc.

2   Marketers should not exceed 30 days in fulfilling orders except in certain circumstances.

3   Marketers should provide customers with written information on payment arrangements, credit instalments, rights to withdraw, cancellation, other terms and conditions, and the most appropriate address for contact.

4   Marketers must refund money promptly (and at the latest within 30 days of notice of cancellation being given) if consumers have not received their goods or services; if damaged goods are returned; if unwanted goods are returned undamaged within seven working days; or if an unconditional money back guarantee is given and the goods are returned within a reasonable period, as well as where the consumer can produce proof of posting for goods that have been returned but are not received.

5   So long as all contractual obligations to customers are met, marketers do not have to provide full refunds on perishable, personalized or made-to-measure products, high-value products, betting, gaming or lottery services or goods that can be copied.

6   If marketers intend to call on respondents personally, advertisements or any follow-up mailing should make this clear. To allow consumers adequate opportunity to refuse a personal visit, marketers should provide a reply-paid postcard or freephone telephone contact.

7   Explicit consumer consent is required *before* marketing by way of fax, e-mail or text message.

Not all of the above (like reply-paid cards) are relevant to the internet, but compliance with the provisions must be ensured.

ICC International Code of Advertising Practice

This Code (similar to the CAP Code) aims to promote high standards of ethics in marketing via self-regulatory codes which are intended to complement existing frameworks of national and international law. The most recent edition of the Code was released in 1997. The Code ties in with the ICC International Code of Practice on Direct Marketing and the ICC Guidelines on Advertising and Marketing on the internet (see below). There is no sanction to enforce the Code; rather it is followed as a matter of good practice.

The Code covers advertisements in their broadest sense, regardless of the medium used, and covers websites which, in essence, aim to promote the website owner. The term 'consumer' refers to any person to whom an advertisement is addressed or who can reasonably be expected to be reached by it, while 'product' refers to any goods or services offered. The Code's basic principle is that all advertising should be legal, decent, honest and truthful, prepared with a due sense of social responsibility and conform to the principles of fair competition. Specific articles in the Code address these topics, as well as truthful presentation, comparisons, testimonials, exploitation of goodwill and imitation.

Article 11 on 'Imitation' is interesting. It suggests that, where advertisers have established distinctive advertising campaigns in one or more countries, other advertisers should not unduly imitate them in the other countries where the former may operate, so as to prevent the initial advertisers from extending their campaigns within a reasonable period of time to such countries. Given the worldwide accessibility of a website, care should be taken that the look, feel and layout of a web page does not imitate any other known web page wherever it may be based and whatever country it may be primarily aimed at.

ICC International Code of Practice on Direct Marketing

Published in 2001, this should be read together with the following additional ICC codes:

- ICC International Code of Advertising Practice
- ICC International Code on Environmental Advertising
- ICC International Code of Sales Promotion
- ICC International Code on Sponsorship
- ICC/ESOMAR International Code of Marketing and Social Research Practice
- ICC Revised Guidelines on Advertising and Marketing on the Internet
- ICC International Code of Direct Selling.

The Code provides individuals and organizations involved in direct marketing with a set of rules generally acceptable nationally and internationally. The Code's purpose is to enhance general confidence in direct marketing and to foster a sense of responsibility towards consumers and the general public.

This Code outlines a number of basic principles dealing with, *inter alia,* truthful presentation, integrity and honesty, clarity, decency, comparison and fair competition, guarantees, etc. There are specific provisions on telemarketing and online communications, with guidelines on bulletin boards. It also says that sellers should have clear, user-friendly privacy policies and post them online. The Code requires sellers to provide a suppression mechanism for those not wishing to receive further online commercial solicitations.

The Code is designed as an international self-regulatory instrument, with prime responsibility for observance on the seller, and is mainly concerned with active marketing organizations making contact with customers.

ICC Guidelines on Advertising and Marketing on the Internet

The Guidelines lay down principles for responsible commercial communication over the internet, world wide web and other online services. This goes *wider* than advertising. Their objective is to enhance the confidence of the public in advertising and marketing provided over the internet, to safeguard optimum freedom of expression for advertisers, to minimize the incentive for governmental and/or inter-governmental regulations, and to meet reasonable consumer privacy expectations. These guidelines should be read in conjunction with the ICC publications listed above.

The Direct Marketing Association Code of Practice

The first edition of this Code was published by the Direct Marketing Association (DMA) in 1993, the second in 1997. The Code sets standards of ethical conduct and best practice to which members, including any agents involved in direct marketing using personal information, must adhere.

The general rules of the Code cover the use of personal information for direct marketing purposes and apply to data owners, data users, list brokers, list managers and data processors, whether or not any payment is made regarding the information. The Rules certainly apply to marketing by telephone.

Institutions intending to be involved in the direct marketing field may wish, for PR reasons, to contract with a direct marketing entity undertaking their marketing which observes the Code.

There is a supplementary code covering electronic commerce, the DMA Code of Practice for Electronic Commerce, to be read in conjunction with this Code.

DMA Online Codes

With the rapid growth of e-commerce and technological advances, the DMA launched an online Code of Practice in July 2000. It comprises the DMA Code of Practice for Commercial Communications to Children Online and the Code of Practice for Electronic Commerce. It sets out standards of ethical conduct and best practice for e-commerce, and applies to online marketing activity in the UK, directed to consumers or business. 'Online marketing' includes advertisements and offers for goods and services taking place online through e-mail, websites, interactive digital television, wireless application protocol (WAP), CD-ROM or interactive kiosks.

Under the Code, members must comply with the CAP Code (see page 200), the rulings of the ASA and any conclusion reached by the DMA. The usual requirements of advertisements being clear and truthful apply, and Article 3 states what information must be provided by members. Article 5 addresses the collection and processing of personal information, and also unsolicited e-mail.

The Code for Commercial Communications to Children Online deals with content of communications, bans most unsolicited e-mailing of children, has much more stringent privacy and information guidelines, and generally requires consent from a parent or teacher before targeting under-18s.

A draft code addressing short message service (SMS) marketing is currently subject to consultation. It will be integrated into the third edition of the DMA's Code of Practice.

The Control of Misleading Advertisements Regulations 1988 (SI 1988/915)

These Regulations cover any form of representation (including via websites) made in connection with a trade, business, craft or profession in order to promote the supply or transfer of goods or services, immovable property, rights or obligations.

The Regulations, as amended,[5] impose a duty upon the OFT Director General, the Independent Television Commission and the Radio Authority to consider complaints about misleading advertisements, unless the complaint appears frivolous or vexatious. If the Director General considers that an advertisement misleads, he may bring injunction proceedings against any person concerned with publication of the advertisement, with powers to obtain information to enable him to carry out the above functions.

The court may grant injunctions on terms it thinks fit, if satisfied that the advertisement the application relates to is misleading. In granting an injunction the court has regard to all interests involved, particularly the public interest, and can require any person appearing to be responsible for publishing the advertisement to provide evidence of the accuracy of any factual claim made. The court will not refuse to grant an injunction for lack of evidence that publication of the advertisement has given rise to loss or damage to any person, or that the person responsible for the advertisement intended it to be misleading or failed to exercise care to prevent it being misleading.

The Consumer Protection (Distance Selling) Regulations 2000 (SI 2334/2000)

The Consumer Protection (Distance Selling) Regulations 2000 are the enactment into English law of the European Union Directive on the Protection of Consumers in Respect of Distance Contracts 97/7/EC (OJ L144/19), published in June 1997.

The Directive standardized Member States' laws on distance contracts between consumers and suppliers. Its aim was to promote free movement of goods and services throughout Member States, so that consumers can access the goods and services of another Member State on the same terms as the consumers of that state. The Directive sets a minimum community level of law required in this area (Recital 4). Member States may introduce more stringent provisions to ensure a higher level of consumer protection, provided they are compatible with the EU treaties (such as the Treaty of Rome). This ability for Member States to introduce higher levels of consumer protection could lead to inconsistency between national laws – rather than a 'level playing field' for those selling goods and services online on a pan-European basis.

Scope

The Regulations apply to distance contracts, these being 'any contract concerning goods or services concluded between a supplier and a consumer under an organized distance sales or service provision scheme run by the supplier who, for the purpose of the contract, makes exclusive use of one or more means of distance communication up to and including the moment at which the contract is concluded.'

'Means of distance communication' is any means which, without the simultaneous physical presence of supplier and consumer, may be used to conclude a contract between those parties. Schedule 1 of the Regulations lists some of these, including electronic mail. The Regulations cover sale of goods or services concluded over the internet or by a mixture of distance communication methods. For example, an advertisement on a CD-ROM which gives a telephone number to ring to conclude a contract could fall under the Regulations as all methods of communication are 'distance' ones, as could advertisements on websites inviting orders to be placed by telephone or e-mail.

Exemptions

The Regulations do not apply to financial services contracts, including investment services and banking services. These are the subject of a separate Directive (see below).

The following contracts are exempted from the Regulations' requirements on prior information (Regulation 7), written confirmation of information (Regulation 8), right of withdrawal (Regulation 10) and time to perform (Regulation 19(1)):

- supply of food, beverages or other goods intended for everyday consumption, supplied to the consumer's residence or to his or her workplace by regular roundsmen
- provision of accommodation, transport, catering or leisure services where the supplier undertakes, when the contract is concluded, to provide these services on a specific date or within a specific period.

Prior information

Regulation 7 requires provision of information to consumers before concluding any distance contract, including:

- the supplier's identity
- his address (where advance payment is required)
- the main characteristics of the goods or services
- the price
- delivery costs
- payment and delivery arrangements
- the existence of a withdrawal right under Regulation 10 onwards
- the cost of using the means of distance communication (where it is calculated other than at the basic rate)
- the period for which the offer or price remains valid
- where appropriate, the minimum duration of the contract, in the case of contracts for the supply of goods or services to be performed permanently or recurrently.

The information must be provided in a clear manner appropriate to the means of distance communication used. It appears that the European Commission's view is that the internet is an acceptable means of providing such information. Regard must be had to the usual principles protecting those unable to give their consent, such as minors.

Written confirmation

Regulation 8 requires that consumers receive confirmation in another durable medium of most of the information referred to in Regulation 7 in good time during the performance of the contract, and at least by the time of delivery, unless the information has already been given to the consumer in an appropriate medium. The following must also be provided:

- written information on how to exercise withdrawal rights
- the address of the supplier's place of business
- information on after-sale service and any guarantees
- and the conditions for cancelling the contract where it is of unspecified duration or a duration exceeding a year.

The DTI has expressed the view that e-mail is a durable medium as it can be printed out by the consumer and is an acceptable form of confirmation. Where a consumer sees the information on a screen but cannot print it – for example, with a WAP telephone or teletext – this is unlikely to be sufficient and the information should be provided in hard copy.

Right of withdrawal

Regulation 10 onwards creates a withdrawal right for the consumer, who will have at least seven working days in which to withdraw from any distance contract without penalty or giving any reason. The only charge that may be made because of the consumer exercising this right is the direct cost of returning goods. For goods, the seven-day period runs from the day of receipt. If the supplier fails to supply the information required by Regulation 8, the period shall be three months instead.

The withdrawal right is not exercisable regarding contracts for:

- provision of services if performance has begun
- supply of goods or services where the price is dependent on market fluctuations the supplier cannot control
- supply of goods made to the consumer's specification or which are liable to deteriorate or expire rapidly
- supply of audio/video recordings/computer software which the consumer has unsealed
- supply of newspapers, periodicals and magazines
- gaming, betting and lottery services.

If the price of goods or services is covered to some extent by credit from the supplier, the credit agreement must be cancellable without penalty if the withdrawal right is exercised.

Other provisions

Regulation 19(1) requires, subject to contrary agreement, suppliers to execute orders within 30 days. Where they fail to do this, the consumer must be informed and be able to obtain a refund as soon as possible. The provision of goods or services of equivalent quality and price may be permitted if provided for in, or prior to, the contract.

Under Regulation 25, consumers cannot waive their rights conferred by the Regulations, nor can they lose the protection of the Regulations by virtue of choice of law of a non-EU country as the applicable law of the contract, if the contract has a close connection with the territory of one or more Member States. So, a supplier cannot circumvent the Directive by stating in an advertisement or contract that the law of a non-Member State is the applicable law of the contract.

The impact of the Regulations on the use of the internet by some commercial organizations is significant.

Distance marketing of financial services

In 2002, the EU adopted a Directive on the Distance Marketing of Financial Services, 2002/65/EC (0J L217/16), published in October 2002 and coming into force in 2004, setting common rules for selling contracts for credit cards, investment funds, pension plans, and so on, to consumers by telephone, fax or over the internet. It fills a gap in the earlier Distance Selling Directive, which excluded financial services. Its main features are:

- a prohibition on abusive marketing practices seeking to oblige consumers to buy services they have not solicited ('inertia selling')
- rules restricting other practices such as unsolicited telephone calls and e-mails ('cold calling' and 'spamming' respectively)
- obligations to give consumers comprehensive information before a contract is concluded
- an obligation to give consumers withdrawal rights from the contract during a 'cooling-off' period – except where there is a risk of price fluctuations in the financial market.

These standards reflect those in the existing Distance Selling Directive.

Other legislation

Many other UK statutes potentially apply to electronic advertisements, including the Trade Descriptions Act 1968, the Consumer Credit Act 1974, the Prices Act 1974, the Consumer Protection Act 1987 and the Trade Marks Act 1994 (to name but a few!).

Examples of some specific regulation – the financial services industry

The Banking Act 1987 (Advertisements) Regulations 1988

These Regulations apply (with certain exceptions) to advertisements containing an invitation to make a deposit. They set requirements for deposit advertisements.

Code of Conduct for the Advertising of Interest Bearing Accounts

This is published by the British Bankers' Association (current edition April 2003) and applies to the advertising of all interest bearing accounts maintained in the UK.

Advertisers must take special care to ensure that members of the general public are fully aware of the nature of any commitment they enter into as a result of responding to an advertisement. The registered or business name of the deposit-taking institution must be clearly stated in the advertisement.

The Banking Code

The 'Banking' Code (current edition March 2003) is drawn up by the British Bankers' Association, the Building Societies' Association and the Association for Payment Clearing Services, to be observed by banks, building societies and card issuers in their relations with *personal* customers only. It is a voluntary code, although most banks active in the UK and building societies comply to a greater or lesser extent with its provisions. It does not expressly mention websites but is clearly looking at new 'electronic' products, as it mentions 'electronic purses' (electronic payment devices).

Clause 8 addresses advertising and marketing services. Clause 8.1 states: 'We will make sure that all advertising and promotional material is clear, fair, reasonable and not misleading.' Clause 2(a) states that signatories to the Code will ensure that their products and services meet relevant laws and regulations.

There is also the voluntary Mortgage Code [6] followed by lenders and mortgage intermediaries regarding their *personal* customers taking out mortgages. It contains almost identical provisions on advertising and compliance with codes of practice.

The Financial Services and Markets Act 2000, Section 21

The Financial Services and Markets Act 2000 (FSMA) replaced the Financial Services Act 1986 and applies to the activities of investment professionals (fund managers, stockbrokers, market makers and other intermediaries) when they carry out 'regulated activities', which will occur amongst other things, when they:

- deal in investments (shares, stocks, options, futures, etc.) as principal or agent
- manage assets belonging to another person, which may include investments
- give advice.

Section 21 of the FSMA regulates advertising and makes it an offence to communicate, or cause the communication of, an 'invitation or inducement' to engage in investment activity in the course of business. This does not apply if the person who makes or causes the communication is an authorized person, or the content of the communication is approved for the purposes of section 21 by an authorized person. The details, and the exemptions, are in the Financial Services and Markets Act 2000 (Financial Promotion) Order 2001[7] (FPO). The prohibition is intended to apply to communications which are clearly promotional in nature, and not just to information that might lead to financial services activity.

A key policy element of the new financial promotion regime is that it should be technology-neutral – able to withstand technological changes without the necessity for amendment. The FPO introduced the idea of 'real-time' and 'non-real-time' communications.[8] This distinction is important when deciding whether any exemptions, some of which are mentioned below, apply.

'Real-time' communications are those made in the course of a personal visit, telephone conversation or other interactive dialogue. 'Non-real-time' communications are any communications not falling within this description, and particularly include communications by letter or e-mail or contained in a publication.

The FPO contains many rules relating to real time solicited and unsolicited communications. Article 8 of the FPO defines a real-time communication as having been solicited if the call, visit or dialogue was initiated by the recipient of the communication, or if it takes place following an express request from the recipient of the communication. Any other real-time communication is unsolicited. The making of a 'cold call' – an unsolicited real-time communication – by an unauthorized person is an offence. An investment agreement entered into resulting from an unsolicited call may be unenforceable against the call's recipient.

Broadly, where authorized persons issue or approve financial promotions, they must apply appropriate expertise and be able to show that they believe on reasonable grounds that the advertisement is fair and not misleading. Guidance on this topic is contained in the appendix to the Financial Services Authority (FSA) Handbook, Authorization Section, which is available on the FSA website.[9] This outlines how certain promotions should be handled, but also lists exceptions to the rules.

Material circulated on the internet or in multimedia form can be a 'financial promotion', and in the FSA Guidelines there is a section relating to this.[10] If a website, or part of a website, operated or maintained in the course of business, invites or induces a person to engage in investment activity, this will be a financial promotion. The FSA's view is that the person who caused the website to be created will be a communicator. An internet service provider who merely manages a website for another and has no control over, or responsibility for, its contents will not be communicating any financial promotion in the website.

The Data Protection Act 1998 (DPA)

The DPA can apply to a host of situations relating to electronic media and is discussed in Chapter 8.

The Telecommunications Data Protection Directive [11]

The Telecommunications Data Protection Directive (TDPD) concerns the processing of personal data and the protection of privacy in the telecommunications sector, and, in particular, in the integrated services digital network (ISDN) and in the public digital mobile networks. It was substantially implemented in the UK by the Telecommunications (Data Protection and Privacy) Regulations 1999, which implement all of the Directive except Article 5 (relating to interception and monitoring of electronic communications). Article 5 was implemented here by the Regulation of Investigatory Powers Act 2000 (RIPA) and the Lawful Business Practice Regulations.[12]

Although much of the TDPD affects Public Telecommunications Operators specifically, some provisions have wider implications. For example, Article 5 mentioned above, Article 12, and Part V of the 1999 Regulations, relate to unsolicited calls for marketing purposes.

The provisions of the 1999 Regulations addressing direct marketing are:

- a ban on the use of automated calling systems for direct marketing purposes – that is, systems which make calls without human intervention and dial numbers sequentially until they find one which is a 'live' number on lines of individual or corporate subscribers without prior consent
- a ban on sending unsolicited direct marketing faxes to individual subscribers without consent
- the ability for corporate subscribers to opt out from receiving unsolicited direct marketing faxes
- the ability for individual subscribers (but not corporate subscribers) to opt out from receiving unsolicited direct marketing telephone calls
- enforcement by the Information Commissioner (IC), who will be advised on technical matters by the Office of the Director General of Telecommunications (the administration of the registers which have been created to allow such opting-out is by the DMA).

Material is not unsolicited where the called line is that of a subscriber who has notified the caller that it does not object to receiving such communications. This could be done by having ticked a box or agreed to this in terms and conditions.

E-mail preference schemes

The TDPD enabled creation of preference schemes for fax and telephone, and the UK now has mandatory schemes. If companies market to individuals who were put on the opt-out list more than a month after they were put on that list, the company could be liable.

The TDPD will be replaced by the new Directive on privacy and electronic communications with effect from November 2003, (the 'E Comms Directive').[13] The E Comms Directive, Article 13, regarding 'unsolicited communications', extends the marketing restrictions to e-mail:

1   The use of automated calling systems without human intervention (automatic calling machines), facsimile machines (fax) or *electronic mail* for the purposes of direct marketing may only be allowed in respect of subscribers *who have given their prior consent*.

2   Notwithstanding paragraph 1, where a natural or legal person obtains from its customers their electronic contact details for electronic mail, in the context of the sale of a product or a service, in accordance with Directive 95/46/EC, the same natural or legal person may use these electronic contact details for direct marketing of its own similar products or services provided that customers clearly and distinctly are given the opportunity to object, free of charge and in an easy manner, to such use of

electronic contact details when they are collected and on the occasion of each message in case the customer has not initially refused such use.

3   Member States shall take appropriate measures to ensure that, free of charge, unsolicited communications for purposes of direct marketing, in cases other than those referred to in paragraphs 1 and 2, are not allowed either without the consent of the subscribers concerned or in respect of subscribers who do not wish to receive these communications, the choice between those options to be determined by national legislation.

4   In any event, the practice of sending electronic mail for purposes of direct marketing disguising or concealing the identity of the sender on whose behalf the communication is made, or without a valid address to which the recipient may send a request that such communications cease, shall be prohibited.

5   Paragraphs 1 and 3 shall apply to subscribers who are natural persons. Member States shall also ensure, in the framework of Community law and applicable national legislation, that the legitimate interests of subscribers other than natural persons with regard to unsolicited communications are sufficiently protected.

This is further explained in one of the preambles to the E Comms Directive:

(41) Within the context of an existing customer relationship, it is reasonable to allow the use of electronic contact details for the offering of similar products or services, but only by the same company that has obtained the electronic contact details in accordance with Directive 95/46/EC. When electronic contact details are obtained, the customer should be informed about their further use for direct marketing in a clear and distinct manner, and be given the opportunity to refuse such usage. This opportunity should continue to be offered with each subsequent direct marketing message, free of charge, except for any costs for the transmission of this refusal.

This is bad news for some Member States, where, at present, all that is required is for consumers to be given an opt-out from unsolicited communications. Those countries must change to an opt-in regime where e-mail is used.

Will this Directive really stop 'spam'? It may prevent spam from other European countries, but in reality, most spam comes from the USA and, increasingly, from Asian countries. This measure will not solve the problem.

A public consultation launched by the Department of Trade and Industry to implement the Directive closed in June 2003. The DTI intends to publish details of the final measures in August 2003. In addition, the EU Commission adopted in June 2003 a proposal for a Directive on Unfair Commercial Practices, that aims to replace the existing multiple volumes of national rules and court rulings on commercial practices with a single set of common rules. A communication on 'spam' by the EU Commission is expected to be adopted in Autumn 2003.

There is already a voluntary e-mail preference service in the UK. The e-mail preference service (EMPS) is administered by Operator Services Limited. Anyone who wishes not to receive unsolicited commercial e-mails can register with EMPS at http://www.emailpreferenceservice.com. Registration is free for consumers and fulfilled within ten working days. A direct marketing company can use the service to check if a receiver of materials on their contact list has made a request not to receive further unsolicited marketing e-mails. The EMPS data check is only available on an *ad hoc* basis and is charged at £85 for a one-off search. It is not obligatory to search it.

The Enterprise Act 2002 – Promoting consumer codes of practice

The Enterprise Act 2002 highlights one of the key functions of the Office of Fair Trading (OFT) as promoting good practice in activities that may affect consumer interests. One of the ways in which the OFT may do this is by giving its approval to (or withdrawing approval from) consumer codes of practice. A code of practice is eligible for approval by the OFT if it is intended to regulate the conduct of businesses that supply goods or services to consumers, with a view to safeguarding or promoting the interests of consumers. So, such a code could cover an area such as unsolicited communications.

A body that administers a voluntary consumer code, and can influence and raise standards within its sector, such as a trade association, may apply for approval of its code. Such a body is known as a 'code sponsor'.

The Enterprise 2002 Act requires the OFT to set criteria for approving codes, and permits it to use an official symbol to signify which codes have OFT approval.

The Regulation of Investigatory Powers Act 2000

The Regulation of Investigatory Powers Act 2000 (RIPA) establishes a basic principle that communications may not be intercepted without consent of the parties to an electronic communication, and specifically prohibits activities such as recording by people other than the users. RIPA establishes offences of unlawful interception on a public or a private telecommunications system and a tort of unlawful interception on a private system by the operator of that system. However, RIPA authorizes interception where the interceptor has reasonable grounds to believe that both the sender and the intended recipient have consented.

The Lawful Business Practice Regulations[14] make exceptions to RIPA and permit businesses to intercept employee communications without consent for certain limited and legitimate purposes. An interception is authorized, for example, if effected with the express or implied consent of the system controller to monitor communications to ascertain compliance with regulatory procedures, or in the interests of national security or for the prevention of detection of crime.

Jurisdictional problems

Jurisdiction is a problematic legal issue relating to the internet. There have been developments in this area of law in Europe, with the introduction of the Brussels Regulation,[15] which has been enacted into UK law by means of The Civil Jurisdiction and Judgements Order 2001.

The Brussels Regulation means that, in a dispute between a consumer and a business, the consumer could take legal action in his *home* state *or* in the home state of the business as regards consumer protection laws. This is dependent on the business pursuing commercial activities in the Member State of the consumer's domicile, *'or, by any means, directing such activities to that Member State'*. The question is whether a website is in any way *'directed'* at the Member State. There are no definite rules regarding this, but the Department of Trade and Industry has offered advice, saying that it would be necessary to look at the nature of the particular website. They add that websites giving information in different Community languages and currencies, and offering to deliver to EU countries would probably count as being directed to the EU, whilst some websites (e.g. a site in English with prices in pounds and restricting orders to UK customers) might be described as targeted only at the UK.

Each case must be considered on its own facts. Potentially, the laws regulating advertising in each country from which the web page can be accessed may apply, which, in essence, is every country in the world. Clearly it is impractical to seek advice to ensure compliance in each jurisdiction, and so it may be an idea to have separate websites for each jurisdiction, specifically targeting that country, in the correct language and using the relevant currency. However, this then restricts the usefulness of the internet to a small number of countries, and is thus not really the way forward.

Prior to the Brussels Regulation, the English courts did not have jurisdiction to try matters which related to activities overseas, as the 1968 Brussels Convention, the predecessor of the Brussels Regulation, provided that the consumer must have taken the steps to conclude the contract whilst in his or her country of domicile. That requirement has now been removed. Previously, for example, a person in Germany who dealt in infringing copies of software could probably not be tried in an English court for his sales in Germany. Now, however, a UK consumer who bought goods in Germany whilst on holiday would be able to sue in the UK courts if the trader had pursued or by any means directed his activities to the UK.

By July 2003, the European Commission had gone through a second consultation period on a revised draft proposal for a Council Regulation known as 'Rome II' (since it extends provision of an existing Rome Convention of 1980 on applicable law in contractual obligations), which has as its goal the harmonization of laws that will apply in non-contractual, cross-border disputes in any situation where there could be a choice between laws of different countries.

Rome II will determine applicable laws in relation to non-contractual matters, such as defamation, product liability and unfair competition. Defamation is covered in Article 7, and provides that the applicable law is that of the country where the victim is habitually resident at the time.

Forming a contract online – general

Whilst there is some debate as to how best to achieve contract formation over the internet, under English law, electronic media should not prove to be an obstacle to a valid contract formation. After all, contracts are formed over the telephone and by fax. The international dimension may complicate matters and it is possible that courts other than the English courts may have jurisdiction in a dispute (for example, where the other contracting party resides overseas and the services or goods are to be provided to him or her there).

Under English law, there are four essential elements to a contract:

- an offer
- acceptance of the offer
- an intention to create legal relations
- consideration.

In many common situations, the four elements are obvious: you see a mobile phone in a show room; you make an offer which is accepted; you tender the purchase price (the consideration), the relevant rental papers are handed over by the seller and a binding contract is formed. However, if the potential purchaser saw the phone advertised in the newspaper and tendered the asking price, a valid contract would not be formed unless the dealer accepted the offer: advertisements are generally only 'invitations to treat', that is, invitations to the world at large to make an offer *to buy*. The distinction between being an *offerer* or an *accepter* is a subtle but important one as it affects their respective abilities to withdraw or reject an offer.

Websites and advertisements

In many cases where a company enters into contracts with customers over the internet, it will do so by way of an advertisement which, if worded correctly, would amount to an 'invitation to treat'. Thus, where a potential customer is applying for some service (an offer), the website owner would be entitled to turn down the application (i.e. not accept). Each case will turn on its own facts and the company's objectives should dictate how the advertisement is worded.

It is important that the terms and conditions underpinning the transaction are referred to and available for the customer to read. These are not the same as the terms and conditions for access to websites (see 'Health Warnings' below). Where services or goods are to be ordered over the internet, the customer must be made aware clearly of the applicable terms and conditions. Views differ on the best way to achieve this. Ideally, customers should be obliged to scroll through the terms and conditions, and then confirm they have read and accept them. It would be difficult, under English law, for customers to deny awareness of the terms if such a procedure *has* to be followed *before* any purchase or order. From a marketing and presentational perspective, this is unattractive. However, if this is not done, a court may hold that the terms and conditions would not apply, especially if they contained unusual or onerous provisions (which should be highlighted to the customer in any event).

The terms and conditions should at least be referred to (prominently) on the first web page relating to the services or goods, with a hypertext link to them. They should also be available from the web page where the order is placed or application made. The objective is to bring the terms and conditions to the customers' attention and to give them every opportunity to read and accept. Immediately before visitors complete transactions, they should be asked to confirm they have read the terms and conditions and accept them. If they do not, they should be offered the opportunity to cancel the transaction or review the terms and conditions. The transaction should not complete without acceptance of the terms and conditions. This should be considered when designing a web page.

Timing and place of formation

Another question to consider is at what time a contract will be deemed formed, and where. There is no specific legislation on this, and no judicial guidance on how the courts would address this in the context of the internet. It is instructive to consider how the law has developed and been applied in the past.

As a general rule in English law, a contract is not formed until *acceptance* of the offer has been communicated to the offerer. As an exception to this, the courts have developed a rule that where an offerer has explicitly or implicitly agreed to the offer being accepted by post, once the letter has been posted, the contract is deemed formed *even if* the offerer does not receive the letter accepting the offer. This rule, the 'postal rule', was developed in the early 19th century as representing the fairest method of allocating the risk and consequence of letters going astray in the post. By analogy, one could argue that where the offerer has expressly (or impliedly) agreed to acceptance by e-mail, once the acceptance has been sent by the accepter into cyberspace, the contract is formed even if the e-mail is never received. Until the courts rule on the point, there must be uncertainty as to whether or not a contract has been formed where the e-mail accepting the offer is not received. To avoid this situation in circumstances where the contract is to be formed without any further approval by the website owner, the relevant terms and conditions should make it clear or a statement seen by the user *before* sending an e-mail should state that the contract is not formed until the website owner has received the e-mail accepting its offer.

Rules have developed regarding use of telex in international commerce. The English courts have held that, where a contract is formed by exchanges of telex, the contract is concluded *in the country where the telex accepting the offer is received*. By analogy, it could be argued that a contract is concluded where the e-mail accepting an offer is received. The significance of this is that English law might recognize that courts overseas could assume jurisdiction merely because the message was received in their jurisdiction.

The offerer could pre-empt matters by specifying in terms and conditions which law applies to the contract and which courts are to have jurisdiction over disputes. However, the effectiveness of these measures could perhaps fall to be determined by the foreign court, and the measures would not bind third parties not a party to the contract (such as a person who had been defamed on an electronic bulletin board run by a website owner), nor would they be effective to avoid regulatory regimes or criminal sanctions.

Health warnings and disclaimers – efficacy in an internet environment?

Many statutes, regulations and rules of regulatory bodies (or prudence) require 'health warnings' to appear on written materials – for example, the standard caveats seen on investment and unit trust advertisements.

Organizations may also wish to include other terms on their website or CD-ROM to protect themselves – for example, a clause restricting those downloading content from their website from replicating it for gain.

Unless terms and conditions are brought clearly to the user's attention, the chances of enforceability are remote. Terms and conditions tucked at the bottom of the home page in small print are less likely to be enforceable than where users must scroll through (with unusual/onerous provisions highlighted or in bold) and click on an 'Accept' icon. In the end, a balance must be struck between sensible risk assessment taking into account the nature of the website, and target audience.

One recommendation would be to discuss the area of 'best practice' on use of the internet with any industry regulators relevant to a website's content to encourage consistent strategies.

Sex and racial discrimination

The principles of sex and racial discrimination apply to electronic media as much as to any other situation. Care must be taken to ensure that the material on such media is not in any way discriminatory between the sexes or racially, applying the same objective thought as with any external publication or information issued by a company.

Illegal material on the internet

There is some self-regulation regarding illegal material on the internet (in particular with reference to child pornography). In September 1996, the Internet Watch Foundation (IWF) was launched to address this. It is an independent organization which implements proposals jointly agreed by the Government, the police and two major UK internet service provider trade associations: the Internet Service Providers Association (ISPA) and The London Internet Exchange Limited (LINX). All internet users are encouraged to report potentially illegal material via a hotline, telephone, fax or e-mail, even if not absolutely certain of legality. The information required is a brief description of what has been seen and details of its location. Reports of something a user personally finds offensive as a matter of personal taste or morality, rather than as a matter of law, cannot be acted upon. The IWF assesses the reported material, traces its origin, and contacts the police and service provider to remove it. The reporter is advised of the progress of his or her report. The IWF stresses there is little it can do about material not liable to prosecution under UK law.

Website owners must be aware that other jurisdictions may have laws on harassment and illegal material which may affect websites accessible in that other jurisdiction.

The dangers of e-mail communications
Liability for defamatory communications

In principle, a company's liability for defamatory e-mail messages sent by its staff does not differ from its liability in respect of any other communication written by its employees. Although the legal status of an e-mail message has not been determined (by the courts or Parliament), the generally accepted view is that it is actionable as a libel – as a publication made in permanent form – because e-mail messages (although seemingly transient) are invariably stored on and retrieved from a computer's hard drive. E-mail messages will accordingly be treated in law as equivalent to letters, faxes and paper documents. To bring a claim for libel based on the publication of such a document, it is not necessary to show any loss or damage has been suffered; the law presumes some damage will flow from publication.

A company will have potential liability on two levels. It may be held vicariously liable if its employees publish e-mail messages through the company's communications system. As the owner and controller of the communications system through which e-mail messages written by its staff are sent, the company may also be directly liable for publishing those messages.

A company will be vicariously liable for defamatory e-mail messages sent by a member of its staff, providing that the employee, when sending the e-mail, was 'acting within the scope of his employment'. Any e-mail sent by a member of staff as part of, or directly incidental to, the carrying out of his or her job will be deemed sent while that person was so acting. This is so even if the member of staff was expressly forbidden from publishing defamatory material. A company will only escape the risk of vicarious liability if the sending of the e-mail message was completely unconnected with the employee's job and could properly be regarded as a wholly private communication.

The fact that an e-mail message is confined to the company's *internal* communications system will not prevent vicarious liability. The courts have held that a communication between two individuals, even where both employed by the same company, can amount to a 'publication' for which the company can be vicariously liable. This arose in *Western Provident Association Limited v. Norwich Union Healthcare Limited and The Norwich Union Life Insurance Company Limited (formerly The Norwich Union Life Insurance Society)*, reported in the *Financial Times* on 18 July 1997. This case did not result in a judgment as it was settled. Norwich Union paid £450,000 in settlement to Western Provident and issued an apology to Western Provident admitting that its staff libelled the private healthcare group by *internal* e-mails. This was the first UK libel action involving messages sent by e-mail. Norwich Union staff spread rumours that Western Provident was being investigated by the Department of Trade and Industry and that the group was close to insolvency. In a statement in open court, Norwich Union admitted the rumours were false, deeply regretted and sincerely apologized to Western Provident for dissemination of the rumours. Norwich Union stated that it had made every effort to ensure that such unacceptable practices would not occur again and undertook not to repeat the allegations.

Although the potential for serious financial or other damage to a third party is greatly increased when e-mails are sent externally, such as to clients or potential clients, a company should not ignore that considerable damage can be caused by a defamatory allegation or rumour circulating internally. Where it can be shown that an employee either intended, or should reasonably have anticipated, that the contents of the e-mail would be passed on to others, within or outside the organization in which he or she worked, the company will be vicariously liable for those further communications.

In 1999 the High Court held that an internet service provider could be liable for defamatory material posted by a third party on one of its newsgroups.[16] Lawrence Godfrey complained to Demon Internet Ltd about allegedly defamatory remarks about him in a posting on a news group hosted by Demon. The posting was made by an unknown person in the USA, who was not a Demon customer. Mr Godfrey informed Demon that it was defamatory and a forgery but, although he demanded that it be removed, it remained there for a month. When Mr Godfrey sued for libel, Demon contended it was not a 'publisher' and could rely on the defence in Section 1 of the Defamation Act 1996. The plaintiff applied to strike out these defences.

The High Court ruled that internet service providers *do* publish the comments which users post on their newsgroups and are liable if these comments are libellous, subject to the defence under Section 1. However, this defence requires that the publisher took 'reasonable care' when publishing the statement and 'did not know' that it was contributing to a defamatory publication. Given that Demon had known the statement might be defamatory but had done nothing to remove it for a month, it could not rely on this defence.

In similar circumstances, a company would have a defence if it could show that it had taken reasonable care in relation to the particular publication and did not know, and had no reason to believe, that what it did caused or contributed to the publication (see Section 1 again). As a general rule, it would be prudent for companies to implement and enforce a strict office policy as to the use which staff make of the company's e-mail facility.

Any company which is sued (as directly liable or vicariously liable, or both) over the contents of an e-mail will be able potentially to rely on the normal libel defences – for example, that the statement is true or is fair comment based on true facts.

The position becomes more complex with e-mail sent to a recipient outside England and Wales. This could occur frequently, particularly in the case of a multinational organization, which has offices or branches worldwide. The question whether such a communication will be actionable here will depend not only on the position under English law but also on the position under the law of the country where the e-mail is received. In some circumstances, liability limits imposed by foreign law may be given effect here.

For these reasons, a company is well advised to ensure that its staff are properly versed in the potential liability to it and to its employees for defamatory e-mail communications. The problem is accentuated because people have tended to treat e-mail as a relaxed and informal mode of communication. A written corporate policy should be implemented, including the following:

1 Staff should be required to confine their e-mail communications to those properly required for business purposes.
2 Staff should be expressly prohibited from publishing any potentially libellous material.
3 Care should be taken to ensure statements are true, could not be misconstrued and are only sent to those with a legitimate interest in the subject matter.
4 Staff should be told to take steps to validate incoming e-mails, as it is possible to 'spoof' the sender's address and change contents *en route*.
5 Staff should be instructed that, if they receive a defamatory e-mail, they should report it to their manager.
6 Staff should *not* repeat the libel, including forwarding it to others.

One hopes such guidelines will help instil a sense of responsibility amongst staff and minimize risks.

Precautions in respect of potential liability for other wrongs

It is recommended also that there be similar restraints on the sending of material which is obscene, discriminatory or might be regarded as harassment of any kind.

Harassment

It is unlikely that harassment issues should arise except where there is use of, say, bulletin boards or live chat. It is perhaps more likely to arise within a corporate's own intranet used by employees. There have been cases in the USA (with astronomical damages claimed) where, for example, employees of companies have claimed they were harassed by sexually or racially discriminatory e-mail.

Probably the most publicized of these actions, *Owens v. Morgan Stanley & Co.*[17] was before the New York Courts in 1996. A law suit was filed by two African-American employees of the firm who claimed they were subjected to a hostile work environment. The original complaint alleged violations of various statutes, including the New York Human Rights Law, and sought $5 million in compensatory damages and $25 million in punitive damages per plaintiff. The basis of the suit was a racist e-mail message which became the subject of office jokes and of ridicule against the plaintiffs, as well as other African-American employees at Morgan Stanley. The plaintiffs even suggested that they were denied promotions despite demonstrating ability although, perhaps, this issue is not linked to the e-mail campaign. The plaintiffs argued that it was directly related to the e-mail campaign, particularly so because, the alleged author of the e-mail message was named in the lawsuit as well as other Morgan Stanley employees accused of further distributing the offending e-mail. The settlement terms of this case are confidential, so it is difficult to know how significant this case was, although the figures bandied around were spectacular.

In English law, it is important for an employer to avoid harassment by e-mail. According to Section 41 of the Discrimination Act 1975, if anything is done by a person in the course of employment, it is treated as having been done by the employer as well as by that person, whether or not done with the employer's knowledge or approval. The exact meaning of 'in the course of employment' in the context of this Act is not entirely clear, but the employer could be liable in certain circumstances. The 1976 Race Relations Act contains similar provisions regarding racial discrimination. It is prudent to have warnings in both situations to assist the employer in attempting to avoid vicarious liability.

Companies Act 1985

Section 349 of this Act provides that:

(1) Every company shall have its *name* mentioned *in legible characters:*
  (a) in all business letters of the company,
  (b) *in all its notices and other official publications,*
  (c) in all bills of exchange, promissory notes, endorsements, cheques and orders for money or goods purporting to be signed by or on behalf of the company, and
  (d) in all its bills of parcels, invoices, receipts and letters of credit.

(2) If a company fails to comply with subsection (1) it is liable to a fine.

(3) If an officer of a company or a person on its behalf:

(a) issues or authorises the issue of any business letter of the company, or any notice or other official publication of the company, in which the company's name is not mentioned as required by subsection (1), or

(b) issues or authorises the issue of any bill of parcels, invoice, receipt or letter of credit of the company in which its name is not so mentioned, he is liable to a fine.

Arguably, e-mail could be used as a notice or receipt. The company's name should therefore appear in all 'official' e-mails.

Confidentiality

Communications sent by e-mail are more easily intercepted, copied and read by strangers than more traditional forms of communication. Best practice is for staff to avoid altogether sending confidential information by e-mail. However, if confidential information has to be so communicated, companies should provide a macro to staff which they are required to use when sending e-mails, particularly externally. The macro should contain a confidentiality warning, similar to that typically appearing on faxes. The macro for external use should also contain any information required by the Business Names Act 1977 to be included on business letters.

The implications of disclosure obligations

At an early stage in litigation, at least after the writ is issued and possibly before, a party comes under an obligation not to destroy documents which might be relevant to the action. If the company has in place a system for the deletion of e-mail files after the expiry of a fixed period of time, it may find itself inadvertently in breach of this obligation. Procedures should be put in place to avoid this. The obligation to preserve documents and to disclose them arises in any litigation, not just libel. Staff should be required to act with caution when sending e-mails, not simply to minimize the company's exposure to a libel claim or other action over the e-mail content, but also to avoid prejudicing the company's position generally with regard to litigation.

Conclusion

The above chapter provides an overview of the main areas of self-regulation and the legal issues that could be relevant to the internet and multimedia products. It is not exhaustive and should act as a reminder to treat the internet no less carefully as a medium than you would any other delivery channel.

Notes

1   Directive 2000/31/EC.
2   [1998] 2 BCLC 282.
3   SI 2001/544.
4   Committee of Advertising Practice (2003) *British Codes of Advertising and Sales Promotion*, 11th edn.
5   Particularly by the Control of Misleading Advertisements (Amendment) Regulations 2000 (SI 2000/914).
6   Second edition April 1998, reprinted January 2003.
7   SI 2001/1335.
8   FPO Article 7.
9   Available at http://www.fsa.gov.uk.
10   AUTH Appendix 1: Financial promotion and related activities 1.22.
11   97/66/EC, OJ L24 published in January 1998.
12   SI 2000/2699.
13   Council of the European Union (2002) Processing of Personal Data and the Protection of Privacy in the Electronic Communications Sector, *Official Journal of the European Communities* (L201), 37.
14   SI 2000/2699.
15   Council Regulation 44/2001 of 22 December, 2000.
16   *Godfrey v. Demon Internet Ltd* [2001] QB 201.
17   96 Civ. 9747.

11

Staying legal: from awareness to action

Laurence W. Bebbington and
Chris Armstrong

Introduction – the current situation

Bad news travels fast. In a wired-up, global community bad news travels even
faster. Increasing reliance on IT systems, software and communications technologies introduces a raft of potential legal risks and liabilities. Consider the
following recent occurrences:

1   In January 2003, 47 employees of Flintshire County Council in Wales were
    investigated for their use of their employer's e-mail system to circulate
    material that was described as being in 'poor taste.'[1] This was merely the lat-
    est, but certainly not the last, in a long succession of stories detailing e-mail
    misuse at work.
2   In December 2002, Cambridgeshire Police Authority sent an unsolicited
    e-mail to over 4000 businesses disclosing all of the recipients' e-mail
    addresses in the CC field. Some received 20 copies of the e-mail. The
    Authority denied breaching data protection legislation but apologized
    unreservedly for any inconvenience caused by what appeared to be 'a
    major technical error.'[2]
3   In November 2002, a 21-year-old university student was sent to prison for
    five months after conducting an online harassment campaign against his for-
    mer girlfriend. His activities included hacking into the girlfriend's personal
    web pages on the Friends Reunited website and posting explicit photographs
    of her. He was convicted of harassment, performing unauthorized modifica-
    tion of a computer program and data protection offences. Two associates,
    employed by the mobile operator O2, who intercepted SMS text messages on

her mobile telephone for him, were dismissed and could be charged with data-protection-related offences.[3]

4   Also in November 2002, the Business Software Alliance announced that two companies, Comojo Holdings (the parent company of London's Metropolitan Hotel) and Amaze Ltd (a Liverpool-based IT solutions company), had agreed financial settlements as a result of the use of unlicensed software. Amaze Ltd also spent £24,000 on appropriate software licences.[4]

5   Over a 24-hour period in July 2002, a UK e-tailer, Foris, offered Sony Vaio laptop computers for sale at £76.17 instead of the usual price of nearly £1000. Other products were offered at a price of 1p.[5] Although orders were placed, Foris announced that these would not be honoured. It argued that no binding contracts had been formed. This online pricing mix-up followed a well-publicized debacle in January 2002 when, after extensive publicity, public pressure and the prospect of legal action, Kodak decided to honour orders placed for its DX3700 digital camera which had been advertised online at a price of £100 instead of £329.[6]

6   In May 2002, a former teacher won £1250 in damages after a former pupil was found to have posted defamatory comments about him on the Friends Reunited website.[7]

7   In the USA in April 2002, a company that allegedly stored thousands of MP3 music files on a network server for downloading and use by its employees paid $1,000,000 to the Recording Industry Association of America in an out-of-court settlement, rather than let the issue of potential copyright infringement go to costly litigation.[8]

Legal and business risk is alive and well – and thriving on the internet. By now, some organizations and companies, but by no means all, are aware that there are significant legal, commercial and reputational risks associated with a presence on the internet and with increasing workplace dependence on IT hardware, software and communications technologies. These risks are likely to increase. Further national and international regulation of online industries and activities will expand in response to a range of needs, for example:

• to enhance even further online protection for consumers and children and other potentially vulnerable groups (e.g. non-professional financial investors)
• to continue the Canute-like struggle against intellectual property theft, piracy and infringement both in the workplace and from homes
• to develop and intensify the fight against organized internet crime, terrorism and information warfare.

Many other areas of online activity could be mentioned. Astonishingly, however, surveys and research continue to suggest that many organizations are failing to identify and address the legal and business risks associated with online activities either properly or in a strategic fashion.

A short report by Fox Williams, a leading UK City law firm specializing in IT and e-commerce law, detailed the findings of a legal compliance survey of the websites of 112 of the 196 companies listed on OFEX, the UK share trading platform for unlisted and unquoted securities.[9] Although 90% of the websites surveyed collected personal data from site visitors, only 35.7% of the companies were registered under the Data Protection Act 1998; 78% of the websites had no privacy policy whatsoever; 80% of the websites had no means of allowing visitors to opt out of receiving marketing material. Nearly 70% of the websites had no terms and conditions of use and only 14% of those that did have them actually required the visitor to accept them as a condition of use of the site. Of 24 websites allowing users to purchase products or services online, only 20.8% of them provided the user with the information required by law under the Consumer Protection (Distance Selling) Regulations 2000. Some 12.5% of the sites incorporated third-party names or trademarks in their meta-tags – thereby exposing them to the risk of legal action for trademark infringement and passing off. A number of companies ran sales promotions or competitions – most of these did not have sufficient safeguards in place to ensure that they did not contravene legislation governing the running of an illegal lottery, nor did they conform to the British Codes of Advertising and Sales Promotion.

The Fox Williams survey was conducted in the first half of 2002. It contains various other interesting findings. Along with many other surveys or reports, it confirms the view that organizations are continuing to expose themselves to major legal risks, liabilities and unnecessary costs in their current use of internet and e-mail technologies and of IT in general. Surveys also confirm consumer scepticism about the trustworthiness of services, products and information provided online. A 2002 international survey of health and finance websites world wide, as well as of price-comparison websites, by Consumers International concluded that many websites are 'failing to provide adequate details . . . leaving consumers potentially at risk from inaccurate, incomplete or even deliberately misleading information.'[10]

These deficiencies in turn expose website operators and service providers to legal action and liabilities, or to reputational damage that can have substantial adverse commercial impact. Staying legal – in terms of managing both external and internal organizational legal issues – does not seem to figure highly on the agenda of many enterprises in the rush to exploit the opportunities offered by the internet, and the latest information and communications technologies.

In October 2002 Brightmail, a leader in anti-spam technology, reported that spam was becoming a significant concern for internet users, with 55% of parents believing that responsibility for dealing with spam lies with their ISP. [11] Brightmail also found that 81% of parents were either concerned or very concerned about the amount of pornographic junk mail on the internet. Research by Star Internet, released the same month, suggested that only 56% of employers were able to determine how much time their employees spent using the internet – despite the significant legal risks that employee internet and e-mail use entails.[12] The study also found that 20% of businesses stated that they could not function after one day without access to e-mail.

While lack of trust about e-commerce among potential consumers is comparatively well-documented, other studies also show dogged unease among businesses concerning business-to-business e-commerce. A European Commission consultation, aimed particularly at small and medium-sized enterprises, documents continuing concerns among businesses and their representative bodies (such as national chambers of commerce) about B2B online commerce, including concerns about information security, the absence of clear guidance on online contracting issues, jurisdictional and applicable law concerns and the protection of sensitive data in using e-business platforms.[13] This consultation has been followed up by a formal Commission working paper as the first step in developing a policy to address these concerns.[14] In November 2002, research by KPMG International indicated that 56% of 134 major listed companies in the UK, USA, Africa, Australia and Europe had experienced failed IT projects in the previous year.[15] The average loss resulting from the failure was £8 million. The highest loss was put at £133 million.

There is a most striking lesson to be learned by all organizations from the legion of internet stories relating to embarrassing corporate e-mail abuses, tales of company copyright and other intellectual property rights infringements, instances of defamation, incidents of online harassment, climb-downs over inadvertent online contract formation, the use of counterfeit or unlicensed software, etc. It is that, while the internet and information and communications technologies present enormous opportunities, these opportunities are generally accompanied by substantial risks. These legal, business and reputational risks must be identified and managed. Even with the best of intentions and best endeavours, mistakes can – and will – happen. Owing to the nature of certain offences it will be difficult or impossible to avoid liability. But good workplace policies might help mitigate some aspects of liability. The pressing need is to audit legal risk areas and liabilities, identify major risks, assess the likelihood of their occurrence and their consequences, to put in place processes and policies to eliminate or reduce risks, and to monitor implementation and success. Legal risks and liabilities are both external and internal. Previous chapters have highlighted in various ways the major areas of concern for legal compliance in managing external relationships.

This chapter will reconsider some of these aspects in terms of more active management of such risks. But it will also focus on a major source of legal risks and liabilities for an organization – its employees. The chapter merely seeks to highlight the major issues and concerns, and outlines a general approach to such issues. It does not seek to provide a total view or approach to risk assessment and management (there is an extensive literature on this subject in a variety of fields – legal, business, computing, etc.), but rather to provide a framework within which to begin examining and thinking about these important problems. The last part of the chapter addresses an often neglected area of discussion about the introduction of policies and procedures to manage employee workplace IT and communications activities – important employment law considerations.

Overview of legal risks posed by employee use of IT and communications technologies

Employee use of IT in the workplace represents very real risks for the employer. Under the doctrine of vicarious liability the employer, in certain circumstances, will be liable for the tortious acts of his employees where these acts can be shown to have occurred in the course of employment. In such circumstances the employer incurs liability and is more likely to be sued on the basis that the employer will be in a better position to pay damages and costs. The employer will also be liable to his own employees for breaches of implied or express terms in the employment relationship – for example, by breaching the employer's duty to provide reasonable protection for employees from racial or sexual harassment. External and internal risks and liabilities cannot be ignored. They must be identified and managed. The major potential risk areas are:

- intellectual property rights infringement
- defamation
- inadvertent contract formation
- data protection
- harassment
- negligent misstatement
- virus communication
- confidentiality.

Intellectual property rights infringement

Infringement of copyright, moral rights, database right and trade marks, and employee use of unlicensed software, are major risk areas. The downloading or distribution of copyright-infringing material by employees using e-mail is a particularly significant risk. Copyright is still not well understood and easily infringed. Non-compliance with licences (such as database licences) or applications software licensing agreements is also an area of concern. The downloading or installation, sharing and use of unlicensed software is a major vulnerability in large organizations – particularly in view of substantially increased criminal penalties and fines for copyright piracy and unlicensed software use as enacted by the Copyright, Trade Marks, etc. (Offences and Enforcement) Act 2002.

Defamation

Employee use of company e-mail systems, bulletin boards, discussion lists and online conferencing and forums is a high-risk area for the publication of material that is potentially defamatory of individuals or other companies. While actual damages awarded may not be high, the costs of the action can be substantial – in *Godfrey v. Demon Internet Ltd*, the award of damages was only £15,000, but the costs awarded against Demon have been estimated at about £250,000.

Inadvertent contract formation

Employees with sufficient ostensible authority constitute risks, since they may unintentionally form new contracts, or modify existing ones, in the course of e-mail correspondence. This could have expensive, even disastrous, consequences.

Data protection

Employees must be properly trained in all aspects of data protection and privacy legislation to ensure that the organization does not breach the rights conferred by this legislation.

Harassment

Sexual and racial harassment – and workplace bullying – by e-mail are a risk. Harassment raises the possibilities of claims for constructive dismissal or action under relevant legislation – Section 41 of the Sex Discrimination Act 1975, for example, states that acts of discrimination committed by an employee will be treated 'as done by his employer as well as by him, whether or not it was done with the employer's knowledge or approval.' Section 31 of the Race Relations Act 1976 contains a similar provision. This Act makes discrimination on the grounds of race, colour, nationality or ethnic and national origin unlawful. It is perfectly possible for such discrimination to include e-mail activities. Conduct, courses of conduct or repeated instances of certain actions are likely to constitute harassment.

Harassment can be broadly described in various contexts – the Commission for Racial Equality describes racial harassment as 'a general term covering a wide range of unacceptable and, often, unlawful behaviour . . . conduct of a racial nature, or other conduct based on race, affecting the dignity of men and women at work.'[16] This appears to be modelled on the European Commission's definition of sexual harassment as 'unwanted conduct of a sexual nature, or conduct based on sex affecting the dignity of men and women at work.'[17] In certain circumstances harassment may be a criminal offence – Section 5(1)(b) of the Public Order Act 1986 (as amended by the Criminal Justice and Public Order Act 1994) makes it a criminal offence 'to display any writing, sign or other visible representation which is threatening, abusive or insulting, within the hearing or sight of a person likely to be caused harassment, alarm or distress thereby.' This could cover the display on a computer screen of obscene material or pornography, or making printouts of such material. The Protection from Harassment Act 1996 is also pertinent here. Cases on some of these subjects are pending in the courts.

Negligent misstatement

This is the obligation for employees to take reasonable care when making statements or giving advice to a third party. Any such advice provided by e-mail could expose the organization to liability where it turns out to be wrong, inaccurate or misleading.

Virus communication

E-mail messages or attachments may contain viruses. The transmission of viruses to the computer systems of other individuals or organizations may cause serious damage or disruption to normal functioning. Liability could arise.

Confidentiality

Breach of confidentiality is a significant risk. Employee disclosure of confidential business information can be highly damaging and embarrassing. An e-mail inadvertently disclosing information about a patentable invention could invalidate a patent application. The ease with which e-mails can be copied, forwarded, misdirected, etc. means that accidental disclosures of confidential information can easily occur.

Staying legal: the management of risk and liabilities

Legal risks and liabilities must be addressed. The risk areas particular to an organization need to be analysed, identified, prioritized and managed. Figure 11.1 suggests several steps that may be useful in thinking about this process. Identification and management of legal risks posed by employees may help reduce the employer's liabilities. The process can also be educational for employees by fostering more responsible use of workplace technologies. One of the most obvious manifestations of a management strategy is the trend towards the creation of well-formulated written policies for employee use of IT and communications technologies. Such policies outline acceptable and unacceptable use, and state the sanctions applicable for breaches. They need to be publicized and distributed to all employees. While such policies may not eliminate liability altogether, they may (especially if supported by other measures) at least reduce it.

Some more detail concerning the steps in Figure 11.1 is given below. This discussion will not merely focus on employee risks – one of the advantages of thinking and reflecting seriously upon risk is that both internal and external risks can be identified. Often they may be related.

1 Risk analysis

A first step might be to analyse and broadly characterize the nature of the risks confronting the business or organization. Thinking in broad terms provides a framework for beginning an analysis that will yield a more detailed list of specific and identifiable legal risks that need to be prioritized. There are several possibilities for broad characterizations. All may need to be addressed. They will vary between organizations and will not be mutually exclusive categories.

For example, legal risks could be characterized as to whether or not their origins are internal or external. Some organizations may need to consider themselves to be major targets of external threats – multinational corporations can be targeted by pressure groups, activists or anarchists, who may attack a corporate or organizational website by a variety of means – denial-of-service attacks, for

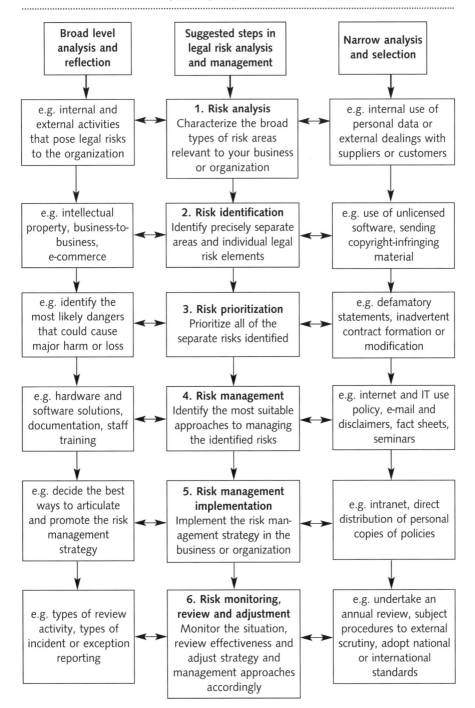

Fig. 11.1 *A multi-step approach to managing business and organizational legal risks*

example. Or any organization may be penetrated by individual hackers challenged by the desire to break into organizational or corporate intranets, customer or financial databases, or other key institutional resources. Such organizations need to protect themselves against the potential legal risks and other consequences that could result from such attacks. This will be a high external threat for some types of organization. They will pose little or no threat to others, such as charities or not-for-profit organizations. But thinking broadly about categorization will allow a potential target organization to move on and identify the precise legal risks associated with a particular external threat.

Internal legal risks obviously originate from employees or other members of the organization (such as students in universities or colleges). However, other internal risks may exist – technology, for example, where the term is used in its broadest sense to include processes or ways of doing things within the organization. Poorly designed processes can lead to legal risks and exposures. The dangers of badly designed processes can be very easily seen where the organization goes on to interact with external suppliers or customers. An example is inadvertent contract formation by automated e-mail responses. Automated dealings with orders from customers using a business website need to be carefully designed and managed internally before external dealings commence. Again, thinking broadly about a typology of risks can assist in moving down to identify the specific legal risks that may need to be addressed as part of a policy.

There may be other ways for an organization to characterize risks – for example, risks that are continuous or ongoing, or those that are more likely to occur at specific times or periods. The danger of employees making a defamatory statement by e-mail or on a bulletin board is an ongoing risk – it could occur at any time. However, a simple omission that concerns a task that is performed very infrequently could also be costly – an organizational failure to renew a domain name registration on time, for example.

Another obvious characterization of legal risk is locational or jurisdictional. Given the global nature of the medium, all organizations or businesses must be aware of the legal risks associated with having an internet presence in many countries. Businesses can fall foul of local legislation and rules governing advertising, consumer rights, prohibitions on selling particular items, etc.

Another characterization may relate to the consequences of a particular risk. Risks can be classified as high, medium or low-risk, and action taken accordingly. As noted above, the likelihood of denial-of-service attacks may be low or non-existent for a respected charity, so that the consequences flowing from such attacks are irrelevant. But it may be a high risk for other organizations, and the legal consequences of such attacks for multinational enterprises such as banks or oil companies could be severe.

Perhaps another important characterization is those legal risks which expose the organization or its employees to criminal charges. The stigma that can attach to an organization where employees are convicted of distributing pornography, for example, can be highly embarrassing and damaging.

2 Risk identification

A broad characterization of relevant risks helps in the more precise identification of separate areas, and the individual legal risks that a business or organization must manage and control. It also helps identify particular employees whose jobs or authority may pose the most serious risks. This is important because such employees could be subject to more extensive training, or tailor-made disclaimers might be written for incorporation in their particular e-mails.

An obvious internal risk is the distribution by employees of copyright-infringing material. This can easily be done by e-mail, or by exchanging floppy diskettes or CD-ROMs, and almost all types of copyright work can be so disseminated. It is an obvious and major internal legal risk.

It is easy to seize on copyright and forget the fact that it forms only one part of the broader area of intellectual property law. Organizations need to be aware of this and consider if, and how, their employees might breach other aspects of intellectual property laws, for example:

- other areas related to copyright such as moral rights or rights conferred by the CDPA 1988 against unauthorized decrypting
- database right
- trade marks
- registered and unregistered design rights
- patents.

Characterization is not mutually exclusive. An organization may wish or need to allocate specific risks to a range of categories. A value of this is that it might then be possible, desirable or indeed essential to select the most important characterization and evolve a risk management strategy based upon that particular major characterization. Online defamation is both an internal and external legal risk. It can also be approached from the standpoint of the consequences that it may have for an organization. The broad characterization of the specific risk may help an organization determine aspects of its policy on the risk area.

This broad characterization of legal risks and the subsequent identification of specific risks within categories are clearly related and overlapping. The process is very important. Firstly, as an approach it introduces some degree of method into identifying major risk areas, assessing the likelihood of their occurrence, and determining weak points in the organization where exposure may be greatest and the types of damage that can be caused. Secondly, there may be several approaches that need to be adopted in response to a risk that has specific legal implications. Characterization assists in the selection of the most appropriate combination of approaches to managing the risk. Thirdly, different approaches will have different resource implications. Again, the characterization of risk assists in the effective allocation of human, financial and other resources in managing the risk.

3 Risk prioritization

Risks, even legal ones, are not all of equal concern. The process of characterization and analysis should, in effect, produce a range of separate, identifiable risks that can be prioritized. Judgement in prioritizing risks and developing responses to particular risks will be called for here. Such judgements will be influenced by a number of factors. A non-exhaustive list would include:

- the type of legal risk
- the likelihood of its occurrence
- the consequences of its occurrence
- the acceptability of the consequences in the absence of action to eliminate or manage the risk.

Prioritization facilitates the effective allocation of resources to eliminate, manage and control the risk. It may not be possible to address all potential areas of concern simultaneously. The range of potential risks often comes as an unpleasant shock to organizations that are only beginning to comprehend the increasing range of legal issues posed by contemporary information and communications technologies. Thus, legal risk areas need to be prioritized for action. There is always the risk that employees might make defamatory statements by e-mail or on external online services. However, an organization might decide that workplace use of the internet and e-mail to download and distribute copyright-infringing music files from online music-swapping services is a greater priority given current major concerns of rights-owners over this issue.

4 Risk management

Various approaches can be adopted to the management of legal risks resulting from the use of IT and communications technologies. Organizations will need to identify the most suitable approaches to manage these. Some common approaches include:

- IT, communications and internet use policy
- software and hardware solutions
- encryption
- e-mail disclaimers
- training and awareness.

IT, communications and internet use policy

An obvious approach is to formulate a formal written policy on workplace use of IT and communications technologies. The development of a full policy, particularly a very strict one, involves many legal issues and may need to be undertaken only with proper legal advice. The content of the policy, and all of the issues that need to be addressed, will vary from organization to organization. Core areas to bear in mind are:

- the general approach to be adopted – strict, liberal or somewhere in between
- background issues and why the policy is needed
- underlying principles that underpin the policy
- guidance on expected good practice in various areas (e.g. e-mail management)
- specific issues:
    — use of e-mail and guidance on legal issues
    — use of the internet and guidance on legal issues
    — data protection and privacy issues
    — intellectual property issues
    — issues relating to unauthorized use of, or access to, facilities
    — policy on disclaimers
    — security issues (e.g. when encryption must be used in e-mails)
    — policy on employee monitoring
    — specific guidance on personal use of facilities
    — the status of the policy, provisions for acceptance and its linkage with disciplinary and grievance procedures.

A formal policy means that all employees know and understand the issues and their obligations.

Software and hardware solutions

Software and hardware solutions that regulate IT and communications use can be adopted. Filtering software can be used to block access to inappropriate sites. Various problems are associated with filtering software (e.g. packages may also block access to useful sites) but nevertheless its use can be considered. Alternatively, perhaps it may be activated only during certain hours of the working day.

Monitoring software can be used in a variety of ways, such as:

- logging sites visited by users
- recording individual keystrokes on a specific machine
- using software that captures materials displayed onscreen
- recording materials downloaded
- screening e-mails for 'stop-words' that could identify inappropriate or illegal content
- monitoring the size of incoming and outgoing e-mail attachments etc.

It is essential to comply with the relevant legislative framework in instituting any screening or monitoring of employee activities.

Virus checking and detection software must be used to limit any risks arising from the accidental transmission of viruses to external suppliers, customers or other organizations. Otherwise liability for damage or loss by another company or organization might arise.

In-house systems or applications can be designed with a compliance philosophy in mind – for example, building in features that will comply with data protection requirements. Firewalls are an important security barrier for most types of organizations. Some organizations may need to implement intruder detection systems.

Encryption

Employees could be encouraged or instructed to use encryption facilities when sending e-mails that may raise legal issues. Thus, it might be made company policy for employees always to encrypt e-mails that contain sensitive personal data or confidential information.

E-mail disclaimers

The legal effect of disclaimers is an area of ambiguity, and their precise legal effectiveness is, as yet, untested in the UK courts. Disclaimers may be effective in some circumstances but certainly not in all. Nevertheless, their use may help to protect an organization or mitigate legal risks in certain circumstances. For example, if it is not possible to encrypt an e-mail that contains confidential information, then a confidentiality notice at the head of an e-mail at least alerts an unintended recipient to the fact that the information enclosed in the e-mail is confidential. A confidentiality notice might lay the grounds for an action for breach of confidence if an unintended recipient discloses or misuses the information.

Disclaimers can be useful because they involve limited 'one-off' costs, which are not excessive for most organizations (but they must be subject to periodic review). Disclaimers may also have a deterrent effect – they may discourage other organizations or individuals from taking legal action if it appears that an organization has a coherent policy for addressing potential legal problems. If legal action is taken, then they can also be useful negotiating tools: repeated dealings with suppliers, customers, etc. who have previously had several opportunities to read an organization's disclaimers might be taken to constitute at least some measure of acceptance of an organization's general approach to dealings. If they had been unacceptable, then the recipient could have elected not to continue dealing with the organization, or could have objected to any of the statements in the disclaimer.

A number of factors are very important in considering the use of disclaimers. Briefly these include:

1   The matter of drafting and language is an important issue. Disclaimers should be drafted by a legal expert in order to ensure that they have legal effect (where possible) and cover all of the areas that need to be covered.
2   The position of the disclaimer is also important. Although many organizations place the disclaimer at the end of an e-mail, the most obvious position is at the head, where it is brought to the attention of unintended recipients immediately. Disclaimers at the end of e-mails are likely to be ineffective.
3   Disclaimers may be needed on internal as well as external e-mails. Confidential information or sensitive personal data can be misrouted to wrong or unintended internal e-mail addresses. Thus, such recipients may also need to be warned by a disclaimer that the e-mail should not be read or routed further.
4   Stylistic issues should be considered – should the disclaimer be in bold or italics, for example? It should be in a font size that is easily readable. All of these factors help to bring the disclaimer to the attention of unintended recipients.

Training and awareness

Much can be done to raise awareness of and control legal risks by addressing the training and awareness needs of employees. A non-exhaustive list of possibilities would be:

- proper coverage of issues and organizational policies during induction and probation periods for new staff
- regular talks or seminars
- fact sheets, guides and coverage of issues in organizational newsletters, e-mail bulletins and other publications (recent incidents in the press or cases from the courts can be highlighted and discussed to illustrate dangers)
- online tutorials or PowerPoint presentations
- small businesses or organizations with limited resources should consider tapping in to local business networks, and liaising with local chambers of commerce or other organizations that offer free but reliable advice, guidance and publications.

Other options may be open to some organizations such as:

- the use of formal and structured approaches to risk identification, assessment and management
- the adoption and implementation of national and international standards in various areas such as BS 7799 on Information Security Management
- the employment of suitably qualified legal and/or it firms or consultants to audit risks and dangers, and to produce a definitive compliance strategy (a number of major legal firms now have considerable expertise in all areas of IT law, while some legal websites and services provide 'off-the-shelf' workplace IT and communications use policies for a very competitive price).

Risk management implementation

Having identified various alternatives to managing legal risks associated with information and communications technologies, a business or organization needs to choose and implement the most appropriate and effective alternatives. Again, the precise combination of these will depend on specific circumstances. A number of important consequences flow from the introduction of approaches to manage legal risks in an organization.

Firstly, policies and procedures must be effectively communicated to all employees. An organization must consider how it should make this information available. Alternatives will include making policies available in printed publications or as documents on an organizational intranet. Major documents such as an IT, internet and communications use policy should also be incorporated into staff manuals or handbooks.

Secondly, an integrated or holistic approach must be taken to implementing approaches – there are, for example, important employment law issues to be addressed. These will be highlighted below.

Risk monitoring, review and adjustment

It is necessary to monitor the situation, review effectiveness, redefine risks and adjust strategy and management approaches accordingly. The nature and acceptability of legal risks may change – something previously regarded as a low-risk area might become medium or even high-risk. Monitoring needs to be focused and conducted in an organized way. Possible options are:

- annual reviews to accommodate new business, legal or technological developments
- incident logs or registers and investigations of incidents, or relevant complaints from customers, users, suppliers, etc.
- creation of a monitoring group to maintain vigilance
- ongoing benchmarking against published standards, industry practices, other organizations, etc.

It is difficult to be too prescriptive about monitoring and review – much will depend on particular circumstances. One thing that organizations must also consider should be an ongoing strategy to monitor and act upon changes and developments in the law.

Employment law issues

References have been made to employers and employees in various aspects of this discussion. The employment relationship provides a crucial and complex context in the management of the legal risks to organizations and businesses posed by employee access to, and use of, information and communications technologies.

The introduction, revision and enforcement of workplace policies and procedures for employees on internet, e-mail and IT use may involve important and far-reaching employment law issues. This must not be forgotten or neglected in introducing, revising or administering such policies.

It is beyond the scope of this book to consider these implications in any depth. The following outline is intended merely to do two things:

- to foster awareness of some employment law issues and guiding principles that need to be considered in regulating use of workplace IT systems and services
- to signal clearly to readers of this book that many potential unforeseen pitfalls and consequences may result from the thoughtless, ill-considered or ill-informed development, introduction, revision or enforcement of such policies.

An employer simply should not act unilaterally and impose entirely new policies, substantially alter existing ones or make changes to 'custom and practice' without proper and fair consultation with employees and their representatives. Expert legal advice may be required before any such action is taken. The unplanned introduction or alteration of such policies could not only damage industrial harmony, but in certain circumstances will expose the employer to actions for breach of contract, constructive unfair dismissal or wrongful dismissal.

Some employment law basics

The employer–employee relationship is governed by a contract of employment. The essential contractual rules on formation of the contract (offer, acceptance, intention to create legal relations and consideration) apply. These need not be discussed for the purposes of this section. The contract need not be in writing, but employers must provide employees with written particulars of their main terms and conditions of employment within two months of starting work.

The terms and conditions that constitute the employment contract are central to an employer's approach to managing employee use of IT and communications technologies at work. An employment contract will usually be composed of the following:

- express terms
- implied terms
- statutory terms
- incorporated terms.

Express terms

These terms have been specifically agreed by the two parties either in writing or orally. Precisely because these terms have been negotiated and agreed, they cannot be altered unilaterally or new terms imposed. Given the organic nature of the employment relationship it is more likely that the employer will wish to introduce new terms. This really must be done by agreement. A change imposed unilaterally by the employer is likely to constitute a breach of contract, allowing the employee to seek damages, or in the case of a fundamental breach, to resign and claim unfair constructive dismissal.

To avoid these problems the employer can ensure that the contract contains an express flexibility clause. This gives the employer the right to vary the terms of employment. Such a clause could specify the employer's right to make changes to a workplace IT and communications policy from time to time in order to take account of developments. Flexibility clauses cannot be used to write a 'blank cheque' to do what the employer wants at some future point. They can be limited by some of the implied terms discussed below. The courts will also interpret them in a restrictive fashion.

An employer who is bent on changing the contract without agreement has two options: he can impose the change (in which case the employee must decide how to respond to the breach of contract), or he can terminate the existing contract and offer a new contract that contains the change (in which case there will be no breach of contract but the employee can claim unfair dismissal while still accepting the new contract). The implications are complex and beyond the scope of this very brief survey.

Implied terms

These have not been agreed in writing but form part of the contract because:

- they are too obvious to need recording
- they are part of 'custom and practice' in the business, sector or industry
- they can be inferred from the conduct of the parties
- or they may be needed to give the contract 'business efficacy'.

Implied terms are binding. In a dispute, a court will only imply terms into a contract if it decides that it would have been the intention of the parties to include the term at the time the contract was made. Over time the courts have already evolved a range of implied terms imposing duties on employees and employers. These can be implied into virtually any employment contract.

For the employee these are the duty to render faithful service, to obey lawful and reasonable orders or instructions, and to exercise reasonable care and skill. For the employer the implied duties are to pay agreed wages and provide work, to provide reasonable support, to provide a safe system of work and a safe workplace, and to provide a suitable working environment. Recently it appears that a further implied duty – to provide a procedure for dealing with employees' grievances – may also be an obligation on the employer. Both employer and employee share an implied term – the duty to maintain mutual trust and confidence. This is potentially extraordinarily wide in scope and is generally relied upon more by the employee than the employer.

Implied terms could be relevant to workplace IT and communications use in various ways. The sudden introduction of a policy which dramatically curtailed personal use of IT and the internet at work could breach custom and practice if such use was moderate and had been tolerated for some time in a sector, business or industry, or by a particular employer. This could apply, for example, in the academic sector. While workplace IT and communications monitoring could certainly contravene the framework created by the Regulation of Investigatory Powers Act 2000, the Human Rights Act 1998 and Data Protection Act 1998, conceivably it could also breach the employer's duty to maintain mutual trust and confidence. An employee could breach the duty to take reasonable care and skill by carelessly making defamatory statements on bulletin boards, or by divulging sensitive personal data or confidential information by e-mail. Sexual or racial harassment at work by e-mail or use of the internet could breach the employer's duty to provide a suitable working environment. Employers could also breach this duty by tolerating or failing to protect an employee against bullying at work (bullying could take many forms, including inappropriate use of e-mail against an employee).

Statutory terms

These are rights given to employees by statute. They automatically form part of every contract of employment. Any attempt to deny an employee any of these rights is unenforceable.

Incorporated terms

Terms can be incorporated from other sources such as collective agreements, a company handbook – or a formal, written IT and communications use policy. Whether such a policy should be incorporated into employment contracts by inserting a clear clause to that effect is not a straightforward decision. Incorporating the policy (and other policies such as a disciplinary and grievance policy) means that a breach of the policy could constitute a breach of contract. The appropriate sanction in the policy can then be invoked by the employer.

Express incorporations cannot be changed without the agreement of both parties. This will limit the employer's freedom to change the policy in the future. Unilateral change raises the problems referred to in the discussion of express terms. In these circumstances the policy becomes merely indicative of the employer's broad approach to the issue. A breach does not necessarily constitute a breach of contract. This may then limit the employer's scope for disciplinary or other action. This creates uncertainty and ambiguity of a rather undesirable nature.

These are important matters to consider in determining how to implement and enforce a workplace IT and communications policy. The employer must be clear about how he wishes important policies to be treated within the employment relationship. The major advantage of clear, written policies together with a clear statement as to their contractual status is that both parties know with some measure of certainty exactly where they stand.

Employment law is extremely complex. This bare and extremely selective outline has only very selectively highlighted some interesting issues related to employee use of IT and communications technologies. It cannot and must not be relied upon to provide sufficient guidance on this very intricate subject. It is merely intended to provide both employers and employees with appropriate food for thought.

Guiding principles

A number of principles should guide the employer in the relationship with employees – and this context is no exception. These are very relevant in the context of managing legal risks and liabilities posed by employee use of workplace IT and communications technologies. This further short review will characterize them as follows:

- consultation
- information
- review and updating
- enforcement
- reasonableness.

Consultation

Consultation is a watchword of employment law. Major new initiatives or significant changes to existing policies should be preceded by meaningful consultation. The employer may come forward with proposals. These should be entirely open to consultation and refinement – if necessary, by direct consultation with all employees, giving opportunities for representations to be made, or through trade union officials or other duly elected representatives. All employees' ideas, views, suggestions, feedback, etc. need to be considered. Proper consultation will result in 'ownership' of policies which are fair, balanced and acceptable to those covered by them. Management should explain clearly why the policy is needed and why particular approaches have been adopted. Failure to consult in a genuine fashion, or to act properly or reasonably, or the unilateral imposition of new policies or major changes to existing policies or practices, could place the employer in breach of the employment contract.

Information

Employees must know exactly where they stand in all aspects of the employment relationship. The employer should provide sufficient information and in appropriate and accessible ways. Thus, employees must be properly informed of workplace policies on use of information and communications technologies. Policies should be unambiguous and understandable, recorded in writing and made available in leaflets, handbooks, on corporate intranets, etc. Best practice suggests that each employee should be furnished with a personal copy. New employees should undergo proper induction and training. Copies of disciplinary procedures should be available, particularly where they have been expressly incorporated into the employment contract.

Review and updating

Unless it is reviewed and updated, a policy is of limited value. Employment, IT and internet law are dynamic areas. Policies and guidance must not stagnate. They should be reviewed and updated in the light of statutory developments, emerging case law and technological developments. As already indicated, change must be properly managed and employees fully appraised of such changes – by re-issuing policies or through newsletters, regular e-mails to staff, etc.

Enforcement

A policy is of limited value (both practically and potentially legally) unless it is enforced on appropriate occasions and in appropriate ways. Any organization's workplace IT and communications policy will be intimately linked with disciplinary procedures. It is a mistake to characterize these policies in merely negative terms – overemphasizing sanctions, for example. They can and should be presented as means of supporting employees, helping them to understand the standards of conduct and performance expected of them. Nevertheless, a policy does need to articulate clearly the sanctions attached to specific policy breaches and the disciplinary procedures that will be adopted in dealing with these. It must also inform employees of all of their rights – such as how to appeal against a warning or disciplinary action taken against them.

Proper procedures and good practice must always be adopted (e.g. oral warnings, written warnings, eventual dismissal, etc.). Enforcement must be applied fairly and consistently, and offences must normally be treated in the same way. Disciplinary procedures are a complex area where the employer must act correctly and reasonably. The rules of natural justice requiring that a fair process is followed must be applied. Any statutory rights must be scrupulously observed –

Section 10 of the Employment Relations Act 1999 provides a statutory right for a worker who has been required or invited by his employer to attend a disciplinary hearing to be accompanied by a companion. The type of disciplinary procedure will depend partly on the size and resources of an organization, but every procedure should conform to basic established principles. The ACAS *Code of Practice on Disciplinary and Grievance Procedures* provides an essential framework for all employers.[18]

A graduated and common-sense response is always called for taking into account all of the circumstances of an infraction – minor infractions may be dealt with informally (in some circumstances additional training or guidance may really be what is needed). More serious ones may need to be dealt with more formally or by an appropriate and properly publicized policy on warnings. Serious offences or gross misconduct might result in summary dismissal.

What constitutes gross misconduct in terms of offences under a workplace IT and communications policy will depend on a range of factors. The distribution of obscene materials, child pornography, etc. will almost certainly fall into this category, as will other activities. An employer should attempt to give employees some indication of the offences which it regards as being so serious as to merit summary dismissal. Again, this is an area where proper legal advice may be needed if such action is contemplated. Successful cases for unfair dismissal result in an award for compensation to be paid to the dismissed employee. Compensation comprises a basic award (currently a maximum of £7500) and a compensatory award (a maximum of £52,600).

Constructive dismissal occurs where the employee resigns, terminating the employment contract in circumstances where the employer has acted in such a way as to justify the employee's action. This could happen on the unilateral imposition of new terms of employment without agreement and where the new terms are such as to amount to a breach of contract. This breach must be very fundamental, totally undermining the employment relationship. The employee's resignation must be as a result of the breach and must occur immediately or very soon after the breach has occurred. If a tribunal determines that an employee has been constructively dismissed, it will then consider whether the dismissal was fair. If the dismissal is not fair then compensation can be awarded.

Both employers and employees should note that during 2003 new statutory disciplinary procedures provided for in the Employment Act 2002 come into force. This means that statutory dispute resolution procedures are implied into all employment contracts. This means that any employee whose contract does not contain disciplinary and grievance procedures that comply with the statutory requirements in Schedule 3 of the Act is able to rely on those procedures. These become contractual terms. Any employer who fails to adhere to them could be faced with an action for breach of contract. Employment tribunals also have the discretion to increase or reduce compensation awards by up to 50% if either an employer or an employee fail to adhere to the procedures laid down.

Reasonableness

In managing the employment relationship, the employer should always be able to demonstrate that he has acted reasonably and fairly whatever the issue. Fairness, transparency, consistency, consultation, adherence to agreed procedures or codes of practice, observance of basic tenets of natural justice, scrupulous observance of statutory responsibilities, etc. are characteristics that will tend to suggest that an employer has acted reasonably. All of these apply to managing the legal risks posed by employees as a result of their workplace use of IT and communications technologies.

Conclusion

This chapter has ranged widely. It does not purport to be a comprehensive survey of all of the relevant areas or issues. That is not the aim of this collection. It does seek to raise awareness of the wider context of many of the legal risks referred to in this chapter and throughout this book. The increasing use of e-mail, the internet, hardware and software, databases and other aspects of IT and communications technologies raises many far-reaching issues for organizations. Much is misunderstood and much is still unclear. The best that organizations can do is to make efforts to inform themselves about the issues, find approaches to identifying and managing risks and as a consequence enhance their opportunities of staying legal in a highly dynamic environment.

Notes

1 Tattum, G. (n.d.) *County Hall staff face e-mail probe*, available at http://icnorthwales.icnetwork.co.uk (visited 3 January 2003).

2 Sturgeon, W. (n.d.) *It's a fair cop as Police admits 'spam attack'*, available at http://news.zdnet.co.uk (visited 6 December 2002).

3 Thomson, I. (n.d.) *Jail for mobile stalker*, available at http://http://www.vnunet.com/News/1137003 (visited 21 November 2002).

4 See 14 November 2002 press releases under News Room on Business Software Alliance, available at http://www.bsa.org/uk.

5 Magee, M. (n.d.) *Foris says it won't process Vaio orders*, available at http://www.theinquirer.net/?article=4684 (visited 30 July 2002).

6 Loney, M. (n.d.) *Kodak snaps under customer pressure*, available at http://news.zdnet.co.uk (visited 31 January 2002).

7   McNamara, M. (n.d.) *Teacher wins damages in Friends Reunited libel case*, available at http://media.guardian.co.uk/newmedia/story/0,7496,719488,00.html (visited 21 May 2002).

8   Ewalt, D. (n.d.) *Tech Firm Pays $1M Penalty in MP3 Sharing Case*, available at http://www.informationweek.com/story/IWK20020410S0002 (visited 10 April 2002).

9   Fox Williams (2002) *Website Legal Compliance: Fox Williams Survey of OFEX Listed Companies*, London, Fox Williams.

10 Consumers International (2002) *Credibility on the Web: an international study of the credibilty of consumer information on the internet*, London, Consumers International, 4.

11 See 17 October 2002 press releases, available at http://www.brightmail.com.

12 See October 2002 media release, available at http://www.star.net.uk.

13 European Commission (n.d.) *Open Consultation on 'Trust Barriers for B2B E-Marketplaces'*, available at http://europa.eu.int/comm/enterprise/ict/policy/b2b/index.htm.

14 European Commission (2002) *Commission Staff Working Paper on B2B Internet Platforms: opportunities and oarriers for SMEs – a first assessment*, SEC (2002) 1217, Brussels, European Commission.

15 KPMG International (2002) Failed IT Projects Cost Business over £8 million a Time, *Assurance*, (25 November), available at http://www.kpmg.co.uk/kpmg/uk.

16 Commission for Racial Equality (1995) *Racial Harassment at Work: what employers can do about it*, London, CRE.

17 *Official Journal*, L49, 24.02, 1992.

18 Advisory Conciliation and Arbitration Service (2001) *Code of Practice on Disciplinary and Grievance Procedures*, London, ACAS.

Conclusion

On 6 April 1780, in the House of Commons, one of the most memorable of British Parliamentary resolutions was moved by John Dunning in a Committee of the Whole House to the effect that 'The influence of the Crown has increased, is increasing and ought to be diminished.' For the purposes of this book and the subjects of the various chapters contained within it, the sentiments behind this famous resolution might be paraphrased to the effect that 'The influence of the law on information work has increased, is increasing and is only likely to increase even further.'

That increasing influence is particularly apparent to the editors in drawing together a few concluding thoughts. Our first thought is that time waits for no man, and neither indeed does the law. The areas covered in this book have moved on and are moving on daily as a result of new laws, new cases and new applications and interpretations of existing laws. There is nothing that can be done about this. It is apparent throughout the book that the law is organic. It grows, it expands, it develops, and in many of the areas we have touched on it is growing particularly rapidly. A few examples might be useful.

In *Durant v. Financial Services Authority* (24 October 2002, unreported) the court considered the very important issue of whether certain paper files held on an individual constituted a 'relevant filing system' as defined by the Data Protection Act 1998. In the particular circumstances of this case the court found that they did not. At the time of writing the case has been appealed to the Court of Appeal. That Court's judgment will provide important guidance on compliance with the Act in this respect. Another case, *P. v. Wozencroft* [2002] EWHC 1724 (Fam), provides guidance on responding to Subject Access Requests, also under the DPA 1998. New regulations, the Race Relations Act 1976 (Amendment) Regulations 2003, now provide a clear definition of what constitutes harassment on the grounds of race, or ethnic or national origin. This is another area touched on in various parts of this book.

Aspects of our legal system are changing – early in 2003 the Government announced that the Appellate Committee of the House of Lords will be replaced as the UK's highest court of appeal by a new Supreme Court. In trying to promote better public access to legal information, a European Judicial Network website (http://europa.eu.int/comm/justice_home/ejn/) went live in the first part of 2003. It provides information about court structures in the EU Member States, and information and guidance on how to apply for legal aid and commence civil actions in each member country – just the type of useful information needed for online consumers in the age of the internet. In May in *Harrod's Limited v. Dow Jones & Company Inc.* [2003] EWHC 1162 (QB), Harrod's Ltd was allowed to proceed with an action in the English courts for defamation following the publication of an allegedly defamatory article in the US edition of the *Wall Street Journal*. Only ten copies of the printed journal were actually distributed in the UK and only a small number of hits on the article were registered on the *Wall Street Journal* website. In June the Organisation for Economic Co-operation and published new international guidelines on combating cross-border fraudulent lottery schemes, prize draws and credit cons as part of a major initiative to combat internet frauds and scams. Mildly amusing perhaps (unless you are one of the people who have been tricked, of course) but internet fraud and internet scams undermine consumer confidence and trust in electronic commerce more generally. Hence the need to target these activities. More rights have been conferred on consumers in their capacity as buyers by the Sale and Supply of Goods to Consumers Regulations 2002, SI 2002 No. 3045. As we have suggested, neither time nor the law wait for any man.

Staying legal is a constant struggle. Understanding this reality is part of the struggle. Another part of the struggle is taking action to maintain awareness. Information specialists are accustomed to keeping abreast of developments in their own fields using commercial databases, free web resources, alerting services, tables of contents services, sharing and exchanging information, etc. This kind of strategy can be adopted to maintain an awareness of key legal developments – especially in areas particularly relevant to the mainstream information profession such as copyright and data protection. To explore possible accessible online and printed resources to achieve this is beyond the scope of this book. But useful starting places include key Government websites such as the Patent Office, which deals with copyright, patents and trade marks; the Lord Chancellor's Department; the Home Office; the Department of Trade and Industry; the Court Service; and the websites of specialist regulators such as the Information Commissioner, the Office of Fair Trading, and so on. Many news services and online magazines (such as *Computer Weekly*) carry features on important legal developments and provide e-mail bulletins. Portals such as Delia Venables' Legal Information Portal (http://www.venables.co.uk) or Sarah Carter's Lawlinks at the University of Kent at Canterbury (http://library.kent.ac.uk/library/lawlinks/) are excellent gateways that will lead those interested in legal current awareness services and legal resources generally to valuable free sources of information.

We have suggested in the Introduction that this book is not about making legal experts out of information professionals but rather about raising awareness of the areas of law that impact on the work of the information professions. Just as information professionals tend to have highly developed skills in current awareness techniques, so they also tend to have highly developed analytical and critical skills in assessing and evaluating information and well developed skills in manipulating and synthesizing information. These valuable skills must also be deployed in the struggle to stay legal. Keeping abreast of developments is crucial. Similarly crucial is evaluating information about these developments and taking appropriate action. Information professionals need to use and act upon information about current legal developments in an appropriate way. This may mean that particular policies – such as a privacy policy or data protection statement on a website – need to be changed as a result of a particular development. Perhaps it means that a guide for students and staff in a university needs to be amended as a result of developments in copyright law. Or it may mean that guidance to staff on some aspect of an internet use policy needs to be changed. In circumstances of major change it may mean setting up a project group to work on and assess the implications of major new legislation in a particular field. An area of major concern for some organizations in 2004 will be intensified preparations for the full coming into force in 2005 of the Freedom of Information Act 2000.[1] We have chosen not to cover this in this collection since so much of this Act is being phased in gradually in 2004. Full implementation of the Act is not required by law until November 2005 but the Government has signalled that it hopes to bring the Act fully into force by the end of January 2005, ten months in advance of the required deadline. Major changes or overhauls of the law may require major initiatives within the organization to cope with them – or may necessitate the need to take full and expert legal advice or engage the services of a suitably qualified consultant.

The crucial point is that keeping abreast of developments needs to be accompanied by appropriate action, where action is needed. Judgements must be made about what new developments do not require any action and those that do. For those that do need action, judgement again needs to be exercised in determining what can be reasonably and safely done without needing to resort to expert legal advice. It is probably simply not possible, and indeed probably may not be necessary, for many organizations to take legal advice every time there is a change to the law of copyright, data protection, patent law, etc But an awareness of basic areas of the law that affect an organization together with intelligent assessments of the impact of new developments should help information professionals in the challenge of staying legal.

An information profession that is more informed about the legal and regulatory framework that affects it, is also a profession that is better placed to represent itself and its user communities in shaping and altering such laws. This is both a professional and an ethical responsibility for information professionals. Arguably the law is out of balance in a number of areas. Perhaps information professionals and users have to 'stay legal' in too many areas, or at least in some areas to unnecessary extents? Perhaps there is a tendency towards over-regulation in some areas?

Developments in the law of copyright appear increasingly unbalanced and excessively protective of copyright owners' interests at the expense of users' rights. There is a pronounced shift towards using the law and technology in ways that lead to greater intrusion and monitoring of individuals and their activities, especially in the digital environment. Does the law place too many burdens on ISPs and other digital information carriers and providers? Does the existing law of defamation truly meet the needs of a wired-up 21st century society where modern publishing technologies are light years removed from the context in which the law of defamation finds its origins? Is the data protection regime too complicated, excessive and burdensome? If information professionals feel over-regulated and over-burdened by excessively protectionist and rigid laws then perhaps we have only ourselves to blame. A profession that is more informed about the legal issues that confront it can only be beneficial to the profession itself, to its users, clients and customers, and to society in general. It may lead to a profession that can comment more authoritatively on proposed new laws, or can respond to consultations on how well existing laws are working, or a profession that is populated with individuals who are prepared to be mobilized by its professional bodies, such as CILIP, to lobby for change and to influence future developments – and, at least as importantly, to understand why the professional association needs this support. It would also be a profession more capable of forging suitable links and alliances with other national professional bodies similarly affected by laws and regulations, and a profession which is better placed to forge further links and alliances with similar bodies overseas to campaign on common and much wider fronts.

In the Introduction we also expressed the hope that this book might be useful to many people engaged in the information profession – a phrase we have used to cover a range of sectors or jobs that are intensively engaged in information creation, dissemination and exploitation. Those involved in information work inevitably approach problems and issues from different perspectives. Publishers, librarians, software designers, web designers, academics, students, computer scientists, etc., might have many differing views about the copyright or patent regimes and how these affect their roles, products, services and professional activities. They might also take differing views about how well each is discharging their responsibilities in staying legal. The same can be said about all of the areas covered in this book. Further, there will be differences within groups - different publishers might take different views about how rigidly they wish to apply or interpret copyright law in controlling the exploitation of their products. Librarians and information managers may differ on how they interpret, implement or apply aspects of the data protection framework to their handling of personal information. Differences of opinion are healthy. Informed differences of opinion are even healthier - and they can also be very constructive. Informed differences of opinion promote understanding, co-operation and mutual support. One of the reasons we hope this book might be read by many different players in the information chain is that we feel that books such as this can help to build bridges and create a dialogue between different sectors of the information profession. This can help us all to shape better solutions to common problems and areas of concern. It is a bit like 'Put yourself in my shoes.' The more we can look beyond our own narrow focus and appreciate that the legal and regulatory regime raises many legitimate issues, concerns and problems from perspectives other than our own, then the better the chance we have of fashioning an information landscape that is relevant, appropriate and fair.

A profession that understands the complexity of the law is also in a better position to campaign for the simplification of the law in key areas. One such area is the law of copyright. It is an area that has expanded remorselessly and an area that is noted for its complexity and ambiguity. In responses to the consultation by the Patent Office on the UK implementation of the 2001 EC copyright directive a number of calls were made by organizations such as the Libraries and Archives Copyright Alliance for the simplification and proper consolidation of copyright law. Copyright law increasingly underpins many work and leisure activities in the information society. Yet its complexity and opacity is daunting. Simplification is not an idle hope. Since the late 1990s the Government has actively been engaged in simplifying another complex area of law – tax law. Simplification of laws is possible, it is desirable and it should be a campaigning goal of our profession for those areas that affect us.

Staying legal is a struggle that is conducted on many levels – on an individual level, on a departmental level, on an organizational level, on a national level and on an international level. It is a struggle that is conducted in different contexts - at work and increasingly at leisure. It is a struggle that is conducted by individuals with varying degrees of knowledge. While it is right for us to emphasize to the information professionals reading through this book that staying legal is a professional, ethical and legal requirement, it is equally as desirable for us to suggest that it is perhaps also a professional and ethical duty for informed professionals to do their best to influence, shape and transform the laws that bind them. On behalf of our contributors and ourselves we hope that this book will assist you in these goals.

Chris Armstrong
Laurence W. Bebbington

Reference

1   Smith, K. (2004) *Freedom of Information: a practical guide to implementation*, Facet Publishing. Awaited early 2004.

Further reading

The following works are provided as a selection of sources that interested readers may wish to consult in order to learn more about many of the areas covered in this book. Inevitably this further reading ranges from accessible introductory texts, or works that can be read by those with a limited knowledge of the law, to more extensive, in-depth treatments of subjects aimed at those with a much fuller grasp of the law in specific fields. Readers should always check for more recently published editions of these books. At the time of writing new editions of some of the books (for example, Rowe, Morcom, Bainbridge) were being listed as due for publication either late in 2003 or early in 2004. Again, it is always useful to emphasize that those who have specific legal issues or problems are always advised to take proper legal advice and not to rely on anything in this book, or any other, to deal with a specific difficulty.

Akdeniz, Y. and Walker, C. (2001) *The Internet, Law and Society*, London, Longman, ISBN 0-582-35656-3.

Bainbridge, D. (2002) *Intellectual Property*, 5th edn, London, Longman, ISBN 0-582-47314-4.

Bainbridge, D. (2002) *Patent Law*, London, EMIS Professional Publishing, ISBN 1-85811-140-4.

Bainbridge, D. (1999) *Introduction to Computer Law*, 4th edn, London, Longman, ISBN 0-582-42334-1.

Beatson, J. (2002) *Anson's Law of Contract*, 28th edn, Oxford, Oxford University Press, ISBN 0-19-876576-2.

Carey, P. (2002) *E-Privacy and Online Data Protection*, London, Butterworths, ISBN 0-406-94588-8.

Carey, P. (2000) *Data Protection in the UK*, London, Blackstone, ISBN 1-84174-127-2.

Carey, P. (1998) *Blackstone's Guide to the Data Protection Act 1998*, London, Blackstone, ISBN 1-85431-866-7.

Chissick, M. and Kelman, A. (2001) *Electronic Commerce: law and practice*, 3rd edn, London, Sweet and Maxwell, ISBN 0-421-76430-9.

Cornish, G. P. (2004) *Copyright: interpreting the law for libraries, archives and information services*, 4th edn, London, Facet Publishing, ISBN 1-85604-508-0 [replaces 3rd rev. edn, ISBN 1-85604-409-2].

De Bruin, R. (2002) *Consumer Trust in Electronic Commerce: time for best practice*, The Hague, Kluwer Law International, ISBN 90-411-1923-X.

Elliott, C. (2002) *Contract Law*, 4th edn, London, Longman, 0-582-47330-6.

Edwards, L. and Waelde, C. (2000) *Law and the Internet: a framework for electronic commerce*, 2nd edn, Oxford, Hart, ISBN 1-84113-141-5.

Furmston, M., Adams, J., Bradgate, R. *et al.* (2003) *The Law of Contract*, 2nd edn, London, Butterworths, ISBN 0-406-94986-7.

Garnett, K., James, J. R. and Davies, G. (1998) *Copinger and Skone James on Copyright*, 14th edn, London, Sweet and Maxwell, ISBN 0-421-58910-8 (updated by periodic supplements).

Gringras, C. (2003) *Laws of the Internet*, 2nd edn, London, Butterworths, ISBN 0-406-90808-7.

Halberstam, S., Brook, J. and Turner, J. D. C. (2000) *Domain Names: a practical guide*, London, Tolley Publishing, ISBN 0-7545-1491-9.

Holborn, G. (2001) *Butterworths Legal Research Guide*, 2nd edn, London, Butterworths, ISBN 0-406-93023-6.

Holyoak, J. and Torremans, P. (2001) *Intellectual Property Law*, 3rd edn, London, Butterworths, ISBN 0-406-93400-2.

Hugenholtz, P. B. (2002) Copyright and Electronic Commerce: legal aspects of electronic copyright management, The Hague, Kluwer Law International, ISBN 90-411-9785-0.

Kitchen, D., Mellor, J. and Meade, R. (2000) *Kerly's Law of Trade Marks and Trade Names*, London, Sweet and Maxwell, ISBN 0-421-45610-8.

Lloyd, I. (2000) *Information Technology Law*, 3rd edn, London, Butterworths, ISBN 0-406-91489-3.

MacDonald, E. (2001) *Managing E-mail and Internet Use: a practical guide to employers' obligations and employees' rights*, London, Tolley Publishing, ISBN 0-7545-1394-7.

MacDonald, E. and Rowland, D. (2000) *Information Technology Law*, 2nd edn, London, Cavendish, ISBN 1-85941-564-4.

Matthews, C. (2002) *The Law of Defamation and the Internet*, Oxford, Oxford University Press, ISBN 0-19-924468-5.

Michaels, A. (2001) *A Practical Guide to Trade Mark Law*, London, Sweet and Maxwell, ISBN 0-421-74760-9.

Morcom, C., Roughton, A. and Graham, J. (2000) *The Modern Law of Trade Marks and Service Marks*, London, Butterworths, ISBN 0-406-06551-9.

Mullock, James and Leigh-Pollitt, P. (2001) *The Data Protection Act Explained*, 3rd edn, The Stationery Office, ISBN 0-11-702754-5.

Oppenheim, C. *The Legal and Regulatory Environment for Electronic Information*, 4th edn, Tetbury, Infonortics, ISBN 1-873699-78-6.

Pedley, P. (2003) *Essential Law for Information Professionals*, London, Facet Publishing, ISBN 1-85604-440-8.

Reed, C. and Angel, J. (2000) *Computer Law*, 4th edn, London, Blackstone Press, ISBN 1-84174-016-0.

Rowe, Heather (1999) *Data Protection Act 1998: a practical guide*, London, Tolley, ISBN 0-7545-0135-3.

Singleton, S. (2002) *Tolley's Data Protection Handbook*, London, Tolley's, ISBN 0-7545-1938-4.

Smith, G. J. H. (2001) *Internet Law and Regulation*, 3rd edn, London, Sweet and Maxwell, ISBN 0-421-70590-6.

Index
to Acts, Agreements, Bills, Conventions, Directives, Orders and Regulations

Index